I
LOVE
ALABAMA

DONALD F. STAFFO

TRIUMPH
BOOKS

Library of Congress Cataloging-in-Publication Data

Staffo, Donald F.
    I love Alabama, I hate Auburn / Donald F. Staffo.
      p. cm.
    ISBN 978-1-60078-724-9
    1. University of Alabama—Football—History. 2. Alabama Crimson Tide (Football team)—History. 3. Auburn University—Football—History. 4. Auburn Tigers (Football team)—History. 5. Sports rivalries—Alabama—History. I. Title.
    GV958.A4S72 2012
    796.332'6309761—dc23

                                        2012005145

This book is available in quantity at special discounts for your group or organization. For further information, contact:

Triumph Books LLC
814 North Franklin Street
Chicago, Illinois 60610
(312) 337-0747
www.triumphbooks.com

Printed in U.S.A.
ISBN: 978-1-60078-724-9
Design and editorial production by Prologue Publishing Services, LLC
Photos courtesy of Paul W. Bryant Museum/The University of Alabama unless otherwise indicated

*To the 'Bama Nation that is so passionately devoted
to its team and so equally detesting of Auburn,
its cross-state rival and nemesis*

*To my wife Marilyn, daughter Andrea and her
husband Brent, and our newborn granddaughter Ava,
who will have no choice but to grow up a 'Bama fan,
and daughter Deanna and her husband Jesse*

CONTENTS

Introduction: I Love Alabama . . . . *vii*

1. **We Love Beating Auburn** *1*

2. **We Love Beating Everybody** *31*

3. **We Love Winning**

   National Championships *47*

4. **Players We Love** *70*

5. **Coaches We Love** *106*

6. **Traditions We Love** *134*

7. **Stories We Love** *157*

Acknowledgments *171*

INTRODUCTION
I LOVE ALABAMA

THIS BOOK IS WRITTEN from the viewpoint of some Alabama fans I know and have observed through my almost three decades of covering the Crimson Tide, and from extensive research relative to the Iron Bowl and Alabama football, especially as it pertains to the Tide's biggest rival.

Make no mistake about it, some diehard Alabama fans really hate Auburn, the school, and everything about it. And the feeling is mutual. However, it must also be understood that whereas most in the 'Bama Nation dislike Auburn, and some very much so, relatively few in the real sense of the word actually *hate* the players who play for the Tigers, the students who attend the institution, or Auburn's traditions. It's nothing personal. It's just that a lot of Alabama fans can't stand the thought of Auburn and its faithful thinking or believing that their football program or their school is on the same level as Alabama. The more the Tiger Nation thinks that and tries so hard to validate that, the more Alabama fans "hate" them.

Now, what fans of both programs really *hate* is losing to each other. And when that happens, sometimes that anger spills over into other areas, and sometimes it crosses the line. It's been that way for a long time, and there are no signs that it's going to be any different in the foreseeable future. Some things never change. And in many ways that's what this book is about.

It is serious in nature about many of the things mentioned because there is a great deal of animosity—yes, even hatred entwined in the Alabama-Auburn rivalry—but it is also meant to be a spoof in other places. The author trusts readers will be able to make the distinctions.

WHY THE IRON BOWL IS THE BEST RIVALRY IN ALL OF SPORTS

There are some great traditional college football rivalries, with Ohio State–Michigan, USC-UCLA, Florida–Florida State, Oklahoma-Texas, and Oklahoma-Nebraska quickly coming to mind, but none evoke the passion of Alabama-Auburn. There is no other way to say it. Alabama and Auburn bring out not only the best, but the worst in their fans. In some circles, because the game is so very important to so many people, the ramifications surrounding the game can be downright nasty.

That's because the Iron Bowl, as the Alabama-Auburn game is called, is between neighbors. It divides the state and separates family and friends, like no other game. The divisions run deep. More than 100 years of hostility between the schools is to some degree always simmering. Children are born into the Tide or Tigers tradition. They inherit a love for one team and a hatred for the other, with this entrenched loyalty passed down from generation to generation.

What makes the Iron Bowl different from other rivalries is that the people so intensely and vicariously involved in it have to live with each other, many times literally in the same house or as part of an extended family. When talk turns to Alabama or Auburn, conversations across the kitchen table can lose some civility and become testy.

The allegiance to one school or the other to some extent defines who you are in the state. In many cases there simply is no choice where a child's allegiance will lie, with the brainwashing beginning at a very early age.

In some families, after a baby learns to say "Mommy" and "Daddy," the next likely words he or she will be taught are "Roll Tide!" And maybe not in that order. Among the bad guys, it might be "War Eagle!"

There is an organization whose membership is in the hundreds and includes people named Bear, Bryant, Paul, and any variation of those names, in honor of the late legendary coach of the Crimson Tide. And that doesn't include people named 'Bama, Crimson, Tide, and names like that. There have been a lot of babies born in the last few years named Nick and Saban, in admiration of the current ruler of the Alabama football dynasty.

Fathers have been known to miss their daughters' weddings if their daughters were foolish enough to plan the wedding on the day of the Alabama-Auburn game. In some families, that applies to any Saturday during football season when the Crimson Tide has a game. During Iron Bowl week it can be difficult if you're in a "mixed marriage," where one spouse is an Alabama alum and the other an Auburn grad.

Some people's happiness quotient for the following year is tied to and dependent upon how their team fared in the Iron Bowl. When one team wins, its hardcore fans celebrate for the next 364 days. Diehard fans of the other team cry for the next 364 days.

A student referred to in Geoffrey Norman's book, *Alabama Showdown: The Football Rivalry Between Alabama and Auburn*, put it this way: "If your team wins, then the rest of the year everything is a little bit easier. If your team loses, then everything you do will just be a little bit harder until they play again."

Speaking about the attitudes of some Alabama fans in the late 1940s and 1950s on the ESPN special *Roll Tide/War Eagle* that was broadcast November 8, 2011, celebrated author and Alabama alumnus Gay Talese said that the perception some Alabama fans had was that the people at Auburn "shouldn't [have] even been in college...that the white outcasts were at Auburn...and with the reenactment every year of the Auburn game, all the elements within the Tuscaloosa community, which is the home city of the University of Alabama, would rise to the occasion of being seemingly superior to these vulgarians and trashy little white folks who represented the college in Auburn." He also stated, "I'm 79 years old and I'm amazed that losing to Auburn still has an effect on me." It's sometimes worse if someone tries to stay neutral. On the same *Roll Tide/War Eagle* broadcast, Greg McElroy, who quarterbacked the Crimson Tide to the 2009 national championship, said, "If you don't pick either one, then both [sides] hate you."

Football in the state of Alabama is serious—very serious. And it's off-the-charts serious when it involves the state's flagship football powerhouse—the University of Alabama Crimson Tide—and its pain-in-the-butt nemesis over yonder.

Instead of saying "hi" or "hello," sometimes people will simply greet each other with "Roll Tide!"—especially during football season. There even was an ESPN-produced video commercial that spoofed the chant, with a state trooper, after writing out a ticket to a speeder, telling the person, "Roll Tide!" To someone from outside the state, all the hullabaloo over the famed Crimson Tide seems insane. To people in the state, it's the norm. It's what they grew up with. It all makes perfect sense.

Now Auburn has its fair share of diehard fans as well, although in the state a much smaller percentage than 'Bama fans. But they are just as rabid, just as loyal, and just as vocal, though they are constantly struggling to be heard over the roar that emanates out of and surrounds the team located across the state in Tuscaloosa. Maybe that's where the burn in Auburn comes from—the frustration and anger of Tigers fans trying to compete with a program that is considered by many the standard by which all college football programs are compared.

It's like in basketball-crazed Kentucky where the Wildcats rule the roost. When the University of Louisville won national championships in 1980 and 1986, bumper stickers immediately came out stating "No. 1 in the nation, No. 2 in the state."

No matter what the Cardinals accomplished, the school's basketball team couldn't escape the huge Big Blue shadow that has forever enveloped the commonwealth. Consequently, just as Louisville is always trying to escape from under the aura that Adolph Rupp constructed in the Bluegrass, Auburn is continuously trying to climb out from under the deep-rooted Alabama tradition and the mystique that Bryant built that engulfs the state to this day.

Therefore, make no mistake about it, the Iron Bowl is much more than a football game. It is a grudge match between two schools that are 160 miles apart that just do not like each other. Alabama and Auburn are in-state schools, but most 'Bama fans would prefer to drop-kick Auburn into Mississippi or somewhere else. And the thing is, they're serious. They have nothing good to say about the school on the other side of the state, or its football team.

To better understand the relationship and the attitude that prevails, it helps to know that the resentment is socially based and stems from the way the students who attend each institution perceive each other. Many Alabama alumni like to remind Auburn faithful that their school was originally called East Alabama Male College (1856–1872), with the first school cheer being, "Rah, rah, rah—Alabama A.M.C."

Then the name of the institution was changed to Alabama Agricultural and Mechanical College (1872–1899) and then to Alabama Polytechnic Institute (1899–1960), which was its official name as late as 1957 when it won the national championship in football. In the minds of some 'Bama fans, Auburn is still A.P.I., and they'd like to keep them that way.

Alabama students consider their University—the Capstone—a combination of city and culture. They look at Auburn as a farm school for hicks and rednecks who ride around in mud-smeared pick-up trucks with gun racks on the back. They think students who go to Auburn are not as smart or as sophisticated as they are. Case in point. On Facebook there's a picture of six guys with orange and blue letters on their chest spelling "ABUURN," with the caption stating, "Where being stupid is a way of life."

That attitude really irked Pat Dye, who was an assistant at UA and later the head coach at AU. He stated somewhat bitterly, "[Alabama fans] talk about Auburn people wearing overalls and driving tractors, when the truth is we also write books and go to the moon," the latter in reference to when in the mid-1980s Auburn was the primary research institution for President Ronald Reagan's "Star Wars" missile defense system and the only school, except for the Service Academies, that put a pilot and a copilot on the same space shuttle.

No matter, Alabama students believe down "on the Plains" really is Nowheresville. 'Bama fans don't necessarily think Auburn is the armpit of the world, only that you can see it from there. Much like Ohio State's Woody Hayes instigated the Michigan rivalry by refusing to buy gasoline there and by referring to it as "that place up North," Bear Bryant fueled the Iron Bowl fires by stating, "Sure I'd like to beat Notre Dame, don't get me wrong. But nothing matters more than beating that cow college on the other side of the state."

Former 'Bama quarterback Scott Hunter likes to refer to Auburn as the "University of East Alabama." Years later, in the early 2000s, Coach Dennis Franchione, refusing to call the school by name, referred to Auburn as "that school down the road."

Auburn students consider the University of Alabama a party school for rich, snobby kids who think they are uppity-uppity and better than Auburn students. The result was that for many years Auburn had an inferiority complex and the resentment and hatred for UA boiled, always looking for an opportunity to erupt, such as on occasions when the Tigers beat hot-shot Alabama in football. Former Auburn hoops star and Basketball Hall of Famer Charles Barkley admitted it, stating, "We have an inferiority complex when it comes to Alabama."

Unlike other rivalries, the Iron Bowl is talked about year-round. Former Alabama coach Gene Stallings, who played and coached at Texas A&M, explained it this way several years ago to Clyde Bolton of the *Birmingham News*: "Talk about the Texas and Texas A&M game will start a week before the game and continue for a week after, but talk about the Alabama-Auburn game never stops. They're talking about it on the Fourth of July. That's what makes this one different from all the other [rivalries]."

Prior to the 1989 game, ESPN's Beano Cook said, "Alabama and Auburn hate each other every day of the year, including Christmas."

Discussions about UA-AU—such as who's better, who's cheating, off-season recruiting—can quickly accelerate into a heated debate and escalate to a full-fledged argument, especially if the talkers have a few beers in them. Insinuations will be made, intelligence questioned, and insults and sometimes objects thrown.

When Auburn beat Alabama one year, the husband, a to-the-bone 'Bama fan, threw the plate of spaghetti he was eating against the wall and then told his wife, who was pulling for Auburn, "Now pick it up."

Bolton tells of an Alabama fan who called in to a talk-radio show offering to sell a couple of Iron Bowl tickets. The caller stated, "Auburn fans need not call. I don't want their money."

Some players also make their feelings known. On the week leading up to the 2011 Iron Bowl, Alabama defensive lineman Josh Chapman was asked by the media if he had any friends who played for Auburn. Chapman shot back, "I don't associate with any people from Auburn."

One proud 'Bama fan stated on the *Roll Tide/War Eagle* documentary, "If Auburn plays Iraq, I want Iraq to win."

Do you get the picture here?

To be fair, Auburn's Corey Lemonier, a defensive lineman and the 2011 team leader with 9½ sacks and 13½ tackles for loss, probably does not have any Crimson Tide players on his Christmas card list. Speaking for himself, his position coach, and his fellow teammates on the defensive line, Lemonier told the media, "I'm not from Alabama, but being here just for one year, I hate them. [Defensive line coach Mike Pelton] says that he hates Alabama, and he's like, 'You should hate them too.' And we do hate them. Everybody in our D-line room hates them."

Although he stated it years earlier, comments like these caused Beano Cook on another occasion to say, "Alabama-Auburn is not just a rivalry. It's Gettysburg South."

Ray Perkins played in three Iron Bowls for Alabama, all victories. Following Bryant as coach of the Crimson Tide in 1983, Perkins stated the week before he was going to coach against Auburn for the first time: "This is *the* week, isn't it? This is the one," he began his Monday morning press conference. "This is the big game of the year. It's bigger than any championship and any bowl game. It's more than [coaching] staff vs. staff, players vs. players. It's [Alabama] people vs. [Auburn] people. It's one of the greatest rivalries in the country. The game is for the bragging rights for the rest of your life. Ask any [Alabama] player who lost [to Auburn] 30 years ago and has had to live with that."

In another interview prior to the Iron Bowl, Perkins emphasized the importance of the bitter intrastate rivalry and what it means to the people who live in Alabama and are obsessed with it 365 days a year by stating, "The season's almost over. Only about 90 percent of it is left."

Perkins also once said that he didn't think Pat Dye, who played for Georgia and later was an assistant coach at Alabama and head coach at Auburn, fully understood the seriousness and intensity of the battle for state superiority in football because he never played in the game. Maybe that's why Auburn's Pelton, who experienced the war in the trenches when he played in the Iron Bowl in the early 1990s, tries to foster a hate for Alabama in the Tigers' defensive linemen he now coaches. Lemonier, Pelton's star player, is from Florida, but it didn't take him long to pick up on Pelton's intense inbred dislike for the Crimson Tide. Living in the state only a short time, he quickly picked up on the culture that surrounds the rivalry and learned to hate Alabama.

Tommy Ford, an Alabama graduate who now works at the University, tries to gain a perspective of the game and writes in his introduction to the book he coauthored with Auburn grad and former AU athletics director David Housel, *Alabama-Auburn Football Rivalry Vault*: "It is indeed a rivalry that transcends all others in all of sports. I like to think I'm a laid-back kind of guy, where wins aren't that big of a deal and losses are not accompanied by the end of the world. Until, that is, I think of 'Punt, 'Bama, Punt' [the 1972 game in which Bill Newton blocked two punts and David Langner scooped both up and ran into the end zone to enable Auburn to come from behind in the last six minutes to beat Alabama 17–16], and then I burn with anger." He also relates that in 1997, when Alabama wasn't very good but came within a minute of upsetting a good Auburn team, he felt so sick he almost threw up on the sideline. The Iron Bowl does that to people who are otherwise well-balanced.

Ford's wife, Robin, is a 1984 Auburn alumna. That makes for an interesting situation when the game is in progress, depending upon which team has the upper hand. Not just in the Ford household, but in many homes and families throughout the state that are divided by what many other people throughout the country think is just a football game. Yeah, right.

Alabama fans not only want their team to win, but want Auburn to lose. With Auburn followers, it's vice versa. The favorite teams of Alabama fans are the Crimson Tide and whoever is playing Auburn. During an Alabama game, when it is announced over the loudspeaker that Auburn has lost, there is a roar that resonates throughout Bryant-Denny Stadium as if the Crimson Tide had just scored a go-ahead touchdown against the No. 1–ranked team in the nation. For Auburn fans, it's the Tigers and any team playing the Crimson Tide. And when the War Eagle crowd is made aware that 'Bama has been beaten, Tigers fans scream and jump for joy in Jordan-Hare Stadium.

Unlike most places, football is king in Alabama. People in the state take a great deal of pride in the success of the state's flagship, championship football team—the University of Alabama Crimson Tide. Whereas the state has been ranked near the bottom in education, behind the times in some other important areas, and ridiculed as being racist, Alabamians can point with pride to the Crimson Tide and say that they are the best in football. And they won't get much of an argument from anyone who has any knowledge of college football. The football tradition that Bear Bryant rebuilt and took to the mountaintop and pretty much kept there for most of two and a half decades instilled pride in the people of the state. And 'Bama fans are not the least bit interested in allowing Auburn to have any success so that they and their fans can share in that pride. No siree.

The magnitude of the game is such that people cannot escape it, even if they are incarcerated. Prisoners remain caught up in it. Jeffrey Addison, an Alabama fan and inmate at the medium security Staton Correctional Facility in Elmore County, told Brad Zimanek of the *Montgomery Advertiser*, "Iron Bowl week here is unreal. It's our version of tailgating," he said in reference to jail-bound fans of both teams eating together to watch the game, with all three televisions tuned in to the contest. Addison estimated that about 70 percent of the inmates are 'Bama fans, about the same proportion as those in the state on the outside. This, despite the fact that Derrick Graves, an Auburn grad and linebacker who played in four and won three Iron Bowls—including in 2004 when the Tigers went undefeated and won the SEC championship—is in Staton serving his fourth year of a 10-year sentence for second-degree rape.

Sometimes an anomaly occurs. Clint Dozier, a huge Alabama fan from Huntsville, said that his father, also a big Tide supporter, has a friend who is an Alabama grad, but his friend's wife went to Auburn. The couple has five children, all of whom are Auburn fans.

Clint and his father wonder, *Where did his friend's father go wrong? How could he let that happen? How did he have so little influence?*

Another factor that magnifies the focus on Alabama and Auburn is that, unlike Ohio State–Michigan, USC-UCLA, and Florida–Florida State, or the Gators and Miami, or the Seminoles-Hurricanes, there is no professional sports team in the state. Football dominates the culture of Alabama in a way unlike other places, affecting the state in ways unimaginable to people who live elsewhere in the country. Some say football is a religion in Alabama. Well, to some people it's more important than religion. To many people it is the biggest, most heated, most hyped rivalry in sports—Yankees–Red Sox and Duke–North Carolina be damned.

People in the state live for the Iron Bowl, a nickname Auburn coach Ralph "Shug" Jordan coined in the 1950s because the Birmingham area was abundant with iron ore. It was a fitting moniker for a game played in Birmingham, at the time a tough, hard-scrabble, working class steel-mill city.

So, in sum, why is the Iron Bowl the best rivalry not only in college football, but in all of sports? The answer is because the hitting on the field is so ferocious, the feelings about the game so intense, and the significance of the outcome so important to the people of the state who are so consumed by it. And they don't apologize for it. They live for it. That and much more makes the Alabama-Auburn rivalry downright nasty and the best in all of sports.

A LITTLE IRON BOWL HISTORY

Football teams from the two schools first played on February 22, 1893, in Birmingham, with Auburn winning 32–22 in front of a little more than 500 people, with 320 from Alabama and 226 from Auburn. See, 'Bama fans say, we had the bigger fan base right from the get-go, and we still control the state. Auburn was and still is second-fiddle.

But trouble began right from the beginning because the schools argued over several things, starting with where the officials would come from, what the per diem stipend would be for players, and how many players would be covered under the per diem. The total per diem difference in the two proposals was only $34, but it was a hurdle that they could not get past. The schools couldn't even agree on whether the game should be counted as part of the 1892 season or the 1893 season, and to this day have it recorded differently in their respective media guides. Alabama lists it as the last game of the 1892 season, and Auburn records it as the first game of the 1893 season. How's that for not seeing eye-to-eye? Future playing dates was another sticky issue that could not be resolved.

On the field, competition was heated from the outset, with the early games marked by roughhouse play and fighting. Auburn enjoyed the upper hand in the early years, winning seven of the first 11 games. But so much bad blood developed that the schools stopped playing each other following a 6–6 stalemate in the 1907 game. Even though Alabama made overtures to resume the series in 1911 and again in 1923, they were rejected by Auburn. The two schools did not play again until 1948.

Between 1907 and 1948, when the schools did not play, Alabama became a national power, while Auburn floundered around in mediocrity. In 1922 the Crimson Tide gained its first national recognition when it defeated the University of Pennsylvania, then an Eastern power, 9–7 in Philadelphia. In 1924 Wallace Wade coached the Crimson Tide to its first Southern Conference Championship and then trumped that the following year by beating Washington 20–19 in the Rose Bowl, giving the University of Alabama its first national championship. In 1926 'Bama won a share of the national championship along with Stanford, Navy, and Lafayette. The Tide squared off against Stanford in the 1927 Rose Bowl, and the two teams battled to a 7–7 deadlock. In 1930 Alabama won its third national championship in six years and again went to the Rose Bowl, where it whitewashed Washington State 24–0.

Meanwhile on the Plains, Auburn was struggling big time, managing only three winning seasons from 1923 through 1931. The Tigers made a huge turnaround in 1932 when they went undefeated (9–0–1) and won the Southern Conference Championship, only to sink back into the pits with only five winning seasons from 1933 through 1948. While the Tigers were wallowing around in the mud, it was high tide across the state where 'Bama was cruising through 14 consecutive winning seasons, capturing four SEC Championships and tacking on two more national titles in 1934 and 1941, the last two under the tutelage of Coach Frank Thomas. The 1934 title was capped with a 29–13 victory over Stanford in the Rose Bowl, and 1941 culminated with a 29–21 win over Texas A&M in the Cotton Bowl.

Whereas Alabama has enjoyed being the dominant football program for decades, Auburn fans suffered and, like red-headed stepchildren, became paranoid.

It took four decades before the two teams finally met again on the football field. And even then legend has it that it took government intervention for the schools to resume play. The Alabama House of Representatives, in December of 1947, passed a resolution that pressured the schools to put aside their differences and compete against each other in football. Less dramatic but closer to reality, Alabama president Dr. John M. Gallalee and Auburn president Dr. Ralph B. Draughon amicably worked out the logistics, agreeing that the game would annually be played in the state's largest stadium, Legion Field in Birmingham, with each school allotted 50 percent of the tickets. A ceremony was held in December 1948 with the presidents of the student bodies of Alabama and Auburn burying

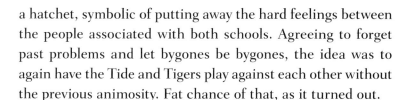

a hatchet, symbolic of putting away the hard feelings between the people associated with both schools. Agreeing to forget past problems and let bygones be bygones, the idea was to again have the Tide and Tigers play against each other without the previous animosity. Fat chance of that, as it turned out.

On December 4, 1948, Alabama and Auburn finally again clashed on the gridiron. Now an established force, the Crimson Tide thrashed the Tigers 55–0, perhaps making Auburn wonder why it ever wanted to again bang heads with 'Bama.

The next year, however, Auburn not only recovered from the thorough beating it received the previous season at the hands of the Tide, but administered a little payback by upsetting UA 14–13. Now that the two state schools were playing each other again, Alabama quickly replaced Georgia Tech as the Tigers' top rival.

After being nipped by the Tigers, the Tide beat Auburn four straight times. After falling to the basement of the SEC, Auburn in 1951 brought in alum Ralph "Shug" Jordan, who turned the program around. Across the state, things had taken a downturn during the "Ears" Whitworth era, enabling Jordan to guide the Tigers to five straight wins, culminating in the national championship in 1957. Auburn was king of the hill, but it's reign as state champion would be brief.

With 'Bama replacing Auburn as a conference bottom-feeder, Alabama reached out to one of its own, Paul Bryant, who had turned around the Texas A&M program. "When Mama called," the Bear returned to Tuscaloosa in 1958. Soon after, there was a changing of the guard.

The year was 1961. John F. Kennedy was president of the United States, Chubby Checker introduced the country to a new dance craze called "the Twist," and Roger Maris broke Babe Ruth's major league home run record. But down in Tuscaloosa, talk was mostly of a football team that week after week was winning football games. The Crimson Tide recorded six shutouts, outscored its opponents 297–25, and beat Arkansas in the Sugar Bowl to win the national championship, Bryant's first. It had been a while, but the Crimson Tide was again sitting squarely on top of the college football world. The rest, as they say, is history, as Bryant went on to dominate the decades of the 1960s and 1970s.

BRYANT ERA COMES TO AN END

In the 1980s, when Bryant was nearing the end of his illustrious career, Pat Dye was starting out at Auburn and Ray Perkins was about to take over in Tuscaloosa. Another shift of power was about to occur.

Dye, a former assistant to Bryant at Alabama, was named head coach at Auburn in 1981. The tide had indeed turned, especially in the heated Alabama-Auburn rivalry. Auburn enjoyed a stretch where they beat the Crimson Tide four consecutive times and six of nine times since Dye took over the Tigers' program. Auburn not only got the best of Alabama during the decade of the '80s, but enjoyed a pretty good run against the rest of the Southeastern Conference as well. Going into the 1991 season, Dye had won four SEC Championships and taken the Tigers to nine bowl games, while compiling an 89–28–3 record.

CONTROVERSY OVER LEGION FIELD

Meanwhile, however, off-the-field tensions mounted as the two schools became embroiled over the site of the Iron Bowl. After Alabama and Auburn resumed play in 1948, the Iron Bowl for many years was played in Birmingham, considered a neutral site. Whereas both teams had once played a few games each season in Legion Field, Auburn had stopped doing so in 1989 when Jordan-Hare Stadium had been expanded to 85,000, making it larger than 75,808-seat Legion Field, even when Legion Field was enlarged to hold 84,000 people. During that era the Tide continued to annually play three or four of its biggest home games there, with Legion Field actually being another home field for Alabama.

A brouhaha developed in 1987 when Auburn proposed playing its home game with Alabama every other year at Jordan-Hare. Alabama balked at the idea. The schools pulled out their contracts for the game and found that the specifics were unclear, since Bear Bryant and longtime friend Shug Jordan more or less made informal agreements. There was a question regarding the legality of the agreement, and lawyers became involved. It seemed to be a matter of interpretation.

Of course, each school interpreted it their own way.

The presidents of the two institutions could get no further than the athletics directors in settling the dispute. Politicians got into the act. It became a stalemate. There were several sides to the issue, which dragged out for a couple of years. Auburn said it had a bigger stadium and had the right to play its home games, including the Alabama game, on campus. UA shot back that Auburn depended upon the Alabama home game to help sell its season-ticket package and thus fill Jordan-Hare. Auburn said Legion Field was no longer a neutral site since the Crimson Tide continued to play there regularly, including their entire 1987 home schedule while Bryant-Denny in Tuscaloosa was being renovated and enlarged. Alabama said the game belonged to the people of the state and argued that the tradition of playing in Birmingham with an evenly split crowd be maintained.

The issue became so hotly contested that UA president Joab Thomas, in an attempt to take the edge off, proposed the series be played on a rotating basis, rather than every year.

The proposal, which didn't get to first base, died because it meant the two teams would meet about four times every six years. It never had a chance. What would some Tide-Tigers psychos live for during the years the two teams did not meet?

After much bickering, which was played out in the press, a compromise was reached. An historic chapter in the Alabama-Auburn football story was written, but the scene was in a boardroom somewhere and not on the gridiron where so many other UA-AU sagas had unfolded.

Auburn won the right to play its home games with Alabama at Jordan-Hare every other year, beginning in 1993. Auburn also got to play its 1989 home game in Auburn, on the condition that the 1990, '91, and '92 games be played in Birmingham. It was called a compromise, but Alabama fans—especially the "Alabama Football Family," considered it a total loss. Apparently

so did the *Birmingham News/Post Herald* that ran a headline: "Auburn Gets Last Laugh in Iron Bowl Dispute."

To get what it wanted, Auburn made a concession by agreeing to play its 1991 home game at Legion Field. Or as Auburn coach Pat Dye purportedly said, "We had to throw them a bone."

With the new arrangement each visiting team would only get 10,900 tickets, instead of the 50-50 split.

Alabama athletics director Steve Sloan took it on the chin from alumni, fans, and especially players, who at the time likened it to selling ammunition to Saddam Hussein. "Playing Auburn in Auburn had to happen sometime, but agreeing to it is what got Steve Sloan in trouble," stated former Alabama star lineman Billy Neighbors.

Alabama fans simply could not fathom playing the game "down on the farm." When the Iron Bowl was played at Legion Field, Birmingham swelled with fans from both teams who flocked to the city. The Tide and the Tiger, the bar across the street from the stadium, used to burst at the seams as supporters from each school crammed the tiny pub, partied, and whooped it up before the game.

Alabama had compiled a 32–15 record in the games played at Legion Field.

During the 1980s, for the most part, Alabama was looking into the eye of the Tiger, and sometimes found itself between its teeth. But Gene Stallings, hired in 1990, grabbed the whip hand, tamed the Tigers, and regained control of the fiercely fought series. That only served as a prelude for what would come—winning the national championship in 1992 and defeating AU five of seven times.

Terry Bowden succeeded Dye and went undefeated in 1993. A little problem was that Auburn was on probation and ineligible for the BCS national championship. 'Bama fans had a good laugh over that one.

Bowden won three of five Iron Bowls, but became embroiled in turmoil and stepped down under pressure toward the end of the 1998 season. Bill "Brother" Oliver, another former Alabama player and assistant coach, replaced Bowden and promptly lost his only game against his alma mater. Across the state, Mike DuBose, also a UA alum, followed Stallings and split four Iron Bowls. Tommy Tuberville replaced Bowden in 1999 and lost two of his first three Iron Bowls, before winning six straight from 2002 through 2007. When he won his fifth consecutive game over Alabama, Tuberville pissed Tide fans off by raising his hand and proclaiming, "One for the thumb."

Nick Saban snapped the streak, but not before losing his first game against Auburn and Tuberville. In his third season in 2009, Saban, with Heisman Trophy winner Mark Ingram leading the way, beat Auburn and then won the national championship by beating Texas.

Gene Chizik, brought on board when Tuberville took the Texas Tech job in 2009, did likewise at Auburn in 2010. With Heisman Trophy winner Cam Newton at the controls, the Tigers, trailing 24–0, came from behind to stick the Tide to the disgust of a full-house in Bryant-Denny Stadium. Auburn then went on to defeat Oregon in the BCS National Championship Game, much to the chagrin of 'Bama fans.

Then last year, Saban, riding Trent Richardson and his stable of running backs, pulverized Chizik and his Plainsmen 42–14, and in doing so reminded them where football superiority in the state rightfully belongs. After dropping Auburn a few—no, make that several—pegs, the Crimson Tide smashed LSU to smithereens to win yet another national championship. The 'Bama Nation could almost hear Auburn fans bellowing, "Oh no, not another run of Alabama Iron Bowl wins and Crimson Tide national championships."

1
WE LOVE BEATING AUBURN

FOLLOWING ARE SOME Iron Bowl games that 'Bama fans particularly love. People in 'Bama Nation will differ on which games are "most loved" and which are their favorites, in part dependent on their age and what they remember. Baby boomers and above are perhaps particularly fond of the Bryant years, whereas younger 'Bama fans identify with and probably relish the more recent Auburn conquests. A couple of colleagues in the media and some members of the Tuscaloosa Quarterback Club assisted in the selection and ranking of the games. It doesn't really make much difference, because Tide fans love it any and every time 'Bama beats Auburn.

1985: ALABAMA 25, AUBURN 23

This game, the 50th installment of the cross-state rivalry, will always be remembered for "the Kick," when Van Tiffin nailed a 52-yard field goal as time ran out to give the Crimson Tide a dramatic 25–23 win over Auburn. It doesn't get much better than that for 'Bama fans who like to see Auburn fans suffer. Beating the Tigers in the final seconds on the final play of the game is like dangling a piece of meat in front of the hungry Tigers and then watching their pain and anguish as you pull the food away at the last second.

"To get an opportunity in a big game like that, and then to come through, that's the dream of every kicker," stated Tiffin. "That's my greatest thrill, one that I'll never forget." Nor will Crimson Tide fans since the moment is forever saved, thanks to a painting by renowned artist Daniel A. Moore simply and succinctly called *The Kick*.

Auburn's Bo Jackson had a good day, carrying the ball 31 times for 142 yards and two touchdowns, but 'Bama's Gene Jelks had a better one, rushing 18 times for 192 yards and one touchdown. Jelks' touchdown, however, was a 74-yard jaunt with just under five minutes left in the game that put the Tide ahead 22–17. Auburn countered with an 11-play, 70-yard march down the field that not only resulted in the go-ahead touchdown, a one-yard blast to paydirt by Reggie Ware, but also ate precious time off the clock.

Crimson Tide quarterback Mike Shula literally threw his way into the school record book. He came through again in 'Bama's biggest of games. The son of former Miami Dolphins Hall of Fame coaching legend Don Shula, Mike completed a 16-yard pass to Jelks and a 19-yard pass to Greg Richardson in a six-play, 45-yard drive that set up Tiffin's game-winning boot.

With the lead changing hands four times in the fourth quarter, the game dripped with drama. "It's one of the greatest games that I've ever been associated with," said ecstatic Alabama coach Ray Perkins, who, as a former player at the Capstone, knew as well as anybody how much a victory over hated Auburn meant.

TOP 5 'BAMA PASSING GAMES OF ALL-TIME

1. **Scott Hunter** | 484 yards | 1969
   vs. Auburn

2. **Jay Barker** | 396 yards | 1994
   vs. Georgia

3. **Gary Hollingsworth** | 379 yards | 1989
   vs. Tennessee

4. **Greg McElroy** | 377 yards | 2010
   vs. Auburn

5. **Mike Shula** | 367 yards | 1985
   vs. Memphis State

ALABAMA

We need to backpedal a little bit here for perspective. In 1984 Alabama had suffered its first losing season in 27 years. The Crimson Tide opened the 1985 season on Labor Day in Athens, Georgia, where UA had a 13–9 lead with under a minute remaining in the game. Then things suddenly turned bleak for 'Bama. Bulldogs linebacker Terrie Webster blocked Chris Mohr's punt, and Georgia's Calvin Ruff fell on the football in the end zone for an apparent 16–13 Georgia win. Samford Stadium rocked with joy, and the jubilant Bulldogs joined in the victory celebration, to the point that Georgia got penalized 15 yards for delay of game.

As it turned out, the celebration was premature. Trailing by three with 50 seconds to go, Shula quarterbacked the Tide 71 yards in five plays to pull the bone out of the Bulldogs' mouth. Shula calmly connected with Richardson on two long passes and then, with 15 seconds showing on the scoreboard clock, found flanker Albert Bell in the end zone for the game-winning touchdown. The sensational win over Georgia jumpstarted 'Bama's season and got the Tide back on the winning track.

After a one-year absence, Alabama was again bowl-bound, this time to sunny Hawaii, where they would dismantle the USC Trojans 24–3 in the Aloha Bowl. And if the loss didn't hurt Southern Cal enough, the Tide salted the bruises by winning its 21st bowl game at the Trojans' expense, tying USC's national record.

TOP 5 LONGEST FIELD GOALS MADE

1. **Van Tiffin** | 57 yards | 1985
   vs. Texas A&M

2. **Ryan Pflugner** | 55 yards | 1998
   vs. Arkansas

3. **Leigh Tiffin** | 54 yards | 2008
   vs. Clemson

4t. **Michael Proctor** | 53 yards | 1993
   vs. Mississippi

   Van Tiffin | 53 yards | 1984
   vs. Penn State

   Philip Doyle | 53 yards | 1988
   vs. Temple

(Pflugner, Leigh Tiffin, and Proctor kicked without a kicking tee.)

ALABAMA

Alabama, beginning with its exciting upset win at Georgia in the season opener and closing with a classic 11th-hour victory over Auburn, endeared itself to Crimson Tide fans everywhere. Even Perkins, who never seemed to be bothered by his critics, had to feel the 9–2–1 season topped off by the big win over Auburn and the bowl win over USC turned down the thermostat a bit.

1967: ALABAMA 7, AUBURN 3

This game is known as "Stabler's Run in the Mud." December 2, 1967, was a miserable day weather-wise and, for the most part, for Alabama on the field. It was a dark, dreary, blustery, stormy day with stinging rain and gusty winds. The field was drenched from heavy downpours that made playing conditions terrible and footing treacherous.

The result was that the Tide and Tigers traded punts for much of the game, although Auburn was in control of the contest, if not on the scoreboard. In the early going the Tigers drove to the Alabama 5-yard line. An incomplete pass and two one-yard runs left them facing a fourth-and-goal situation at the 3-yard line. Rather than kick a field goal, Auburn ran Richard Plagge, who was stopped at the 2-yard line by Dickie Thompson and Mike Hall. On its next possession, Auburn tried a field goal, which was short and wide. Auburn squandered another scoring opportunity when, again forgoing a field goal from chip-shot range, it went for it on fourth-and-2 from the 6-yard line. Roger Griffin ran the ball but came up a yard short. Despite Auburn getting inside the red zone three times, the game was scoreless at the half.

Auburn managed to get on the scoreboard in the third quarter when Mike Riley kicked a 38-yard field goal. The Tigers then failed to take advantage of still another scoring opportunity when they recovered a fumble at the Alabama 23-yard line, but couldn't make a first down. A fumbled snap botched a field-goal attempt.

Meanwhile, Alabama's offense was dormant. It was the third quarter, the Tide only had two first downs, and had only just advanced the ball past midfield. Yet 'Bama only trailed by three points.

Auburn threatened again, getting to the Alabama 12-yard line before the drive was stalled by a 15-yard penalty. Instead of a first down at the 15, it was third down at the 32. Auburn tried to punt, but because of a low snap the punter was smothered by the Crimson Tide.

With 11:29 left in the fourth quarter and Alabama's chances of winning looking as bleak as the weather, quarterback Kenny Stabler, confronted with a third-and-3 situation, called an option sweep, and took off on his famous 47-yard touchdown "run in the mud" that for War Eagle fans must have felt like surreal, slow-motion agony.

Auburn, in complete command of the game up to that point, now found itself behind 7–3. 'Bama hung on to win, and for Crimson Tide fans it seemed like the sun popped out from behind the dark clouds. Under the circumstances, the loss was a bitter pill for Auburn to swallow, especially for its seniors who over their four-year careers not only failed to

TOP 5 RUSHING GAMES OF ALL-TIME

1. **Shaun Alexander** | 291 yards | 1996
   vs. LSU

2. **Bobby Humphrey** | 284 yards | 1986
   vs. Mississippi State

3. **Mark Ingram** | 246 yards | 2009
   vs. South Carolina

4. **Bobby Marlow** | 233 yards | 1951
   vs. Auburn

5. **Johnny Musso** | 221 yards | 1970
   vs. Auburn

ALABAMA

beat Alabama, but couldn't even score a touchdown against the Crimson Tide.

After the game a disappointed Shug Jordan remarked, "I don't think the best team won today." Bear Bryant agreed that the Tide was very fortunate to come out on top. "Yes, we were lucky to win the game," he admitted. "What else do you want me to say?"

The Tide managed only four first downs to Auburn's 13, and punted 13 times to the Tigers' 10. But the only numbers that counted—and mattered—to Alabama fans were 7 and 3, the final score.

What makes the game so satisfying for 'Bama fans is not just that Alabama won, but the way they won. It was like punching Auburn in the stomach. Stealing the game just added misery to the War Eagle woes, making Tide fans everywhere all the more merrier.

Alabama went to the Cotton Bowl and finished 8–2–1, while Auburn settled for a 6–4 campaign.

1971: ALABAMA 31, AUBURN 7

This was the only time that both teams entered the Iron Bowl undefeated and untied. On a Thursday night, Auburn's Pat Sullivan was awarded the Heisman Trophy. He, his Tigers teammates, and War Eagle fans were as happy as a pig in poop. Two days later it was as if the pig had become the bacon that Alabama had for breakfast as Johnny Musso and Alabama's wishbone offense annihilated Auburn 31–7. Musso rushed for

ALABAMA

TOP 5 TOUCHDOWNS SCORED *IN A* SEASON

1. **Shaun Alexander** | 24 | 1999
2. **Trent Richardson** | 21 | 2011
3. **Mark Ingram** | 20 | 2009
4. **Siran Stacy** | 18 | 1989
5*t.* **Shaun Alexander** | 17 | 1998
    Bobby Humphrey | 17 | 1986

Johnny Musso picks up yardage against Auburn.

167 yards and completely outplayed Sullivan as the Crimson Tide cruised to an unexpectedly easy romp over the Tigers.

Well, for Auburn fans, the lopsided score at least quickly put them out of their misery.

However, both teams lost in their bowl games, Alabama getting embarrassed by Nebraska 38–6 in the Orange Bowl and Auburn 40–22 by Oklahoma in the Sugar Bowl. Still, the Crimson Tide won the Iron Bowl.

1981: ALABAMA 28, AUBURN 17

Alabama fans especially love this game because it gave Bear Bryant his 315th win, which enabled the iconic coach to become the winningest coach in NCAA Division I-A history. They get added joy because the historic victory came at the expense of Auburn. That's two good reasons to love this game.

This was Pat Dye's first year as Auburn's head coach. He had served as an assistant on Bryant's staff for eight years. The protégé was facing the master in what would be a notable game. Alabama was 8–1–1 and ranked fourth in the country. Auburn was mediocre at 5–5.

Similar to 1967 when Auburn threatened on several occasions and had little or nothing to show for it, the Tigers in 1981 got inside the Alabama 10-yard line four times but came away with only 10 points. The game was tied at the half 7–7, and again at 14–14 in the third quarter. Al Del Greco made a field goal to give the War Eagles a 17–14 lead going into the fourth quarter.

A 38-yard touchdown pass from Walter Lewis to Jesse Bendross put 'Bama back in front 21–17. Alabama hung on to win 28–17 to give Bryant the victory that broke Amos Alonzo Stagg's all-time win mark. Following the game, Bryant took congratulatory telephone calls from President Ronald Reagan and former President Jimmy Carter.

The Crimson Tide went to the Cotton Bowl, where after leading Texas 10–0 entering the fourth quarter, it fell to the Longhorns 14–12. Alabama finished 9–2–1 and No. 7 nationally. Auburn was finished after the loss to 'Bama, ending the season with a losing 5–6 record.

1974: ALABAMA 17, AUBURN 13

The 1974 Iron Bowl was a matchup of top 10 teams, undefeated and No. 2 ranked Alabama (10–0) against once-beaten and seventh-ranked Auburn (9–1). Moreover, the game was for the SEC title and a Sugar Bowl berth. It was played on Friday of Thanksgiving weekend.

With Richard Todd directing the Tide attack and Calvin Culliver running the football, Alabama built a 17–7 halftime lead. However, with just under two minutes remaining in the game, AU closed the gap by scoring a touchdown on a fake field goal to pull within 17–13.

With 1:07 to go, Alabama lined up in punt formation. Seeing flashbacks of the "Punt, 'Bama, Punt" game of just two years earlier, 'Bama fans were biting their nails. For those fans who forgot, they were quickly reminded as some Auburn fans serenaded them with "Punt, 'Bama, Punt!"

Auburn wasn't able to block the punt, but the pressure the Tigers applied forced a 27-yard punt. Following a three-yard return to the AU 49-yard line, Auburn had time for one play. An end around by Dan Nugent blew up when Mike DuBose knocked the ball loose and then fell on it to preserve the win.

Alabama went to the Orange Bowl for a rematch with Notre Dame, the Fighting Irish having edged the Crimson Tide 24–23 the year before in the Sugar Bowl. Notre Dame again came out on top with another narrow victory, 13–11. The win tarnished the national title that had already been bestowed upon the Crimson Tide by UPI prior to the bowl season. It was also Alabama's eighth straight bowl game without a victory, again tarnishing the sterling 43–1 regular season record that 'Bama had compiled over the previous four years. Auburn played Texas in the Gator Bowl and won 27–3.

2011: ALABAMA 42, AUBURN 14

The Iron Bowl is always a huge game, and the events that occurred the previous week made this one even bigger. The Crimson Tide entered the previous week ranked behind LSU and Oklahoma State in the BCS poll, but that Friday night Alabama got the help that it needed when double-digit underdog Iowa State stunned the Cowboys 37–31 in two overtimes, setting up 'Bama for a likely rematch with LSU in the BCS Championship Game if only they could get by the Tigers.

The only thing between Alabama and the probable national championship game against LSU was hated Auburn. As long as the Tide didn't stub its toe against the Tigers, it would most likely get another shot at the team that a few weeks earlier defeated them 9–6 in overtime in Tuscaloosa.

But first things first. There was that little matter of that game coming up on the Plains. The game for the "state championship" is a year-round obsession for people living in the state,

Alabama running back Trent Richardson (3) puts a move on an Auburn defensive back in the second half of the Tide's 42–14 victory in the 2011 Iron Bowl at Auburn's Jordan-Hare Stadium. Photo courtesy of AP Images

anyway, but for the fourth year in a row the outcome of the game could derail the title hopes of one of the contestants. ESPN's *College GameDay* was coming to Auburn, and the all-sports network had recently ran the documentary *Roll Tide/War Eagle.*

Auburn coach Gene Chizik put it this way: "In-state [the Iron Bowl] is always about as big as you can get. I think from a national perspective, you know the fact that we both won a national championship in the last two years has probably given it some extra attention."

UA linebacker Dont'a Hightower said the game just revs you up and can catapult you on to bigger and better things. "You get all the energy up for that game, and then you win that game, so you go off and have so much steam [that it carries over to] the SEC championship and then the national championship."

In addition, signs posted around the UA football complex reading "Never Again" constantly reminded the Crimson Tide players of the colossal collapse that they experienced the year before when 'Bama blew a 24–0 lead and lost.

In the week leading up to the game, there were also signs posted in Auburn around Toomer's Corner. With a picture of Harvey Updyke, the man who angered Auburn fans by poisoning the oak trees there, the signs stated: "Wanted: For

ALABAMA

TOP 5 PASSING YARDS IN A SEASON

1. **Greg McElroy** | 2,987 yards | 2010

2. **John Parker Wilson** | 2,846 yards | 2007

3. **John Parker Wilson** | 2,707 yards | 2006

4. **A.J. McCarron** | 2,634 yards | 2011

5. **Greg McElroy** | 2,508 yards | 2009

Murder of Our Beloved Oak Trees. Also Wanted for Having Too Much 'Bama in Him, and for Six Other Felony Charges but He Claims 13"—the latter a dig at the Crimson Tide's claim of 13 national championships.

All that just added to the buildup.

Whereas the Tide was again riding high, Auburn was only a shell of the team that had won the national championship the year before. The Tigers were 7–4 and nowhere near the force they were when Heisman Trophy winner Cam Newton led the offense and Lombardi winner Nick Fairley spearheaded the defense that beat everybody, including UA in that shocking 28–27 come-from-behind win over the Crimson Tide. Eighteen starters were gone from that team.

Consequently the Tigers had already taken it on the chin to the tune of 45–10 against LSU, 38–14 against Arkansas, and 45–7 against Georgia. The three losses were on the road when the Razorbacks were ranked No. 10, the Bayou Tigers No. 1, and the Bulldogs No. 14. In addition to losing, Auburn wasn't even competitive.

Regardless, as it did the three previous years, the Iron Bowl had BCS national championship implications for one of the teams. In 2009 Auburn was set on ruining Alabama's season until late in the fourth quarter when Roy Upchurch scored to put the nail in the Tigers' coffin. In 2010 UA shot out to a 24–0 first-half lead and appeared set to blow up Auburn's dream season before Cam Newton rallied the Tigers to an improbable comeback victory.

In the 2011 Iron Bowl, the score at the half was Alabama 24, Auburn 7, the same as it was the year before. But in 2011 the Tigers didn't have Newton, Fairley, and the others to bring them back, so they went down hard to the Tide, 42–14, in the most lopsided Iron Bowl played in Jordan-Hare Stadium.

Auburn's offense was inept against Alabama's No. 1–ranked run defense, which had allowed only three rushing touchdowns all season. The Plainsmen got their two touchdowns when Kenneth Carter fell on AJ McCarron's fumble in the end zone and when Onterio McCalebb raced 83 yards with a kickoff return.

Clint Moseley, who passed for only 62 yards, summed up the Tigers' offensive effort in futility when he said, "As a quarterback, when the bright spot of your day is a punt, it's never a good thing."

Trent Richardson rambled for a career-high 203 yards and caught a five-yard touchdown pass to bolster his Heisman chances, and AJ McCarron completed 18 of 23 passes for 184 yards and a school Iron Bowl record–tying three touchdown passes as the No. 2 Crimson Tide destroyed the Tigers. In doing so, 'Bama also ended Auburn's 14-game home winning streak.

Besides improving Alabama's lead in the Iron Bowl series to 41–34–1, 'Bama fans love this game because it also propelled the Crimson Tide into the BCS National Championship Game against LSU. Also because it's the latest Iron Bowl, memories are fresh, and it again gave Tide fans bragging rights heading into next year.

TOP 5 FIELD GOALS MADE IN A CAREER

1. **Leigh Tiffin** | 83 | 2006–2009
2. **Philip Doyle** | 78 | 1987–1990
3. **Michael Proctor** | 65 | 1992–1995
4. **Van Tiffin** | 59 | 1983–1986
5. **Brian Bostick** | 38 | 2002–2004

ALABAMA

1994: ALABAMA 21, AUBURN 14

This was a showdown game that would have national repercussions. Alabama and Auburn both came into the game undefeated, Alabama sporting a No. 4 national ranking and Auburn No. 6. The Crimson Tide bolted to a commanding 21–0 lead at the half. However, the Tigers came back to make a game of it as Patrick Nix guided AU to two second-half touchdowns. The game went down to the wire. Auburn advanced the ball to the Tide 40-yard line. With less than a minute to go, Auburn was behind and needed a touchdown to win. On fourth down and needing three yards for a first down, Auburn called for a pass. 'Bama's defense stiffened as the Tide's Sam Shade drilled the Auburn receiver right at the first-down marker. The spot was crucial, and the officials ruled the Tigers were stopped an inch short. Shade's tackle preserved a 21–14 victory.

Another fun day for Tide fans.

1996: ALABAMA 24, AUBURN 23

In a seesaw affair, Alabama shot out to a 17-point lead in the first half, only to watch Auburn score 23 unanswered points to go out in front. Embattled Alabama quarterback Freddie Kitchens threw a six-yard touchdown pass to Dennis Riddle with 26 seconds to go to tie the score. Jon Brock then booted the all-important extra point for a topsy-turvy 24–23 victory at Legion Field that enabled the Crimson Tide to continue on to the SEC Championship Game.

After the game, Gene Stallings announced that he would resign following 'Bama's bowl game against Michigan. The Tide defeated the Wolverines 17–14 in the Outback Bowl to send Stallings out a winner.

2001: ALABAMA 31, AUBURN 7

This was Dennis Franchione's first season as Alabama coach. The Crimson Tide, 4–5, was a heavy underdog, so much so that only one sportswriter in the entire state predicted an Alabama victory. And rightfully so, since Auburn had a 7–2 record, was playing at home, and only needed to beat 'Bama to win the SEC West and advance to the SEC title game.

Long story short. Andrew Zow started for an injured Tyler Watts and had a big game, Santonio Beard rushed for 199 yards, and Ahmaad Galloway added another 127 yards as Alabama trounced the Plainsmen 31–7.

Alabama fans loved this one because most didn't expect it. Therefore it was a very pleasant surprise.

Gene Stallings looks on as Alabama's Jon Brock kicks the extra point to give the Tide a 24–23 win over Auburn at Legion Field on November 23, 1996. Stallings announced his retirement after the game. Photo courtesy of AP Images

1984: ALABAMA 17, AUBURN 15

Alabama had a 4–6 record in 1984 and was looking to beat Auburn in order to salvage some satisfaction from the season at the expense of the Tigers, who were preseason favorites to win the national championship before Bo Jackson got hurt and a few other things went wrong. Alabama did just that, beating Auburn 17–15 and thus relegating the Tigers to the Liberty Bowl.

Almost as much as they get giddy over 'Bama victories and successes, Tide fans revel in Auburn losses and in any disappointments that the losses may incur. So this was a double bonus of sorts, sticking the Tigers plus helping send Auburn to a bottom-of-the-barrel bowl after they were projected to be the best team in the country at the beginning of the season.

Late in the fourth quarter, Auburn, trailing 17–15, got the turnover it needed on an interception, giving the Tigers the ball on the Alabama 17-yard line. The Tigers were now in a position to win. Six plays later and with 3:27 left in the game, Auburn had a fourth-and-goal situation from the Alabama 1-yard line. Rejecting a chip-shot field goal, Auburn coach Pat Dye decided to go for the touchdown. The call was for Brent Fullwood to skirt right end, with Jackson the lead blocker. The only problem was that Jackson, who had rushed for 118 yards, went left instead of right. With nobody there to pick him up, 'Bama defensive back Rory Turner flattened Fullwood for a three-yard loss.

After the game, an elated Turner stated, in words that would be in headlines in Sunday morning's *Tuscaloosa News*, "I waxed that dude!"

"If I had known Bo was going to go the wrong way on the sweep, I'd have called for a field goal," said Dye in his postgame remarks. In the minds of Alabama fans, Iron Bowl 2 A.B. (After Bryant) will always be identified and remembered as "Wrong Way Bo."

TOP 5 INTERCEPTIONS *IN A* SEASON

1. **Cecil "Hootie" Ingram** | 10 | 1952
2t. **Harry Gilmer** | 8 | 1946

    Robert Lester | 8 | 2010

4t. **Steve Higginbotham** | 7 | 1971

    Jeremiah Castile | 7 | 1982

    Antonio Langham | 7 | 1993

    Kevin Jackson | 7 | 1996

    Mark Barron | 7 | 2009

A L A B A M A

A joke came out after the game: "Did you hear about the new Bo Jackson doll? Just wind it up and it runs the wrong way." Another had Coach Pat Dye, before the play, looking up to God and asking, "Lord, which way should we run, left or right?" God answered, "Run right." After Fullwood got smashed, Dye asked, "God, why did you tell me to run right?" God said He didn't know and turned to the gentleman seated next to him and asked, "Bear, why did we tell Pat to run right?"

Another joke, a zinger at Auburn being relegated to the Liberty Bowl where they went and beat Arkansas 21–15, went: "Want to get to Memphis? Go to the 1-yard line at Legion Field and take a right."

Such things are part of this classic intrastate rivalry.

1992: ALABAMA 17, AUBURN 0

With the game scoreless, Antonio Langham got a pick-six when he intercepted a pass thrown by AU quarterback Stan White and returned it 61 yards for a touchdown. The Crimson Tide went on to win 17–0, giving Gene Stallings his third consecutive win in the Iron Bowl.

The 'Bama Nation loved it because that was something previous coach Bill Curry couldn't do, having gone 0–3 against the War Eagles prior to Stallings' arrival at the Capstone. Crimson Tide fans also loved it because it kept Alabama undefeated and enabled UA go to the SEC Championship Game where it defeated Florida 28–21, and then on to the Sugar Bowl where it mauled top-ranked Miami 34–13. Since it was Alabama's first national championship since 1978, 'Bama Nation loved that a lot!

WE LOVE TO SHUT OUT OTHER TEAMS

MOST SHUTOUTS IN A SEASON:

8 1930, 1925, 1920

7 1924, 1919

6 1966, 1961, 1937, 1933, 1926, 1923, 1909, 1905

5 1979, 1960, 1954, 1942, 1938, 1936, 1934, 1931, 1928, 1917, 1915, 1914, 1913, 1907, 1904

4 1975, 1973, 1962, 1959, 1944, 1940, 1939, 1935

ALABAMA

1964: ALABAMA 21, AUBURN 14

The 1964 Iron Bowl was a thriller with Alabama winning a 21–14 decision and, in so doing, winning its second national championship for Bryant. The Crimson Tide came into the contest undefeated, winning its games pretty decisively, with its closest game being a 17–14 win over Florida. Auburn entered with a 6–3 record.

The better team won. Alabama went to the Orange Bowl where they lost to Texas 21–17. That's still better than the Tigers, who stayed home for the holidays.

1965: ALABAMA 30, AUBURN 3

'Bama Nation loves this game because the Crimson Tide soundly defeated the Tigers 30–3 en route to winning its third national championship under Bryant. It took a 39–28 victory over Nebraska in the Orange Bowl to ensure the Tide another national title since the Associated Press voted for the national champion after the bowl games. Auburn finished with a 5–5–1 record, 4–2–1 in the SEC. That was good enough to go to the Liberty Bowl, where the Tigers lost to Ole Miss 13–7.

1973: ALABAMA 35, AUBURN 0

The Crimson Tide came into the game with an 10–0 record. Auburn had a 6–4 record. The Tide was No. 1 in the nation, and the Tigers were eighth in the Southeastern Conference. The year after "Punt, 'Bama, Punt," behind the quarter-backing of Richard Todd, the 'Bama Nation took delight in crushing Auburn 35–0.

ALABAMA

TOP 5 RUSHING YARDS IN A SEASON

1. **Trent Richardson** | 1,679 yards | 2011
2. **Mark Ingram** | 1,658 yards | 2009
3. **Bobby Humphrey** | 1,471 yards | 1986
4. **Shaun Alexander** | 1,383 yards | 1999
5. **Glenn Coffee** | 1,383 yards | 2008

The score was 14–0 at the half, and things only got worse for the War Eagles in the second half. During the season Alabama scored 454 points and only gave up 89 points en route to the UPI national championship. Notre Dame put a blemish on the season, however, saddling the Crimson Tide with a 24–23 loss in the Sugar Bowl.

Noteworthy is that Bill Davis, who kicked from 1971 through 1973, became the third of the place-kicking Davis brothers to score points against Auburn. Tim kicked from 1961 through 1963, Steve from 1965 through 1967, and Mike kicked in 1975. Combined, the Davis brothers were a pain in the butt for Auburn, accounting for 36 points against the Plainsmen by converting six field goals and 24 extra points.

2008: ALABAMA 36, AUBURN 0

Besides walloping the War Eagles, what made this another biggie was that it was Alabama's first victory over Auburn at Bryant-Denny Stadium. Furthermore, the convincing shutout ended a six-year losing streak in the series. On top of that, the victory clinched a spot in the SEC title game.

A lot of reasons for 'Bama faithful to love this victory.

1999: ALABAMA 28, AUBURN 17

Alabama had lost to Auburn four straight times in Jordan-Hare Stadium. And with the Tide trailing 14–6 in the third quarter, it looked like it might be five straight times. But Tyler Watts replaced Andrew Zow at quarterback and guided UA to the Auburn 6-yard line. Star running back Shaun Alexander, however, was stopped short of the end zone on four consecutive carries, and it looked like the Plainsmen had taken the air out of UA. But, on the very next play, 'Bama sacked Auburn quarterback Ben Leard in the end zone for a safety, and suddenly 'Bama was back in business.

After Alabama received the ball following the safety, Alexander took over the game. He spearheaded a touchdown drive that put the Crimson Tide in front 15–14 and scored two more touchdowns in the fourth quarter to give UA a 28–17 win. Alexander completed his day's work with 182 yards rushing and three touchdowns. After four losses, Alabama had finally beat Auburn in Jordan-Hare Stadium. The Crimson Tide then defeated Florida to finish as SEC champions.

1948: ALABAMA 55, AUBURN 0

The significance of this game is that it was the first game played between Alabama and Auburn in 41 years. After years of political bickering, the highly anticipated contest took place at Legion Field in Birmingham. Alabama fans who remember this game include it in their "love" list because the Crimson Tide torched the Tigers 55–0, slapping the War Eagles with their worst loss since 1917. 'Bama beat Auburn so convincingly that Auburn probably wished that the series had stayed dormant. So what is there not to like about that?

1950: ALABAMA 30, AUBURN 0

Bobby Marlow scored three touchdowns in Alabama's 34–0 win that avenged the 14–13 upset loss to Auburn the year before. The Tigers finished 0–10 for the only time in school history. 'Bama fans were happy about that as well.

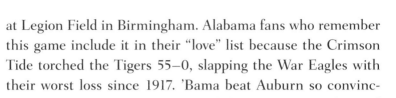

WE LOVE THE IRON BOWL RESULTS
ALABAMA LEADS THE SERIES OVER AUBURN 41–34–1

Date	Winner	Score	Site
2/22/1893	Auburn	32–22	Lakeview Baseball Park, Birmg.
11/30/1893	Auburn	40–16	Riverside Park, Montgomery
11/29/1894	**Alabama**	18–0	Riverside Park, Montgomery
11/23/1895	Auburn	48–0	Tuscaloosa
11/17/1900	Auburn	53–5	Montgomery
11/15/1901	Auburn	17–0	Tuscaloosa
10/18/1902	Auburn	23–0	West End Park, Birmingham
10/23/1903	**Alabama**	18–6	Highland Park, Montgomery
11/12/1904	Auburn	29–5	West End Park, Birmingham
11/18/1905	**Alabama**	30–0	West End Park, Birmingham
11/17/1906	**Alabama**	10–0	Birmingham Fair Grounds
11/16/1907	(Tie)	6–6	Birmingham Fair Grounds
12/4/1948	**Alabama**	55–0	Legion Field, Birmingham
12/3/1949	Auburn	14–13	Legion Field
12/2/1950	**Alabama**	34–0	Legion Field
12/1/1951	**Alabama**	25–7	Legion Field

1953: ALABAMA 10, AUBURN 7

Shug Jordan came out with his famous X and Y teams, and for the first time since 1949 Auburn scored first. Alabama knotted it up at 7–7. With a minute left in the game, a piling-on penalty against Auburn proved costly because it set up Bobby Luna's 28-yard, game-winning field goal. It was the first field goal in the Iron Bowl since 1906.

1903: ALABAMA 18, AUBURN 6

Auburn's players were bigger than Alabama's players. The average weight of the AU players was 161 pounds, while the average weight of UA players was 148 pounds. Auburn came into the

11/29/1952	**Alabama**	21–0	Legion Field	
11/28/1953	**Alabama**	10–7	Legion Field	
11/27/1954	Auburn	28–0	Legion Field	
11/26/1955	Auburn	26–0	Legion Field	
12/1/1956	Auburn	34–7	Legion Field	
11/30/1957	Auburn	40–0	Legion Field	
11/29/1958	Auburn	14–8	Legion Field	
11/28/1959	**Alabama**	10–0	Legion Field	
11/26/1960	**Alabama**	3–0	Legion Field	
12/2/1961	**Alabama**	34–0	Legion Field	
12/1/1962	**Alabama**	38–0	Legion Field	
11/30/1963	Auburn	10–8	Legion Field	
11/26/1964	**Alabama**	21–14	Legion Field	
11/27/1965	**Alabama**	30–3	Legion Field	
12/3/1966	**Alabama**	31–0	Legion Field	
12/2/1967	**Alabama**	7–3	Legion Field	
11/30/1968	**Alabama**	24–16	Legion Field	
11/29/1969	Auburn	49–26	Legion Field	
11/28/1970	Auburn	33–28	Legion Field	*Continues*
11/27/1971	**Alabama**	31–7	Legion Field	*on next page*

ALABAMA

game a 5-to-1 favorite, but Alabama again upset the Tigers, 18–6, in a game played at Highland Park in Montgomery.

1977: ALABAMA 48, AUBURN 21

Alabama entered the game on an eight-game winning streak. Auburn was in the midst of a mediocre 5–6 season, but the Tigers did finish with a 4–2 record in the SEC. Running the wishbone offense, Jeff Rutledge tacked 48 points on the Tigers in a 48–21 win. Alabama finished 11–1 and undefeated in the SEC to win the conference championship. 'Bama capped the campaign with a 35–6 demolition of Ohio State in the Sugar Bowl in a game that featured two coaching legends, Bryant and Woody Hayes.

12/2/1972	Auburn	17–16	Legion Field
12/1/1973	**Alabama**	35–0	Legion Field
11/29/1974	**Alabama**	17–13	Legion Field
11/29/1975	**Alabama**	28–0	Legion Field
11/27/1976	**Alabama**	38–7	Legion Field
11/26/1977	**Alabama**	48–21	Legion Field
12/2/1978	**Alabama**	34–16	Legion Field
12/1/1979	**Alabama**	25–18	Legion Field
11/29/1980	**Alabama**	34–18	Legion Field
11/28/1981	**Alabama**	28–17	Legion Field
11/27/1982	Auburn	23–22	Legion Field
12/3/1983	Auburn	23–20	Legion Field
12/1/1984	**Alabama**	17–15	Legion Field
11/30/1985	**Alabama**	25–23	Legion Field
11/29/1986	Auburn	21–17	Legion Field
11/27/1987	Auburn	10–0	Legion Field
11/25/1988	Auburn	15–10	Legion Field
12/2/1989	Auburn	30–20	Jordan-Hare Stadium, Auburn
12/1/1990	**Alabama**	16–7	Legion Field
11/30/1991	**Alabama**	13–6	Legion Field

1960: ALABAMA 3, AUBURN 0

Tommy Brooker booted a 23-yard field goal in the second quarter to give Alabama all the points it needed in a 3–0 win over the Tigers. The Crimson Tide defense held Auburn to 63 yards rushing. The victory clinched a bid to the Bluebonnet Bowl in Houston, where 'Bama played Texas to a 3–3 tie. Again, Alabama's points came on a field goal by Brooker. What do 'Bama fans like about this Iron Bowl the most? The final score.

1894: ALABAMA 18, AUBURN 0

Alabama followers, especially those alive at the time, love this win, because after losing the first two games against Auburn,

11/26/1992	**Alabama**	17–0	Legion Field
11/20/1993	Auburn	22–14	Jordan-Hare Stadium
11/19/1994	**Alabama**	21–14	Legion Field
11/18/1995	Auburn	31–27	Jordan-Hare Stadium
11/23/1996	**Alabama**	24–23	Legion Field
11/22/1997	Auburn	18–17	Jordan-Hare Stadium
11/21/1998	**Alabama**	31–17	Legion Field
11/20/1999	**Alabama**	28–17	Jordan-Hare Stadium
11/18/2000	Auburn	9–0	Bryant-Denny Stadium, Tuscal.
11/17/2001	**Alabama**	31–7	Jordan-Hare Stadium
11/23/2002	Auburn	17–7	Bryant-Denny Stadium
11/22/2003	Auburn	28–23	Jordan-Hare Stadium
11/20/2004	Auburn	21–13	Bryant-Denny Stadium
11/19/2005	Auburn	28–18	Jordan-Hare Stadium
11/18/2006	Auburn	22–15	Bryant-Denny Stadium
11/24/2007	Auburn	17–10	Jordan-Hare Stadium
11/29/2008	**Alabama**	36–0	Bryant-Denny Stadium
11/27/2009	**Alabama**	26–21	Jordan-Hare Stadium
11/26/2010	Auburn	28–27	Bryant-Denny Stadium
11/26/2011	**Alabama**	42–14	Jordan-Hare Stadium

ALABAMA

this was the first of what would be many wins over the Tigers. The Crimson Tide won 18–0, but the victory was not without controversy. Auburn said Alabama cheated by paying two players.

"The first argument between Alabama and Auburn occurred prior to this game," according to Auburn football expert David Housel. "Auburn claimed that two Alabama players, whose last names were Shelly and Abbott, were not bona fide students. Alabama denied the claim, and the players played in the game. They dominated the game. The next week Shelly and Abbott began a prize-fighting exhibition tour of the South, which verified Auburn's claim," writes Housel.

The Alabama victory, however, stood. The Alabama-Auburn game was taken very seriously, even back then.

2

WE LOVE BEATING EVERYBODY

'BAMA ESPECIALLY LOVES
SQUASHING THE BIG ORANGE!

Long before Auburn became Alabama's biggest rival, Tennessee was the Tide's biggest rival. In fact, the Alabama-Tennessee game was the biggest game in the South.

UA-UT is a storied series dating back to 1901. But like the Auburn rivalry, because fans of both teams got out of control, competition between Alabama and Tennessee was suspended for two years (1910 and 1911).

The Crimson Tide has played more games against the Volunteers than against any other team. Since 1928 'Bama and the Big Orange have met on the gridiron every year except 1943, when World War II caused cancelation of the game. In the Southeastern Conference, Alabama and Tennessee together have dominated the league, winning 35 championships in the SEC's 79-year history.

Alabama fans don't remember the games, but they love the scores from 1903 through 1913 when, except for 1904,

Alabama won every year and didn't let the Vols score for nine years. More specifically, UA notched seven straight shutouts and eight in nine years. They really liked the 1906 score when 'Bama squashed the Big Orange 51–0.

The rivalry has seen both teams string together long winning streaks, with 'Bama fans enjoying the run from 1961 through 1966 when the good guys won four in a row, played to a 7–7 tie in 1965, and then won again in 1966, 11–10. The Crimson Tide then won 11 straight from 1971 through 1981, and had a nine-game unbeaten streak from 1986 through 1994. Tennessee came out on top seven straight times from 1995 through 2001 and 10 of 11 times through 2006, excluding the victory that Alabama had to vacate in 2005. Alabama has won the last five games and maintains a 48–37–8 lead in the series. 'Bama has led the series continuously, except in 1960 when

MOST SEC TITLES

Alabama (22)
Tennessee (13)
Georgia (12)
LSU (11)
Florida (8)
Auburn (7)
Mississippi (6)
Kentucky (2)
Mississippi State (1)
Arkansas (0)
South Carolina (0)
Vanderbilt (0)

Tennessee briefly held a 19–18–6 advantage following a 20–7 win that year.

Alabama fans of all generations love to beat Tennessee, some almost as much as they love beating Auburn. Some older fans love deflating the Big Orange even more than pounding the Plainsmen.

"When Coach Bryant was at Kentucky, he never beat Tennessee, and when he came here he at first had a hard time beating Tennessee. Back then the game was bigger than Auburn," stated longtime Bryant assistant coach Clem Gryska, who passed away in 2012. "The Alabama-Tennessee game is a big, big game with the alumni of both universities," stated the late Bert Bank, who had been involved with Alabama athletics going all the way back to 1952, when he began broadcasting the games.

Dave Hart played basketball at Alabama and, after stints as athletics director at East Carolina and Florida State, returned to his alma mater in 2008 to become executive athletics director. In the fall of 2011, a month before the UA-UT football game, Hart was appointed athletics director at Tennessee. He told the *Tuscaloosa News*, "I've followed this rivalry since I was an athlete in this conference myself. I've always thought, before I came back to Alabama three years ago and before I came to Tennessee, that this is one of the great rivalries in college athletics. The third Saturday in October, it gives me chills to even talk about it. To me, it's what college football is all about."

Dont'a Hightower, a junior linebacker on the 2011 Tide team, has been schooled about the significance of the UA-UT game.

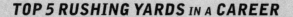

TOP 5 RUSHING YARDS *IN A* CAREER

1. **Shaun Alexander** | 3,565 yards | 1996–1999
2. **Bobby Humphrey** | 3,420 yards | 1985–1988
3. **Kenneth Darby** | 3,324 yards | 2003–2006
4. **Mark Ingram** | 3,261 yards | 2009–2010
5. **Trent Richardson** | 3,130 yards | 2009–2011

"This game brings up a lot. It's a good rivalry, maybe even better than the Iron Bowl. A lot of people, they don't ever really ask, 'What's your record in the Iron Bowl?' They ask, 'What's your record against Tennessee?'"

Derrick Oden, a linebacker and captain of Alabama's 1992 national championship team, recalled that playing in Knoxville was "such an intimidating environment. You see a sea of orange, and you just keep hearing 'Rocky Top' over and over. When we were preparing to play at Tennessee, Coach Stallings miked the practice field with 'Rocky Top.' I heard it so much that I remember sitting in class and whistling 'Rocky Top.' One of my friends said, 'Do you know you're whistling "Rocky Top?"' I didn't even realize it, but it was just so ingrained in my mind.

"It's a great rivalry. You have to look at the traditions, the championships behind your name [UA has a conference-leading 22; UT is second with 13]. The game against Tennessee is so much more relevant because of who they are. I loved playing

Tennessee, and I loved going to Knoxville. I can say with pride that I never lost to Tennessee."

Nose guard Josh Chapman, a member of the 2011 Alabama team, told the *Tuscaloosa News*, "Tennessee's a great rival. It means more to not just us, [but also] to people in the state and people who played here at the university. I mean, it's a great rivalry. I love playing in this game."

Guard Chance Warmack added, "You come in as a freshman, and they're already telling you about the rivalry. So you pretty much already know what you have to do to get ready for Tennessee as a team. It's been like this for a long time. You just get used to it."

Like the Iron Bowl, there have been many big games in the Tide-Vols series. Following are a few.

October 24, 2009: Alabama 12, Tennessee 10

Alabama had just played seven straight games, and the strain was beginning to tell. The team was tired. Straight ahead was Tennessee. With the Crimson Tide ahead 12–10, on the last play of the game, the Volunteers faced a third-and-11 on the Alabama 28-yard line. Daniel Lincoln attempted a 44-yard, game-winning field goal, and the game became an instant classic when Terrence "Mount" Cody, a 6'5", 355-pound UA nose tackle blocked the kick to seal the deal as time expired. The play will be forever imprinted in 'Bama folklore as acclaimed artist Daniel A. Moore immediately planned another in his long line of Alabama football paintings—this one called *Maximum*

Block, the title of the work derived from the play that was called in which all 11 players are sent to try and block the kick.

The win enabled Alabama to remain unbeaten (8–0, 5–0), albeit by the skin of its teeth, get a rest with an upcoming bye week, and continue on its march toward what would be its 13th national championship.

October 20, 1990: Alabama 9, Tennessee 6

Tennessee was ranked No. 3 in the nation, and the Crimson Tide was unranked when the teams met at Neyland Stadium. With the score tied 6–6 and only four ticks of the clock left in the game, Philip Doyle nailed a 48-yard field goal to give Alabama its fifth straight victory in the series. Since Van Tiffin's field goal to beat archrival Auburn is called "the Kick," this beauty over archrival No. 2 should be called "Kick II."

"Every kicker wants a kick like this one," said Doyle after the game. "It was an SEC game against the No. 3 team in the nation, and it was on ESPN. The scenario couldn't get any better for a kicker."

Seconds before Doyle's game-winning boot, Tennessee's Greg Burke, who had booted a 51-yard field goal earlier, was prepared to kick what he hoped would be a game-winning field goal. With 1:35 to go, Burke's 50-yard attempt was blocked by the Tide's Stacy Harrison, with 'Bama getting a very good roll as the ball bounced off Burke's face-masked helmet all the way back to the Tennessee 37-yard line. Alabama advanced it seven yards closer in order to give Doyle a reasonable chance to put it between the uprights. Harrison's block may not be

TOP 5 PASSING YARDS IN A CAREER

1. **John Parker Wilson** | 7,924 yards | 2005–2008
2. **Brodie Croyle** | 6,382 yards | 2002–2005
3. **Andrew Zow** | 5,983 yards | 1998–2001
4. **Greg McElroy** | 5,691 yards | 2007–2010
5. **Jay Barker** | 5,689 yards | 1991–1994

ALABAMA

as dramatic as Thomas Rayam's blocked field goal on the last play of the game that preserved the victory over Penn State ("the Block"), but considering it came in a conference game against an archrival that was ranked third in the country, it was relished just as much.

"This has to rank up there with the biggest wins I've ever had in my career," stated an elated Gene Stallings. "We had terrible field position throughout the game, but we got great effort from the defense. This was a great win."

Doyle was rewarded by being named ESPN's Player of the Game.

The win was important not only because it came over the Big Orange in what many traditionally regard as the biggest game in the South, but because it also brought new hope to a season some people considered almost beyond repair. Suddenly talk turned to the possibility of a bowl game, something some had prematurely given up on.

October 22, 2005: Alabama 6, Tennessee 3

With 13 seconds left, Jamie Christensen made a 34-yard field goal to give Alabama a 6–3 victory over a Tennessee team that had won nine of the 10 previous games in the series.

October 22, 2011: Alabama 37, Tennessee 6

Alabama fans love this game, especially the second half. 'Bama, No. 2 in the nation, came into the contest a four-touchdown favorite against a substandard Tennessee team that was plodding along with a 3–3 record, including 0–3 in the conference. But the Tide put forth a lackluster effort during the first 30 minutes, and the Volunteers managed to make it a 6–6 game at the half.

What 'Bama fans will remember is the way the Crimson Tide, a run-oriented team, came out passing after intermission and scored 31 unanswered points in the second half to demolish the Vols. UA notched its fifth consecutive win in the series,

TOP 5 TDs *SCORED IN A* CAREER

1. **Shaun Alexander** | 50 | 1996–1999

2. **Mark Ingram** | 46 | 2008–2010

3. **Trent Richardson** | 42 | 2009–2011

4. **Bobby Humphrey** | 40 | 1985–1988

5. **Johnny Musso** | 38 | 1969–1971

the first time it won that many in a row over the Big Orange since the 1986 through 1992 seasons.

"This game means a lot to a lot of people," said head coach Nick Saban, recognizing the matchup of traditional southern powerhouse programs. "It means a lot to me."

The 'Bama second-half surge was reminiscent of the win over Tennessee the year before, when a recharged Crimson Tide team exploded in a 41–10 drubbing of UT. Beyond annihilating Tennessee, the win kept Alabama on a collision course with LSU in a game that would match the No. 1 Bayou Bengals and the No. 2 Crimson Tide. The winner almost assuredly was going to the BCS national championship game.

A little earlier in the day, two states away in Tiger Stadium, when the home team was making mincemeat out of Auburn, the LSU fans started screaming, "We want 'Bama, We want 'Bama."

With under a minute to go, the crowd in Bryant-Denny Stadium began chanting, "LSU, LSU, LSU!"

With both teams having a bye week before what amounted to a national championship–type matchup, fans of both schools got their wish.

WE WANT TO BEAT LSU!

Since Nick Saban's arrival at Alabama, LSU has become another hated rival, right behind Auburn and Tennessee.

November 8, 2008: Alabama 27, LSU 21 (OT)

During Nick Saban's second year at Alabama, the LSU game was one that Tigers' fans had circled ever since Saban left Baton Rouge. The Tide ventured into Tiger Stadium, where a hostile crowd awaited the return of the coach who took LSU to its first national championship since the Paul Dietzel–coached, Billy Cannon–led "Chinese Bandits" of 1958. It was bad enough that Saban left Baton Rouge, but the situation was significantly exacerbated when, after his short foray into the NFL, he resurfaced at SEC rival Alabama.

As if Saban's return to the Bayou weren't enough to excite the Cajuns, Saban was bringing to town the No. 1–ranked team in the country to take on the No. 15–rated Tigers. Rising to

Alabama head coach Nick Saban

the occasion, Alabama (10–0, 6–0), though severely tested, survived in overtime, 27–21. The win clinched the Crimson Tide's first SEC Western Division Championship since 1999 and, in doing so, a spot in the SEC Championship Game.

'Bama had a chance to win the game in regulation, but with the scored tied 21–21, a 29-yard Tide field-goal attempt was blocked as time expired. In OT the Tigers got the ball first, but Rashad Johnson intercepted a pass in the end zone, his third pick of the game. On Alabama's first play from scrimmage, quarterback John Parker Wilson fired a 23-yard pass to star freshman wide receiver Julio Jones, setting up the ball at the LSU 2-yard line. Wilson scored the winning touchdown on a quarterback sneak.

While Crimson Tide fans rejoiced in the victory, no doubt the loss sent many LSU fans into various degrees of depression.

November 7, 2009: Alabama 24, LSU 15

In game three of Saban vs. LSU, the school he once coached, No. 1 Alabama (8–0, 5–0) entertained the No. 9 Bayou Tigers (7–1, 4–1) in what was becoming an annual game for the lead in the SEC West. For only the second time in the season, Alabama was behind at the half, 7–3, and trailed 15–13 early in the fourth quarter before Julio Jones sprinted 73 yards down the sideline as the Tide defeated the Tigers 24–15. The win gave 'Bama its second straight SEC Western Division title and kept the Tide in contention for the national championship, which they went on to win.

* * *

The Alabama victory over LSU that Tide fans love the most, of course, happened in the 2012 BCS Championship Game. Don't worry, we'll get to that in chapter 3.

NONCONFERENCE GAMES WE LOVE

January 1, 1979: Alabama 14, Penn State 7

A favorite game for many fans is the "Goal-Line Stand" against Penn State that helped the Crimson Tide win the 1979 Sugar Bowl and the national championship. The contest in the Superdome was a defensive struggle between undefeated and untied Alabama, ranked No. 1 in the nation, and unbeaten Penn State.

With eight seconds left in the first half, quarterback Jeff Rutledge hit Bruce Bolton with a 30-yard touchdown pass to give 'Bama a 7–0 lead at intermission. With 4:25 left in the third quarter, a Chuck Fusina scoring pass to Scott Fitzkee tied the score. Shortly thereafter the Tide's Lou Ikner returned a Penn State punt 62 yards to the Nittany Lion 11-yard line, where three plays later Major Ogilvie scored what proved to be the winning touchdown on an eight-yard run.

Alabama was in front 14–7 when the Nittany Lions recovered a fumble inside the Alabama 20-yard line. Penn State drove for a first down at the 8-yard line. A run picked up two yards and a short pass advanced the ball to the 1-yard line.

With under seven minutes remaining, Penn State had two plays to gain three feet and pull within an extra point of a tie. On third down, PSU's Matt Suhey tried to dive over the top but was stopped one foot short of the end zone.

An Alabama lineman chided Penn State, "You got a foot to go, so you'd better pass." Fullback Mike Guman then tried to dive over the top but was stood up an inch from the goal line by a 'Bama brick wall led by linebacker Barry Krauss.

"That goal-line stand was something I'll never forget," said Bear Bryant after the game. The play is preserved in Crimson Tide history by a Daniel A. Moore painting, appropriately titled *Goal-Line Stand*.

October 4, 1986: Alabama 28, Notre Dame 10

Alabama and Notre Dame rarely play, so it was special when the Fighting Irish came to Birmingham on October 4, 1985. It was a game everyone was waiting for. The game didn't need any hype. A record number of press credentials were handed out, and the game was being carried on national television, although that isn't anything unusual for Alabama football games. There was just a feeling of anticipation, more so than for other games. The Irish had beaten Alabama in all four of their previous meetings, and leading up to this game there was a feeling of determination among Alabama players to do something about that.

The Tide did do something about it, although statistically the game was a lot closer than the 28–10 score would indicate.

Another play that will always be etched in the minds of those who saw it was Cornelius Bennett's blindsiding Notre Dame quarterback Steve Beuerlein. Moore's painting titled *The Hit* is another that 'Bama fans have in their growing collection. Upon entering Bryant Museum, turn right, and *The Hit* hangs prominently in a place where no visitor can miss it.

"That was as vicious a hit as you will ever see," said then–Alabama sports information director Wayne Atcheson. "But it was clean. It was one of those plays that Cornelius has become famous for, a big play that sets the tone of the game against a big-time opponent.

"For me as SID, beating Notre Dame was one of the happiest days I've ever experienced. It was Alabama–Notre Dame. We hadn't played the Irish that many times, and we just had a feeling that we were going to win. It was my biggest thrill as SID."

October 28, 1989: Alabama 17, Penn State 16

Alabama was ranked No. 6 and Penn State No. 14 when the Crimson Tide traveled to State College, Pennsylvania, to play the Nittany Lions. With 'Bama ahead 17–16 and 13 seconds left, a loss looked imminent as Penn State's Ray Tarasi lined up to kick a chip-shot field goal. Tarasi had earlier kicked field goals of 22, 26, and 46 yards, and was set to boot a game-winning three-pointer from extra-point distance.

However, Thomas Rayam stormed in to block it and became the answer to the trivia question: in 1989 who blocked the field goal to preserve the win over Penn State?

Ranking among the single biggest plays in Crimson Tide history, the moment is saved in people's minds because Daniel A. Moore, who had produced dramatic portraits of *Goal-Line Stand*, *The Kick*, and *The Hit*, soon added *The Block*. "When I heard that double-thump, I don't think I've ever seen a team so emotional," said Coach Bill Curry of Rayam's block, which was selected SEC Play of the Week.

MOST INTERCEPTIONS *IN A* CAREER

1. **Antonio Langham** | 19 | 1990–1993
2t. **Harry Gilmer** | 16 | 1944–1947
   Jeremiah Castile | 16 | 1979–1982
   John Mangum | 16 | 1986–1989
5t. **Steve Higginbotham** | 14 | 1969–1971
   Kermit Kendrick | 14 | 1985–1988
   George Teague | 14 | 1989–1992

ALABAMA

The win was the Crimson Tide's second straight over a ranked opponent on national television. It was also Curry's third straight win over legendary coach Joe Paterno, a coach he admired and studied.

October 1, 2005: Alabama 31, Florida 3

The 2005 season started with Alabama winning its first nine games. The fifth win of the season was huge, however, when the No. 15–ranked Crimson Tide throttled No. 5 Florida 31–3 in a battle of undefeated teams on national television in what was Coach Mike Shula's signature win. The game was called Alabama's biggest win ever in Tuscaloosa. The victory was significant because, not only was it 'Bama's first-ever win over a top 5 team in Bryant-Denny Stadium, but it validated that Alabama was close to being back after five years burdened by probation and problems. It was also bittersweet since star junior wide receiver/kick returner Tyrone Prothro sustained what would turn out to be a horrific career-ending broken left leg in the fourth quarter.

The win catapulted the Crimson Tide to No. 7 in the AP poll, its highest ranking since being third in the August 27, 2000, poll. The Tide kept winning, and late in the season was one of three remaining unbeaten teams in the country, ranked No. 3 in the USA Today Poll and No. 4 in the AP and Harris Polls.

October 11, 1958: Alabama 29, Furman 6

At first glance, readers may wonder why this game is included in games 'Bama fans love. Very simple, really. This is the game in which the legend began. After returning to his alma mater from Texas A&M, Bear Bryant notched his first win as Alabama's coach. The Crimson Tide defeated Furman 29–6. Based on his reputation at Kentucky and with the Aggies, everyone knew that Bryant was going to be a winner at Alabama, but no one could really imagine just how much of a winner he would become.

This was not the first game Bryant coached at Alabama. In his first game, UA lost to LSU 13–3. In his second game 'Bama battled to a 0–0 tie with Vanderbilt. It was in his third game, the 29–6 win over the Paladins, that he got what would be the first of 232 wins at Alabama and his first in what was then Denny Stadium, where he would go 72–2. That's why the 'Bama Nation loves this game so much. It was the start of something that gave the fans of Crimson Tide football, the University, and the state something to be proud of.

3

WE LOVE WINNING NATIONAL CHAMPIONSHIPS

LET'S GET STRAIGHT to the point. *This is Ala-Bam-a Football!* Seriously, what is there not to love? It just doesn't get any better than Alabama football. The Alabama football tradition is the best, bar none. Alabama fans love national championships. One of the reasons they love national championships so much is because the Crimson Tide has won a lot of them. Alabama's 14 national championships are the most in the nation. It never gets olds. The more the merrier.

Of Alabama's 14 national championships, nine are recognized universally. Trailing the Crimson Tide are Notre Dame with eight and Oklahoma and Southern Cal, which have seven each. Further evidence of Alabama's excellence throughout the 20th century is that the Tide has won national titles in the 1920s, '30s, '40s, '60s, '70s, and '90s, and has opened this century with national championships in the first two decades. Try topping that!

THE TIDE'S NATIONAL CHAMPIONSHIP SEASONS

1925

Alabama fans love this one, even if most of us weren't even born yet, because it was 'Bama's first. It set the precedent for what was to come. Wallace Wade guided the Crimson Tide to a perfect 10–0 season in which 'Bama shut out all nine of its opponents and then capped it off with a 20–19 squeaker over Washington in the Rose Bowl—a game that earned national respect for southern football.

Stars on the team included Johnny Mack Brown, Grant Gillis, and Bruce Jones. Johnny Mack Brown not only was a star on the football field but, following the exposure he received in Pasadena, became an actor in Hollywood starring mostly in cowboy movies.

1926

Alabama followed up its first national championship season by winning another national championship. Coach Wallace Wade took a team that was missing many of its first-string players from the year before and still went undefeated (9–0) during the regular season. Led by All-American Hoyt "Wu" Winslett, the Tide made a return trip to Pasadena where it played a Stanford team coached by Glenn "Pop" Warner to a 7–7 tie in the Rose Bowl.

Stanford jumped out to a 7–0 lead, and the score stayed that way until center Clarke "Babe" Pearce blocked a Stanford punt with four minutes left in the game, setting up the Tide at the Stanford 14-yard line. Four running plays advanced the

Star halfback Johnny Mack Brown, who was nicknamed the "Dothan Antelope," went on to become a Hollywood actor.

ball to the 1-yard line, where Jimmy Johnson plunged into the end zone for the touchdown. Herschel Caldwell kicked the PAT, and the Crimson Tide salvaged a 7–7 tie. The tie was the only blemish on a 9–0–1 campaign.

1930

In 1930 Alabama made its third trip to the Rose Bowl and won its third national championship under Wade. The culmination of the 10–0 season was a 24–0 waxing of Washington State. Wade didn't think the 1930 team had as many outstanding individual players as his 1925 team, but said what it had was a lot of depth. So much so that Wade started every game, including the Rose Bowl, with his second-team playing the first quarter. His reasoning was psychological, explaining that the opposition became psyched out after being held scoreless by the Tide's second-team because it knew that it would get even tougher when Alabama's best players entered the game.

1934

Frank Thomas was the head coach when Alabama won its fourth national championship. 'Bama was 9–0 and again Rose Bowl–bound, where they whupped Stanford 29–13.

ALABAMA'S NATIONAL CHAMPIONSHIPS (14)
MOST IN DIVISION I

1925	1965
1926	1973
1930	1978
1934	1979
1941	1992
1961	2009
1964	2011

ALABAMA

Dixie Howell rushed for 111 yards, completed nine of 12 passes for 160 yards, and averaged 43.8 yards on six punts. When his day's work was done, Howell trotted off the field to what was called "the noisiest ovation ever given a visiting player on a California gridiron."

Famed sportswriter Grantland Rice opened his story by writing, "Dixie Howell, the human howitzer from Hartford, Alabama, blasted the Rose Bowl dreams of Stanford with one of the greatest all-around exhibitions football has ever known."

End Don Hutson caught two 20-something-yard passes and added runs that turned them into 50-something-yard touchdowns, with Rice calling him "incomparable." Accolades also came from Ralph McGill of the *Atlanta Constitution* who wrote, "No team in the history of football, anywhere, anytime, has passed the ball as Alabama passed it today. And no man ever passed as did Dixie Howell, the swift sword of the Crimson attack."

Hyperbole or not, Howell, Hutson, and their teammates stole the show in the 1935 Rose Bowl.

1941

Despite losing to Mississippi State and Vanderbilt, in 1941 the Houlgate system designated Alabama (9–2) the best team in the country. This time UA ventured to the Cotton Bowl where they proved their worth by defeating Southwestern Conference champion Texas A&M 29–21, giving Thomas his second national title. 'Bama shared the national championship with Minnesota and Texas.

The Aggies won the statistical battle, 13 first downs to one, 13 pass completions to one, 79 plays to 32, and 309 total yards to 75, but the Crimson Tide prevailed where it counted the most—on the scoreboard. 'Bama overcame all of its offensive futility by capitalizing on 12 turnovers—seven pass interceptions and five fumble recoveries.

A bizarre and unlikely win for sure, but a victory nonetheless. Fitting for a team that was declared national champions despite losing two games.

1961

After a 20-year drought, Bear Bryant got Alabama back in the national championship business. All-America tackle Billy Neighbors and linebacker Lee Roy Jordan, also a center on offense, were the stars of a bone-jarring defense that notched six shutouts, held opponents to only three touchdowns, and allowed only 25 points all season. Quarterback Pat Trammell was a leader. Tommy Brooker was a good defensive end who also won games with his foot as a place-kicker.

Alabama put the finishing touches on an outstanding season by beating Arkansas 10–3 in the Sugar Bowl. In 2011 the group gathered to celebrate the 50th anniversary of the school's sixth national championship, and Bryant's first.

1964

Unlike some national championship years when the Crimson Tide cruised through its regular season, Alabama in 1964 won some close, hard-fought games, with the 17–14 victory over

Joe Namath (12) and Ray Perkins (88) congratulate each other after a pass completion.

Florida, the 17–9 triumph over LSU, and the 21–14 win over Auburn coming to mind.

Alabama went 10–0 and was named national champions at a time when the title was awarded prior to bowl games. In the Orange Bowl, Alabama squared off against a Texas team led by All-America linebacker and Maxwell and Outland Award winner Tommy Nobis.

When an Alabama fan thinks of 1964, the first thing that comes to mind is Joe Namath, the Tide's All-America quarterback. Texas had taken a two-touchdown lead before Namath threw a seven-yard scoring pass to Wayne Trimble. The Longhorns scored again to make it 21–7. A 20-yard touchdown pass from Namath to Ray Perkins followed by a David Ray field goal pulled 'Bama to within four.

Trailing Texas 21–17 in the fourth quarter, Namath, following an interception by Jimmy Fuller, drove 'Bama to within inches of the goal line. Facing a fourth-and-inches, similar to 'Bama's "Goal-Line Stand" that would come years later in 1979 against Penn State, except that the script was flipped, Nobis and his Longhorns linemen and linebackers stopped the gimpy-legged Namath short of the end zone to preserve the victory.

Namath to this day still feels that he scored, but the officials ruled he didn't, so the score stands. The loss to the Longhorns was the only blemish on that 10–1 season. "We had a bunch of great guys, I remember that," Namath recalled. "The 1964 team was determined. It was not a gifted team. We had a lot of big hearts, with Coach Bryant leading the way. We played Texas in the Orange Bowl and missed by that much," he said, raising his hand with thumb and forefinger about an inch apart.

"When you go through things together, fellows don't forget that. The camaraderie and the togetherness is something that Coach Bryant built."

The national champion Crimson Tide's loss to Texas resulted in controversy because Arkansas won its bowl game and finished undefeated. As a result, the following season the Associated Press began designating national champions after the bowl games.

1965

Despite opening the 1965 season with an 18–17 loss at Georgia, playing Tennessee to a 7–7 stalemate, and struggling with the Mississippi teams—barely escaping with a 17–16 win over the Rebels and a 10–7 victory over the Bulldogs—the 9–1–1 and fourth-ranked Crimson Tide parlayed a 39–28 victory over third-ranked Nebraska in the Orange Bowl to win the school's eighth national championship.

Prior to the Orange Bowl game, Alabama was aware that upsets had occurred earlier in the day, and beating Nebraska would give Alabama its second straight national championship. The Crimson Tide, quicker and faster than the larger Cornhuskers, prevailed in the high-scoring affair that enabled 'Bama to jump over No. 1 Michigan State and No. 2 Arkansas because the Spartans had lost to UCLA in the Rose Bowl and the Razorbacks fell to LSU in the Cotton Bowl.

1973

In 1973 Alabama ran roughshod through its regular season without really being challenged. The Tide opened the campaign with a 66–0 annihilation of California, and it was all downhill from there. Easy wins over Kentucky (28–14), Vanderbilt (44–0), Georgia (28–14), Florida (35–14), Tennessee (42–21), Virginia Tech (77–6), Mississippi State (35–0), Miami (43–13), LSU (21–7), and Auburn (35–0) followed.

Bear Bryant is carried off the field by his team after they defeated Auburn 35–0 at Legion Field on December 1, 1973. The Crimson Tide remained undefeated on its way to Alabama's ninth national championship. Photo courtesy of AP Images

Then it was off to the Sugar Bowl, where the Crimson Tide would play Notre Dame in a first-ever meeting of two of the most storied programs in college football history. It was Bear Bryant vs. Ara Parseghian.

As expected, the pregame hype was off the charts and the hotly contested game more than lived up to its billing. The Fighting Irish managed a 24–23 win that enabled Notre Dame to win all the national championships except those declared by the UPI and Dunkel. Alabama won the UPI national championship, and Oklahoma claimed the Dunkel national championship.

A national championship is a national championship, and this was the Crimson Tide's ninth.

1978

The only setback during the regular season was in the third game to Southern Cal, a 24–14 loss. The famous "Goal-Line Stand," where Barry Krauss and company stopped Penn State on two consecutive plays inside the 1-yard line to preserve a 14–7 win over the No. 1–ranked Nittany Lions in the Sugar Bowl, enabled Alabama (11–1) to rack up its 10th national championship.

1979

Alabama ripped through its regular season schedule with ease, except for a 3–0 escape over LSU in the ninth game of the season. The Tide outscored its opponents 383–67 in recording the first 12-win season in school history. The total included a 24–9 win over No. 6 Arkansas in the Sugar Bowl that gave the Crimson Tide back-to-back national championships.

The Steadman Shealy–quarterbacked wishbone offense averaged 32.6 points a game, while the Don McNeal and E.J. Junior–led defense surrendered only 5.3 points a game.

Major Ogilvie, with two touchdown runs and a 50-yard punt return that set up another 'Bama score, was named MVP of the Sugar Bowl as the Crimson Tide defeated a Razorbacks team coached by Lou Holtz to complete an unbeaten season.

1992

It had been 13 years since Alabama won its last national championship, and Bear Bryant was long gone, but Bryant's protégé, Gene Stallings, guided the Crimson Tide to its 12th national title.

Led by the nation's top-ranked defense, which only allowed 9.4 points a game, Alabama was unbeaten during the regular season. The first-ever Southeastern Conference Championship Game matched Western Division champion Alabama against Eastern Division kingpin Florida. On the line was a berth in the Sugar Bowl, and for the Crimson Tide a chance to play Miami for the national championship.

The Gators were beaten the week before by archrival and No. 3 Florida State, 45–24. 'Bama dispatched Florida 28–21 and earned the right to play for the national championship against the No. 1–ranked Miami Hurricanes and their Heisman Trophy–winning quarterback Gino Torretta. The Tide went into the game as decided underdogs.

On December 10 the Football Writers of American selected Gene Stallings to receive the Paul W. Bryant Award as National Coach of the Year. "It meant so much to me because it has his name on it. It was sort of an emotional moment," said Stallings, one of "the Junction Boys" who played for Bryant at Texas A&M, served as his assistant at Alabama, and then, as the Aggies' coach, beat his mentor in the 1968 Cotton Bowl.

NATIONAL CHAMPIONSHIP COACHES

Coach	Year	Record	Bowl
Wallace Wade	1925	10–0	Rose Bowl: UA 20, Wash. 19
	1926	9–0–1	Rose Bowl: UA 7, Stanford 7 (tie)
	1930	10–0	Rose Bowl: UA 24, Wash. St. 0
Frank Thomas	1934	10–0	Rose Bowl: UA 29, Stanford 13
	1941	9–2	Cotton Bowl: UA 29, Texas A&M 21
Bear Bryant	1961	11–0	Sugar Bowl: UA 10, Arkansas 3
	1964	10–1	Orange Bowl: Texas 21, UA 17
	1965	9–1–1	Orange Bowl: UA 39, Nebraska 28
	1973	11–1	Sugar Bowl: Notre Dame 24, UA 23
	1978	11–1	Sugar Bowl: UA 14, Penn St. 7
	1979	12–0	Sugar Bowl: UA 24, Arkansas 9
Gene Stallings	1992	13–0	Sugar Bowl: UA 34, Miami 13
Nick Saban	2009	14–0	BCS Title Game: UA 37, Texas 21
	2011	12–1	BCS Title Game: UA 21, LSU 0

A L A B A M A

The table was set. No. 1 vs. No. 2 for all the marbles. The USF&G Sugar Bowl in New Orleans hosted the national championship game that featured two undefeated teams. Miami, 11–0 and on a 28-game winning streak, entered the game as an 8½-point favorite, the largest point spread in Sugar Bowl history. The Crimson Tide came in at 12–0 with victories in its last 22 contests. The mighty Hurricanes, cocky and bragging in the days leading up to the game, were expecting to win their second straight national championship to become the first team in college football history to win four titles in six years and five in 10 years and, in doing so, solidify the program as a dynasty.

Somebody forgot to tell Alabama of Miami's mission, because the Crimson Tide, confident and not the least bit intimidated by Miami's trademark braggadocio, stunned the 'Canes 34–14.

Alabama dominated Miami and, in doing so, shut the Hurricanes up, similar in a way to what Ken Norton temporarily did to Muhammad Ali when he broke the legendary but loquacious champion's jaw in the third round to win the heavyweight title in 1973.

"The Miami players did a lot of talking about how we hadn't faced anyone like them," defensive back Sam Shade told reporters after the game. "Somewhere in the third quarter they stopped telling us how good they were and how they were going to beat us."

Alabama's defense played a big part in the victory. Knocking the Hurricanes off their high horse was, of course, the highlight of a season that was full of highlights. One play from the game, although it was nullified because of a five-yard offside penalty, continues to excite fans before every home game. When the big screen in Bryant-Denny Stadium replays George Teague racing down the sideline to catch Miami receiver LaMar Thomas from behind and rip the ball away seven yards shy of a Hurricanes touchdown, and then attempt to take it back the other way, the crowd roars. No matter, the play was still designated by ESPN as its Play of the Day and instantly made Teague a part of Alabama history, with "the Strip" immortalized in a painting by Daniel A. Moore.

"That play [even though it didn't count] George Teague made when he took the ball away may be the finest play an Alabama

*Gene Stallings with the
National Championship
Trophy in 1992*

player ever made," stated Bill Oliver, the defensive coordinator who masterminded the scheme that shutdown the Hurricanes. It was only fitting that Alabama won its 12th national championship in its 100th year of football. In doing so, the Crimson Tide became the first team in school history and the third team in college football history, along with BYU and Nebraska, to go undefeated in 13 games en route to the national championship. With the victory over Miami in Stallings' third year as coach, Alabama also extended its winning streak to 23 games, the longest in the nation.

Hardly anyone expected Alabama to win the national championship, with Corky Simpson the only writer in the Associated Press Top 25 poll to every week pick the Crimson Tide No. 1. "I took my share of flack from people around the country," he wrote in his column following the season. "But I knew that this Alabama team was special because I did something that other [voters] apparently failed to do. Homework."

Winning the national championship did something else. It set off a feeling of euphoria among 'Bama fans who hadn't experienced that kind of satisfaction since Bear Bryant won the school's last NCAA title in 1979.

'Bama fans did more than enjoy the 1992 season. They loved it. To them, 'Bama football was back, big-time.

2009

Alabama started the season ranked fifth in the nation, but those who follow the Tide for a living believed that there were many question marks and that the high ranking was predicated

ALABAMA'S BOWL GAMES (59)
MOST IN DIVISION I

13	Sugar Bowls
8	Orange Bowls
7	Cotton Bowls
6	Rose Bowls
4	Liberty Bowls
3	Independence Bowls
3	Sun Bowls
2	BCS Title Games
2	Bluebonnet Bowls
2	Capital One/Citrus Bowls
2	Gator Bowls
2	Music City Bowls
1	Blockbuster Bowl
1	Aloha Bowl
1	Hall of Fame Bowl
1	Fiesta Bowl
1	Outback Bowl

ALABAMA

on the success that 'Bama had had the year before. Concerns included an unproven quarterback, an unknown running back, and replacing virtually the entire offensive line.

But the Crimson Tide opened the season by beating No. 7 Virginia Tech 34–24 in a matchup of top 10 teams in the Chick-fil-A Kickoff Classic. The Tide then beat everyone else it played with relative ease, with the exception of a 12–10 squeaker over Tennessee that was decided on a game-saving block and a 26–21 win over Auburn in a game in which the Tigers used some trickery to jump out to a quick 14–0 lead. Down 21–20 in the Iron Bowl with 1:24 to go and confronted with a third-and-3 at the AU 4-yard line, Greg McElroy ran a play-action fake and tossed a game-winning touchdown pass to Roy Upchurch that enabled the Tide to escape with the victory.

"Only the strong survive, but the strong still get their asses whipped. That was my message to the team," stated Nick Saban after salvaging a victory where the only time the Tide led was at the end. "That last drive in the fourth quarter to win the game may have been one of the greatest that I have ever been associated with."

Throughout most of the season the two best teams, according to the polls, had been Florida and Alabama. The two Southeastern Conference powers met not for the national championship, but for the SEC Championship with the winner advancing to the BCS National Championship Game at the Rose Bowl to likely play the next highest ranked team, No. 3 Texas.

While the Crimson Tide decisively beat the Gators 32–13 to earn its trip to California, the Longhorns punched their ticket for Pasadena by pulling out a last-second 13–12 win over Nebraska in the Big 12 Championship Game.

The stage was set, with No. 1 again going against No. 2, but this time 'Bama was on top. Two tradition-rich programs going head-to-head for the national championship.

Two early field goals gave Texas a 6–0 lead, but 'Bama soon thereafter took control of the contest to grab a 24–6 advantage at the half. The 'Horns got back to within 24–21 with 6:15 remaining in the game.

When Texas got the ball back on its own 7-yard line with 3:14 to go, 'Bama fans got a little queasy. Not for long, though, as a blitzing Eryk Anders, coming from the blind side, smashed into Longhorns quarterback Garrett Gilbert, causing a fumble that Courtney Upshaw recovered at the UT 3-yard line. Three plays later, Heisman Trophy winner Mark Ingram barreled into the end zone, sealing Alabama's first national championship under Nick Saban and the school's first in 17 years.

With 'Bama back on top of the college football world, Crimson Tide fans rejoiced.

2011

Except for an overtime 9–6 loss to No. 1 LSU on November 5 in Tuscaloosa, Alabama steamrolled everyone else. Although the Crimson Tide had a national championship–caliber team, the heartbreaking loss to LSU made it unlikely that UA would get a chance to play for the national title. Left out of the SEC

Miniature four-foot replica statue of Nick Saban that is in the Bryant Museum.
A nine-foot statue of Saban is included along with other Alabama national
championship coaches in the Walk of Champions plaza in front of Bryant-
Denny Stadium.

Championship Game, Alabama was not even conference champion.

Then some improbable events occurred. Two higher ranked teams, Stanford and Oklahoma State, lost, reopening the door for 'Bama. LSU, the undefeated and undisputed No. 1 team in the nation, had earned a spot in the BCS National Championship Game January 9 in New Orleans after demolishing Georgia 42–10 in the SEC Championship Game. Meanwhile, Oklahoma State, ranked No. 3, routed No. 13 Oklahoma, to also finish with an 11–1 record that matched the Tide's.

The BCS format is designed to have the two best teams in the country play for the national championship. 'Bama Nation had to wait until 7:15 Sunday evening when ESPN announced who the combination of human and computer polls had determined was going to play for the national title.

The Tide had maintained its No. 2 ranking. Provided with a second chance, the Tide took full advantage of the opportunity it was given. Called by some "The Game of the Century II," since the first meeting between LSU and UA had been dubbed "The Game of the Century," and "The Rematch of the Century" by others, Alabama dominated the Tigers, drubbing

ALABAMA'S BOWL VICTORIES (34)
MOST IN DIVISION I

1926 Rose Bowl	Alabama 20, Washington 19
1931 Rose Bowl	Alabama 24, Washington State 0
1935 Rose Bowl	Alabama 29, Stanford 13
1942 Cotton Bowl	Alabama 29, Texas A&M 21
1943 Orange Bowl	Alabama 37, Boston College 21
1946 Rose Bowl	Alabama 34, Southern Cal 14
1953 Orange Bowl	Alabama 61, Syracuse 6
1962 Sugar Bowl	Alabama 10, Arkansas 3
1963 Orange Bowl	Alabama 17, Oklahoma 10
1964 Sugar Bowl	Alabama 12, Mississippi 7
1966 Orange Bowl	Alabama 39, Nebraska 28
1967 Sugar Bowl	Alabama 34, Nebraska 7
1975 Sugar Bowl	Alabama 13, Penn State 6
1976 Liberty Bowl	Alabama 36, UCLA 6
1978 Sugar Bowl	Alabama 35, Ohio State 6
1979 Sugar Bowl	Alabama 14, Penn State 7

ALABAMA

LSU 21–0. Whereas LSU won the field-goal-kicking contest in the regular season game, the championship game started out like it was going to be more of the same. The Crimson Tide built a 15–0 lead on five field goals and then gave the Tigers a real kick in the gut when Trent Richardson burst into the end zone on a 34-yard run that gave 'Bama its final points and saddled an LSU team headed for greatness with an embarrassing loss to win the BCS national championship.

LSU finished with only 92 yards of total offense and five first downs. The Tigers didn't cross midfield until midway through the fourth quarter. In a game featuring two of college

1980 Sugar Bowl	Alabama 24, Arkansas 9
1981 Cotton Bowl	Alabama 30, Baylor 2
1982 Liberty Bowl	Alabama 21, Illinois 15
1983 Sun Bowl	Alabama 28, SMU 7
1985 Aloha Bowl	Alabama 24, Southern Cal 3
1986 Sun Bowl	Alabama 28, Washington 6
1988 Sun Bowl	Alabama 29, Army 28
1991 Blockbuster Bowl	Alabama 30, Colorado 25
1993 Sugar Bowl	Alabama 34, Miami 13
1993 Gator Bowl	Alabama 24, North Carolina 10
1995 Citrus Bowl	Alabama 24, Ohio State 17
1997 Outback Bowl	Alabama 17, Michigan 14
2001 Independence Bowl	Alabama 14, Iowa State 13
2006 Cotton Bowl	Alabama 13, Texas Tech 10
2007 Independence Bowl	Alabama 30, Colorado 24
2010 BCS Title Game	Alabama 37, Texas 21
2011 Capital One Bowl	Alabama 49, Michigan State 7
2012 BCS Title Game	Alabama 21, LSU 0

ALABAMA

football's best defenses, Richardson's run came after neither team had scored a touchdown against each other in the two confrontations—that is, after banging heads for four quarters plus an overtime in November and going into the fourth quarter in New Orleans.

Richardson rushed for 92 yards and finished the season with a school single-season record 1,679 yards. Quarterback AJ McCarron completed 23 of 34 passes for 234 yards to win Offensive Player of the Game honors. Jeremy Shelley set a BCS bowl record with five field goals.

Alabama-LSU "Round 2" was a knockout. Battered and bewildered, LSU was punch-drunk from the pummeling administered by the Crimson Tide. It was as if the Tigers were hit by so many lefts that they were begging for a right.

In the same Superdome in the Big Easy where Alabama had won a national championship in 1992 when the Crimson Tide's defense destroyed Miami, 'Bama unleashed a defensive fury that was even more ferocious than the 1992 version in completely overwhelming LSU. The Tide made Tigers quarterback Jordan Jefferson look as flabbergasted and inept as the 1992 team made Miami QB Gino Torretta look confused and useless as he floundered around. Again a higher-rated, overconfident, and cocky team that had been doing a little trash-talking, got trashed by the Tide. LSU should have learned the lesson that the Hurricanes learned the hard way years earlier: don't piss off the Tide! If you do, you're likely to get a nationally televised ass-whuppin'.

Alabama won national championship trophies awarded by the BCS, Associated Press, MacArthur Bowl, and Grantland Rice.

Soon after the game, jokes appeared on Facebook. Here are a few:

Last time a Tiger got beat that badly, his wife was holding a golf club.

(Relative to LSU's All-American and Heisman Trophy finalist cornerback Tyrann Mathieu, nicknamed the "Honey Badger" for his ferocious hitting and for an animal that is considered fearless:) Know how you make a Honey Badger cookie? Put him in a bowl and whip for three hours.

Did you hear that the LSU team is still stuck in New Orleans? Somebody painted a 50-yard line on the interstate, and they can't get across.

[In a little jab at LSU coach Les Miles]: Nick Saban traded in his vehicle for a new one because he wanted *Les*(s) *Miles* on it.

4

PLAYERS WE LOVE

ALABAMA HAS HAD a slew of first-team All-Americans, and most could be included here. However, due to space restrictions, only a few will be. Again, this listing is subjective, and readers may have different opinions, especially if they are from different generations of 'Bama fans. As with the selection of games, friends in the media and from the Tuscaloosa Quarterback Club provided suggestions for what follows.

PRE-BRYANT ERA

Harry Gilmer

Harry Gilmer was a three-time All-SEC performer, an All-American in 1945, and MVP in the 1946 Rose Bowl. An all-around player, Gilmer ran, jumped, passed, kicked, and tackled. He did everything but peel oranges at halftime. In 1946, when he was designated SEC Player of the Year, he led the Tide in rushing, passing, interceptions, and punt and kickoff returns.

"Gilmer was a great triple threat," recalled Clem Gryska, one of his teammates. "I remember watching kids on the playgrounds when everybody was trying to run and jump and throw like him. They were all trying to emulate him."

Harry Gilmer (52) with coach Frank Thomas

Bert Bank, who had long been affiliated with Alabama football going back well before Gilmer played, called Gilmer "one of the all-time greats. Just a great athlete. He's one of the top five players at Alabama during the era that I'm familiar with, which is 1933 through the present," Bank said in 1992.

Playing offense and defense back in the one-platoon days of college football, Gilmer set several Alabama records, some of which still stand. He accounted for a school-best 52 touchdowns and 436 punt-return yards. His 16 career interceptions still ranks second in school annals.

Asked how he feels when someone breaks one of his Alabama records, Gilmer modestly said, "That's something that I get asked the most. When it happens, I don't feel like something is being taken away from me, but that someone has just done something better than me."

He even joked about when Chris Anderson raced 96 yards for a touchdown against Temple, beating Gilmer's record by one

ALABAMA

CRIMSON TIDE IN THE
COLLEGE FOOTBALL HALL OF FAME (23)

Cornelius Bennett	Marty Lyons
Johnny Mack Brown	Vaughn Mancha
Paul "Bear" Bryant (coach)	Johnny Musso
Johnny Cain	Billy Neighbors
Harry Gilmer	Ozzie Newsome
John Hannah	Fred Sington
Frank Howard	Riley Smith
Dixie Howell	Gene Stallings (coach)
Pooley Hubert	Frank Thomas (coach)
Don Hutson	Wallace Wade (coach)
Lee Roy Jordan	Don Whitmire
Woodrow Lowe	

yard for the longest touchdown run. "Chris Anderson runs the 40 in 4.2 to 4.35 seconds, whereas my best 40-time was probably 4.75, so I enjoyed my run longer than he did.

"Records are meant to be broken. I'm pleased and happy for the players who break my records. Until people told me, I didn't even know I had some of those records."

When Gilmer was a single-wing tailback, the Tide rolled to a 30–9–2 record, winning all 10 of its contests in 1945. Gilmer had numerous outstanding games for 'Bama, with many believing that his best was when he rushed for 216 yards on only six carries and threw two passes for over 50 yards in a 60–19 win over Kentucky in 1945. Not Gilmer, however.

"The game I remember the most was a game we lost in 1946, 12–0, to Tennessee in Knoxville. It was the roughest, most physical game I ever played in. There were a lot of games that we won, but I look back on that one because I put forth my ultimate effort. That's why I say it was probably my best game."

Gilmer was voted to the Alabama Team of the Century as a first-team defensive back.

A legend among the old-timers, Gilmer gives the impression that he wonders what all the fuss is about. "I don't know how to respond to what people think," he said. "I don't feel I'm anything special. I'm not in conversations about these things every day. I live in St. Louis, where people don't even know who I am. They don't know I'm from Alabama, and I don't tell them. I enjoy doing my own thing."

Gilmer spent four decades working in the NFL where he concluded his career as a scout for the Phoenix Cardinals. He was inducted into the College Football Hall of Fame in 1993.

Don Hutson

A unanimous All-American in 1934, Hutson was a charter member of both the College and Pro Football Halls of Fame. ESPN voted Hutson to its all-time college football team in 1989. He was named to Alabama's all-time team for the first 50 years of football and then to the All-Century Team 50 years later. The star end when Bear Bryant played, Bryant was referred to as "the other end," one of the few times Bryant ever played second fiddle to anyone.

As a member of the Green Bay Packers, Hutson led the NFL in receiving in eight of his 11 seasons and in scoring five straight years. A nine-time All-Pro, Hutson won back-to-back MVP Awards in 1941 and 1942. When he retired from pro football in 1945, Hutson held 18 NFL records, including most receptions with 488.

Johnny Mack Brown

Johnny Mack Brown was one of the early stars of Alabama football, earning the nickname "the Dothan Antelope" for the way he gracefully maneuvered and weaved through tacklers on his way to touchdowns.

He was an outstanding halfback on Tide teams that went 25–3–1 and went undefeated (10–0) in 1925, the year 'Bama won its first national championship. He hauled in two long

Johnny Mack Brown (at left) with Allison T. "Pooley" Hubert (right)

touchdown passes and was named Most Valuable Player as 'Bama beat Washington in the 1926 Rose Bowl, a win that put Alabama on the national football map.

Being in California near Hollywood, Brown's fame catapulted him to a post-football career as a movie star who was featured in more than 160 films and a few television shows, mostly westerns, over a 40-year career that saw him play opposite some of the leading actresses of that era, including Mary Pickford, Greta Garbo, and Joan Crawford. In addition to the awards he won as a football player, Brown received a star on the Walk of Fame on Hollywood Boulevard.

Bart Starr

Bart Starr is much more famous for his stellar career as the quarterback for the Green Bay Packers during their glory years under Vince Lombardi. However, as a sophomore at Alabama in 1953, he led the Crimson Tide to the Cotton Bowl, was ranked second nationally as a punter with a 41.1-yard average, and was named to the first-ever All-Academic SEC Team. In the pros, Starr guided the Green Bay dynasty to six division, five NFL, and the first two Super Bowl championships. In the 1967 NFL Championship Game against the Dallas Cowboys, called "The Ice Bowl" because it was played in freezing weather conditions with a wind-chill factor that drove the temperature down to −17°, Starr ran into the end zone behind the blocking of Jerry Kramer to give the Packers the victory. That sent them to Super Bowl II, where they defeated the Oakland Raiders 33–14.

Alabama quarterback Bart Starr went on to NFL fame with the Green Bay Packers.

A four-time Pro Bowler, Starr played 16 years in the NFL, led the league in passing three times, and passed for 24,718 yards and 152 touchdowns. He was the MVP in Super Bowls I and II and was inducted into the Pro Football Hall of Fame in 1977.

BEAR BRYANT ERA

Joe Namath

Throughout most of the 1960s and into the 1970s, Joe Willie Namath was as famous as Michael Jordan and Tiger Woods would later become. Almost everyone in the country knew Namath's face, and many still do. If he leaves home, there probably is not a day that he is not asked to sign an autograph for someone. Namath became, along with Muhammad Ali, the most high-profile, recognizable athlete of his time. Namath is one of only a very, very few athletes whose fame transcended the game they played in such a way that even the biggest celebrities wanted to meet them.

This is not your ordinary Joe. This Joe can always go home again, whether that is Beaver Falls, Pennsylvania, where he grew up; Tuscaloosa, where he played for the Crimson Tide; New York City, where he starred for the Jets; or West Palm Beach, Florida, where he resides.

A highly publicized three-sport star at Beaver Falls High School, where he excelled as a rifle-armed and accurate quarterback on the football team, as a double-figure scoring point guard who could dunk on the basketball team, and as a pitcher and line-drive-hitting outfielder on the baseball team good enough to attract the attention of major league scouts, Namath ventured into the Deep South to play for the legendary coach Paul "Bear" Bryant.

Assistant coach Clem Gryska said that Namath, when only a freshman, was the only player ever to go up on Bryant's famed coaching tower, making Namath special right from the get-go. Early on, Bryant called Namath "the best athlete I have ever seen." Bryant also did what Namath's high school basketball coach could not do—instill discipline in the young athlete who sometimes did as he pleased, which included walking off the court and quitting his high school team in the middle of a game.

Grabbing Namath by the face mask and chewing him out, Namath said that Bryant "could put the fear of God in me." After that, Bryant could do no wrong in Namath's eyes. But Namath could still do wrong in the coach's eyes, as he did when he was a junior and got caught breaking training rules toward the end of the season, resulting in his suspension for the last regular season game against Miami and the 1964 Sugar Bowl.

About Bryant he said, "It was in later years that you recognized what you learned [relative to] the things that he told us when we were 18, 19, 20 years old. We trusted Coach Bryant a great deal. There was a lot of animosity when I entered pro football. The one thing that carried me through was that I played for Paul Bryant at the University of Alabama."

Namath already was a household name by the time he finished his career at Alabama. He spurred the NFL to sign a

CRIMSON TIDE IN THE PRO FOOTBALL HALL OF FAME (7)

	Inducted
Don Hutson	1963
Bart Starr	1977
Joe Namath	1985
John Hannah	1991
Dwight Stephenson	1998
Ozzie Newsome	1999
Derrick Thomas	2008

ALABAMA

then unheard of $427,000 contract that included a Jets green Lincoln Continental convertible to play for the New York Jets of the American Football League and became the first mega-salaried athletic media star.

"It came down to listening to Coach Bryant. He didn't tell me to go with a certain team," Namath explained. "He said to get to know the owners and the people that you are going to be working with. It wasn't ever about playing in New York City. It was just to play football. It came down to what Coach Bryant told me."

With the Jets, the young, flamboyant quarterback sported a Fu Manchu mustache and wore white shoes, picking up the nickname "Broadway Joe" for his well-documented big-city carousing. Then he shocked not only fans, but also his coach when he promised that the Jets would beat the Baltimore Colts in Super Bowl III.

Vince Lombardi's Green Bay Packers had dominated the AFL's teams in the first two Super Bowls, and the Colts were three-touchdown favorites over the Jets. Namath said his guarantee victory statement was spontaneous, and was triggered by a remark made during a gathering in Miami.

"We had a bunch of guys who played hard and accomplished something, and then there were a bunch of guys telling us we were going to lose by three touchdowns," he clarified. "Then I got up to speak in Miami, and some guy called out, 'We're going to beat your asses!' I got angry.

"Coach [Weeb] Eubank got very angry with me for making that statement. He said, 'What are you doing? Now you're giving them ammunition to get them fired up.' I said, 'If they need that kind of motivation to beat us, they're in trouble.'" Namath delivered when New York beat Baltimore 16–7 to give the fledging AFL its first Super Bowl victory and what is still the Jets' only title. The win forced the NFL to respect the AFL and hastened the merger of the two leagues.

Namath became the toast of New York City while still in his twenties, a superstar who became one of the Big Apple's biggest celebrities. Guys idolized him, girls fawned over him, and even the biggest movie stars wanted to hang out with him. A jet-setting ladies man and New York's most eligible bachelor, the charismatic quarterback opened up a string of popular Bachelor III nightclubs, including one in Tuscaloosa, with patrons hoping Namath would show up so that they could get a glimpse of "Broadway Joe," the moniker Namath picked up after *Sports Illustrated* ran a cover of Namath at the intersection of Broadway and Seventh Avenue.

Joe Namath is arguably the most famous player to ever play for Alabama.

It was during this time that Namath, who then lived his life in the fast lane, also said, "I can't wait until tomorrow because I get better looking every day," and that "I'd rather fight in Vietnam than get married," statements that only perpetuated and magnified his playboy image.

"My high school teammates in Pennsylvania came up with the first quote," Namath said.

Then there was the panty hose commercial to which Namath had a simple response: "That was business."

When it was mentioned that in the 1970s he had an aura around him similar to what Jordan and Woods had later on, Namath had a modest reply: "I don't know about that, but that image did work in New York City. A lot of it was because we did win a championship. That's part of it because you never see anybody get tired of winning."

During his heyday, Namath was as successful partying in the trendiest nightclubs on Saturday nights as he was throwing touchdown passes on Sunday afternoons. The Hall of Fame quarterback was widely known for his conquests on and off the field. The Namath legend, spawned in Tuscaloosa, where his teammates and friends remember his fondness for hanging around The Jungle Club, has grown through the years. Namath visits Tuscaloosa periodically and said that he makes it a point to visit those he is close to. When he returns, it's purposely unpublicized and without fanfare.

Almost 50 years after Namath's star shined so brightly in T-town, Tuscaloosa residents continue to embrace one of its most famous adopted sons. "Some of the people here, we go back a long time. The more you live life, the more you realize that what it is all about is your associations with people. When you think of the things you miss, it's the people that you've been with," he said.

Joe Namath is an interesting person who has lived an extraordinary life that not many people can identify with. In two interviews, one exclusive and one for about an hour with another sportswriter and a TV reporter, Namath was extremely cooperative and cordial, even when answering questions on some touchy subjects.

Despite chronic knee problems that were first encountered in the fourth game of his senior year against North Carolina State, Namath in his 13-year NFL career completed 1,886 passes for 12,663 yards and 173 touchdowns, numbers that helped get him inducted into the Pro Football Hall of Fame.

Lee Roy Jordan, Namath's teammate at Alabama and his opponent in the NFL, said, "I thought Joe was the best athlete that I played with or against, college or pro."

Besides Bear Bryant, Joe Namath is the biggest star to play football at Alabama.

Lee Roy Jordan

Lee Roy Jordan, who played on Bear Bryant's first national championship team in 1961 and was an All-American in 1962, is a legendary linebacker who played a key role in helping Bryant turn around the fortunes of the Alabama football program.

Jordan was a stabilizing factor on defense for Tide teams that went 8–1–2, 11–0, and 10–1. A unanimous All-American as a senior, Jordan recorded an astonishing 30 tackles in a 17–0

Lee Roy Jordan with coach Bear Bryant

win over Oklahoma. Bryant once said of Jordan, "If they stay inside the boundaries, Lee Roy will get them."

Jordan was voted Alabama's Player of the Decade for the 1960s.

In addition to playing for Bryant, Jordan also played 14 years in the NFL for legendary Dallas Cowboys coach Tom Landry, where he was part of the "Doomsday Defense" on teams from 1966 to 1976 that made the playoffs 10 out of 11 years, reaching the Super Bowl three times, and winning Super Bowl VI over the Miami Dolphins. In comparing Landry with Bryant, Jordan said, "[Landry] was a great person, a great Christian, and a great leader. He had a different way of leading than Coach Bryant, but both were effective and both won."

Jordan, a five-time Pro Bowler, played in the famous "Ice Bowl" NFL Championship Game against Green Bay in frigid sub-zero weather when Lombardi's Packers beat the Cowboys on the last play of the game. Guard Jerry Kramer made the block that allowed Alabama alumnus Bart Starr to sneak into the end zone for the game-winning touchdown.

Johnny Musso

"The Italian Stallion" was a three-year starter and a two-time All-American who led the SEC in rushing in 1970 and 1971. He rushed for 167 yards and outplayed soon-to-be-named Heisman Trophy winner Pat Sullivan as the Crimson Tide overwhelmed Auburn 31–7 in a marquee Iron Bowl game where, for the first time, both teams entered the game undefeated.

Johnny Musso gets some instruction from Bear Bryant.

In his three games against Auburn from 1969 through 1971, Musso accounted for 569 yards, 467 by rushing and 102 on eight receptions. His 467 rushing yards was 10 short of Bobby Marlow's Iron Bowl record 477 yards.

Musso graduated as the Crimson Tide's career leader in rushing with 2,741 yards and rushing touchdowns with 36, the latter a record that stood for 16 years. He caught 61 passes for 495 yards and four touchdowns, and passed five times for 88 yards and two more touchdowns. Altogether, the 5'11", 200-pound Musso amassed 3,328 yards of total offense and scored 40 touchdowns. He was voted to the 1970s All-Decade Team and to UA's Team of the Century. He finished fourth in Heisman Trophy voting in 1971.

Musso was "the Italian Stallion" a few years before Sylvester Stallone made the moniker famous in his original *Rocky* movie in 1976.

John Hannah

After being a two-time All-American at Alabama, a 10-time All-Pro in 13 seasons with the New England Patriots, and in 1991 being inducted into both the College Football Hall of Fame and the Pro Football Hall of Fame, John Hannah has been called by many the best offensive lineman to ever play football.

Despite being elected to the all-time college football team by ESPN in 1989, Hannah feels that he was more suited for professional football. "That's because I matured later in life," he explained. "And the pro game is much more wide open, where

I could do a lot more offensively than I could do at Alabama. The pro game is a lot more fun for offensive linemen."

Hannah and the Patriots in 1985 played in Super Bowl XX, but Hannah said that he did not enjoy the game, and not just because the Patriots were handily defeated by the Chicago Bears. "The Super Bowl is not a football game as much as it is a theatrical show," he said. "Nobody can keep their adrenaline pumping for five or six hours that it takes to play the game. I didn't enjoy it at all. It was awful. I wanted to go and play football, not see a rock show and movie stars. I wished it were like a regular season game. The lengthy halftime and all the hoopla completely destroyed your tempo and game rhythm."

Hannah said that the Super Bowl, because of its circus atmosphere, "then boils down to talent," which he said was completely different from what he experienced at Alabama. "At Alabama we knew the other team was physically better than us, but we knew we were going to beat them. Coach Bryant got the adrenaline going and got us up for games. The Super Bowl takes that out of the equation."

Hannah said the biggest thing he learned from Bryant was "that you could learn more and push yourself more than you thought that you could. I learned that I could make myself do things that I never thought that I could do."

Hannah said the highlights of his college career were beating Southern Cal his junior year when 'Bama unveiled its wishbone—an offense that completely surprised the Trojans—and beating Auburn in the last regular season game that year.

Another memorable moment came his senior year when the Crimson Tide came from behind to win at Tennessee.

An SEC champion in track in the shot-put and discus and an undefeated wrestler in the heavyweight division, Hannah said that he really enjoyed playing for the Crimson Tide on national television and in front of crowds that were larger than in the NFL. "When I went to New England, a sportswriter asked me what it's going to be like playing in front of 55,000 people, and I said it won't be too disappointing."

Hannah hails from a family deeply steeped in Alabama football. His father Herb was an offensive lineman for UA and played a year with the New York Giants. His Uncle Bill was a guard and linebacker on Bear Bryant's first 'Bama team, and his brothers Charles and David were also all-conference linemen for the Crimson Tide.

Hannah, at the time of this interview, said the last chance for another Hannah playing football rests with his brother Charles' son, John David, named after the two football-playing siblings. Asked what grade he's in, John said, "He's in first grade."

Kenny Stabler

Following Joe Namath and Steve Sloan, Kenny Stabler continued the Crimson Tide's tradition of outstanding quarterbacks. An All-American, Stabler quarterbacked the 1966 undefeated and untied Tide team. He was named Most Valuable Player in 'Bama's 34–7 rout of Nebraska in the Sugar Bowl. Although the team did not win the national championship, Bear Bryant

Crimson Tide QB Kenny Stabler runs with the ball on a keeper play to score the first touchdown in the 1968 Cotton Bowl against Texas A&M in Dallas. But 'Bama lost to the Gene Stallings–coached Aggies 20–16. Photo courtesy of AP Images

called the 1966 squad his best team. "Coming from him, that's all I need," said Stabler about his famed coach's assessment.

Stabler is named, along with Namath, for the quarterback position on UA's 1960s Team of the Decade as well as on the University's Team of the Century.

Nicknamed "Snake," Stabler was drafted in the second round and went on to star in the NFL, where he won the 1976 passing title when he guided the Oakland Raiders to the Super

Bowl championship with a 32–14 victory over the Minnesota Vikings. He completed 60 percent of his passes over the course of a 15-year professional career.

Stabler said his most memorable games were the 1967 "run in the mud" Iron Bowl win over Auburn, Oakland's 1974 playoff win over the Miami Dolphins, and of course the Raiders' Super Bowl victory over the Vikings.

Like Namath, Stabler had a longtime and well-earned reputation as a party person and a night owl. In his heyday in the off-season he was known to come back and hang around his old stomping grounds, frequenting the bars at Gulf Shores. Legend has it that he was at least in part responsible for the area becoming known as the "Redneck Riviera."

Steve Sloan

Sandwiched between Namath and Stabler was Steve Sloan, another All-American. Often overlooked because he played between two legends, Sloan was a star in his own right, leading the nation in passer efficiency in 1965. He was in the top 10 in Heisman Trophy voting and capped his career by being named MVP in 'Bama's 39–28 victory over Nebraska in the 1966 Orange Bowl. Sloan returned to Alabama as athletics director in the late 1980s.

Ozzie Newsome

From 1974 to 1977 Ozzie Newsome caught 102 passes for 2,070 yards, setting an SEC record by averaging 20.3 yards per reception. A four-year starter and an All-American his senior year, Newsome was named to Alabama's All-Decade Team for the 1970s and to the Crimson Tide's Team of the Century.

After college, Newsome enjoyed a Hall of Fame career in the NFL. Following his professional playing career, Newsome became a longtime and well-respected executive with the Baltimore Ravens. Prior to being inducted into the Pro Football Hall of Fame in 1999, Newsome was inducted into the College Football Hall of Fame and the NCAA Hall of Fame in 1994,

NCAA INDIVIDUAL STATISTICAL CHAMPIONS

Kickers

Hugh Morrow	1945	46/46 PATs

Punt Returns

Harry Gilmer	1946	11.8 yards/return

Interceptions

Hootie Ingram	1952	10 for 63 yards

Kickers

David Ray	1964	52/53 PATs, 12 FGs

Passer Rating

Steve Sloan	1965	153.8

Field-Goal Percentage

Kicker	Year	Made /Att.	Pct.
Philip Doyle	1989	22/25	.880
	1990	24/29	.828
Michael Proctor	1993	22/29	.759

Scoring

Shaun Alexander	1999	13.1 ppg

ALABAMA

and the Alabama Sports Hall of Fame in 1995. That's how good he was.

Billy Neighbors

Billy Neighbors was a two-way tackle and co-captain on Bear Bryant's first national championship team in 1961. An all-conference performer who was named the top lineman in the SEC and MVP of the Senior Bowl, Neighbors was a consensus All-American who would later be named to 'Bama's All-Decade Team of the 1960s, the Crimson Tide's All-Century Team, and in 2003 was elected to the College Football Hall of Fame.

When Neighbors played, Alabama shut out Auburn three straight times, 10–0, 3–0, and 34–0. "They never scored a point against us," he said proudly. "The turning point to us winning the national championship was when we beat Auburn 34–0. Then we beat Arkansas 10–3 in the Sugar Bowl. The best thing that ever happened to me was when we won the national championship. I've got the University of Alabama to thank for that."

Neighbors entered Alabama the year before Bryant arrived and began resurrecting the program that had fallen on hard times.

After playing every play on offense, defense, and special teams for the Crimson Tide, Neighbors went on to the American Football League, where he made the All-Star team in 1963 and became a three-time All-Pro before retiring in 1969.

Neighbors grew up in the small Alabama community of Taylorsville. "I went from Taylorsville to New York City, where I was on *The Ed Sullivan Show* and *The Bob Hope Show*," he related. "Playing at Alabama changed my life. I'd never been on an airplane before, I'd never seen an escalator before, I'd never seen doors that opened by themselves before.

"I was just a country boy playing in New York City, in Boston, in San Francisco, and in those other big cities. But those were just Sunday afternoons. Except for that, I'd rather have been right here in Alabama."

Neighbors was one of several in his family who played for the Crimson Tide, the others being his older brother, Sid, who played in the 1950s; his sons, Wes, who played center for Ray Perkins, and Keith, a linebacker on Gene Stallings' national championship team in 1992; and his grandson, Wesley, who in 2011 was a redshirt freshman free safety for Nick Saban.

Pat Trammell

Pat Trammell will always have a special place in the hearts of Alabama fans. For one thing, he was the quarterback on Bear Bryant's first national championship team in 1961. For another, he was one of Bryant's favorite players.

A second-team All-American and an Academic All-American, Trammell was the first Alabama quarterback to pass for more than 1,000 yards in a season. As a senior, he was named SEC Most Valuable Player and scored the only touchdown in the Crimson Tide's 10–3 victory over Arkansas in the Sugar Bowl.

Pat Trammell (12) with Bear Bryant

After graduating, Trammell became a medical doctor. Unfortunately, he passed away at the age of 28 of cancer. When he learned that Trammell had passed away, Bryant stated, "This is the saddest day of my life."

Barry Krauss

A two-time All-America linebacker and a member of the Tide's All-Decade (1970s) and All-Century Teams, Krauss will always be remembered for stopping Mike Guman short of the end zone in the 1979 Sugar Bowl win over Penn State. His famous tackle, known as "the Goal-Line Stand," helped earn him Sugar Bowl Most Valuable Player accolades.

Krauss, who served as a team captain, said about that play, "I don't think there is any picture that depicts Alabama football any better than [*The Goal-Line Stand* painting by Daniel Moore]. Mike Guman tried to go over the top, and we stopped him. That was about a group of guys who had the same commitment and passion who came together at the right time, right place, in the right situation, to win the national championship."

Krauss, who was also MVP of the 1976 Liberty Bowl, played 11 years in the NFL with the Baltimore Colts and Miami Dolphins. He later served as the sideline reporter for 'Bama football broadcasts.

POST-BRYANT ERA

Mark Ingram

The school's first Heisman Trophy winner, Ingram left the Capstone as Alabama's single-season rushing leader with 1,658 yards. As a sophomore in 2009, he won the Heisman, college football's most prestigious individual award that goes to the best player in the country. The 5′10″, 215-pound running back rushed for 118.4 yards a game and added 30 catches for 322

ALABAMA

MAJOR AWARD WINNERS

Heisman Trophy
Mark Ingram (2009)

Butkus Award (Nation's Top Linebacker)
Derrick Thomas (1988)
Rolando McClain (2009)

Outland Trophy (Nation's Top Interior Lineman)
Chris Samuels (1999)
Andre Smith (2008)
Barrett Jones (2011)

Lombardi Award (Nation's Best Lineman)
Cornelius Bennett (1986)

**Johnny Unitas Golden Arm Award
(Nation's Best Senior Quarterback)**
Jay Barker (1994)

Jim Thorpe Award (Nation's Top Defensive Back)
Antonio Langham (1993)

Lott Trophy (Defensive Impact Player of the Year)
Demeco Ryans (2005)

Doak Walker Award (Nation's Best Running Back)
Trent Richardson (2011)

yards that season. He led the Crimson Tide to a 14–0 record that included a 37–21 win over Texas in the BCS National Championship Game. Against the Longhorns, Ingram carried the ball 22 times for 116 yards and two touchdowns to earn Offensive Most Valuable Player honors. Ingram was at his best against the best teams, averaging 189 all-purpose yards against six top 25 teams, including four top 10 teams.

In the closest vote in the 75-year history of the Heisman Trophy, Ingram edged out Stanford's Toby Gerhart to finally bring a Heisman Trophy to Alabama.

Despite leaving prior to his senior year for the NFL, Ingram played in 39 games for Alabama, running the ball 572 times for 3,261 yards, a 5.7 yards-per-carry average, and 42 touchdowns. He also caught 60 passes for 670 additional yards and four more touchdowns.

That, his modesty, and his ever-present ear-to-ear smile, what's not to like?

Trent Richardson

In Ingram's Heisman Trophy–winning season, Richardson was content to be the backup running back. When Ingram left early for the NFL, Richardson shot out from underneath Ingram's shadow to become Alabama's marquee rushing threat. In 2011 Richardson tied a school record by rushing for more than 100 yards in nine games. He gained an SEC-leading 1,583 yards and scored 20 touchdowns during the regular season. His 131.9 rushing yards per game ranked fifth in the nation. Richardson was a Heisman Trophy finalist, and although he didn't win the award like his former teammate, Richardson rushed for a single-season school record 1,679 yards, shattering Ingram's mark of 1,658 yards.

He also caught 29 passes for 338 yards and three more touchdowns. Furthermore, Richardson was rock-tough, having not fumbled at all during the 2011 season and only once in 614 career touches.

Whereas Ingram struggled in two Iron Bowl games, Richardson in 2011 ran through, over, and around Auburn for a career-high 203 yards, including rambling 57 yards on a breakaway run in the fourth quarter.

In saying that he thought Richardson was the best player in the nation, Saban added, "You love saying that about someone who's such a good person, who does so much to serve other people. He's a great teammate. He's a leader. He cares about everyone around him."

Richardson was Associated Press SEC Offensive Player of the Year and a first-team pick for the 2011 American Football Coaches Association and the Walter Camp All-America teams. He became the first player from Alabama to win the Doak Walker Award, given to the nation's best running back. He was also a finalist for the Maxwell Award, given to the best football player selected by coaches and sports journalists. Like Ingram in 2009, Richardson in 2011 led the Crimson Tide to the national championship.

Cornelius Bennett

A dominant linebacker, Cornelius Bennett was a three-time All-SEC selection, a three-time All-American, and Alabama's first winner of the Lombardi Award, which is given to the best lineman in the nation. While playing for Alabama, Bennett was credited with 287 tackles, 15 sacks, and three fumble recoveries.

"Biscuit," as he was fondly called, was named Player of the Decade for the 1980s and was selected to Alabama's All-Century Team. He was also named Defensive Player of the Game for both the 1985 Aloha Bowl and the 1986 Sun Bowl.

Cornelius Bennett (97) with Derrick Thomas (55) to his left, two of Alabama's greatest linebackers.

Bennett is perhaps best remembered for a play against Notre Dame when he made a ferocious sack on Fighting Irish quarterback Steve Beuerlein, who acknowledged that it was the hardest that he'd ever been hit. Captured in a painting appropriately named *The Sack* by artist Daniel A. Moore, a giant portrait of the vicious tackle hangs on a wall to the right when a visitor enters Bryant Museum. It is a favorite backdrop for visitors taking pictures. Bennett played in five Super Bowls during his NFL career.

Derrick Thomas

Derrick Thomas followed Cornelius Bennett as an Alabama linebacker and in some ways surpassed him. The first SEC player to win the Butkus Award (given to the nation's best linebacker), Thomas recorded a school-record 27 sacks in one season (1988) and totaled 52 in his college career. In 1988 he was a unanimous All-American, the Butkus Award winner, CBS Player of the Year, and Washington Pigskin Club's Defensive Player of the Year. Thomas was voted Defensive Player of the Decade for the 1980s and selected for Alabama's Team of the Century.

Thomas played in the NFL for the Kansas City Chiefs and was named Defensive Rookie of the Year in 1989. One of the best linebackers to ever play the game, his career and his life were tragically cut short at the age of 33, when he was involved in an automobile accident that paralyzed him from the chest down. He died a couple of weeks later due to complications from a blood clot. A nine-time All-Pro, Thomas, despite a shortened career, notched 126½ sacks, recovered 18 fumbles, forced 45 fumbles, and registered three safeties, all Kansas City records.

Derrick Thomas, one of the greatest linebackers to ever play the game

He established an NFL single-game record for sacks with seven. In a game that was played on Veterans Day, he dedicated his performance to his father, an Air Force pilot who was killed in Vietnam in a mission ironically dubbed "Linebacker II."

Thomas is considered one of the best linebackers of all time.

Jay Barker

Jay Barker will always have a special place in the hearts of Alabama fans because he quarterbacked Alabama to the 1992 national championship. He notched a 35–2–1 record as a starter and completed his career as the winningest quarterback in the storied history of the program, although use of an ineligible player later caused the Crimson Tide to forfeit all of the 1993 regular season victories.

Besides leading the Tide to the national championship, Barker is also remembered for the big day he had on October 1, 1994, when he rallied 'Bama, after trailing by nine points in the fourth quarter, to a 29–28 win over Georgia. Michael Proctor booted a 32-yard field goal with a little over a minute remaining to give UA the win. Barker threw for a Bryant-Denny Stadium–record 396 yards in the contest, and the Tide went on to finish the regular season with a perfect record.

Barker completed 402 of 706 passes for 5,689 yards, all school records. He received the Johnny Unitas Golden Arm Award in

ALABAMA'S WINNINGEST QBs

QB	Record	Pct.	Years
Jay Barker	35–2–1	.934	1991–1994
Millard "Dixie" Howell*	22–2–1	.900	1934–1937
Greg McElroy	24–3–0	.889	2009–2010
Joe Namath	21–3–0	.875	1962–1964
Terry Davis	21–3–0	.875	1971–1972
Pat Trammell	26–2–4	.875	1959–1961

*Howell played in a single-wing formation in which he did not line up as a quarterback, but was the team's primary passer.

ALABAMA

1994 and was a finalist for the Heisman Trophy and the Davey O'Brien Award. He was an All-American and consensus All-Conference QB as a senior. A devout Christian who includes his favorite biblical passage when he signs autographs, Barker was and still is recognized by many as an outstanding role model.

Shaun Alexander

An All-American and SEC Player of the Year in 1999, Alexander also is a devout and outspoken Christian who always has a big smile, which along with his many accomplishments, endeared him to 'Bama fans. He established three SEC records and 15 Alabama records and finished seventh in Heisman voting his senior year.

Among his records, Alexander holds the Alabama career rushing standard with 3,565 yards. He averaged 4.9 yards a carry and scored 41 touchdowns. He also caught 62 passes for 798 yards and eight touchdowns. In 1999 he averaged 125.7 yards a game and gained 1,383 yards on the ground.

In his nine-year NFL career, Alexander rushed for 9,453 yards and 100 touchdowns and was on the receiving end of 215 passes for 1,520 yards and 12 touchdowns. As a member of the Seattle Seahawks in 2005, Alexander had a season for the ages, rushing for an NFL-high 1,880 yards that included 11 games with 100 or more yards, both team records, and an NFL record 28 touchdowns. The performance earned Alexander the NFL's Most Valuable Player Award as he led the Seahawks to Super Bowl XL.

After starring at Alabama, Shaun Alexander went on to the NFL to star for the Seattle Seahawks.

Eric Curry and John Copeland

Called "the Bookends," Curry and Copeland were All-America defensive ends on the Crimson Tide's 1992 national championship team. Named UPI Lineman of the Year and Chevrolet

Defensive Player of the Year, Curry was a Lombardi Award finalist as a senior. Copeland was a consensus All-American who played on Tide teams that went 24–1. Most teams were smart enough not to try to run around end when Curry and Copeland played, and few opponents were able to successfully turn the corner and pick up positive yardage against "the Bookends."

David Palmer

An all-around threat as a receiver who occasionally played quarterback and running back in certain situations, and as a kickoff and punt returner, David Palmer was an All-American who in 1993 finished third in Heisman Trophy voting. That season he set school single-season records for receiving yards (1,000) and receptions (61). Wearing jersey No. 2, when he played and broke free for one of his characteristic long gainers, the saying was, "The Deuce is loose."

As a sophomore, he set school records for most punt-return yardage (409), and for returning three punts for touchdowns during the regular season.

5

COACHES WE LOVE

BEAR BRYANT

Alabama football is, of course, synonymous with Bear Bryant. Bryant is the yardstick by which all college coaches are measured. He set an unparalleled standard for Crimson Tide football. In college football circles, the Bear Bryant legacy—the mystique—will live forever. Bryant's record-breaking, on-the-sideline accomplishments and what he did for the Crimson Tide and college football as well as what he did off-the-field for the University of Alabama and the state of Alabama are well documented and burned forever in the minds and hearts of the Alabama faithful. Bear Bryant stories will be forever told, and retold. Alabama fans and Bryant fans never tire of them. They continue to flourish, rekindling memories of the man they're about.

Bryant's impact, larger-than-life legend, and mystique are still felt throughout the South and, to a lesser degree, the nation. Bryant's 25-year stamp on the UA program set it apart from every other program in the country, Notre Dame notwithstanding. The man's presence still looms large over the community, the campus, and especially the head coach's office.

Legendary Alabama
coach Paul "Bear"
Bryant, whose 323 career
victories were at the time
of his retirement the most
ever by a college football
coach

Bryant's 323 career victories—at the time of his retirement
the most ever by a college football coach—only begin to tell
the story of Bear Bryant. It only scratches the surface of what
he meant to the University of Alabama, Tuscaloosa, the state,
the South, and beyond.

As a young college student in upstate New York during the
1960s, I remember hearing quips like, "Down in Alabama the
Bear walks on water," and, "They say the sun doesn't get up in
Alabama until the Bear gets up." And that was *before* Bryant
made his final—and arguably his greatest—glory run, going
116–15–1 from 1971 through 1981!

Bryant's 323–85–17 record, 29 bowl appearances, 13 Southeastern Conference championships, and six national championships over a 36-year career are unmatched. He was National Coach of the Year three times, SEC Coach of the Year eight times, and National Coach of the Decade for both the 1960s and 1970s.

He turned out 68 All-Americans, including a Heisman Trophy winner, although the latter—John David Crow—was coached by Bryant at Texas A&M. He paved the way for 46 of his players or assistant coaches to go on and become head coaches. When later competing against them on 49 occasions, he beat them 43 times.

Clearly the numbers are testimony to Bryant's coaching ability. Bryant won virtually every award and honor that can be bestowed upon a man in his profession, but his greatness stemmed not so much from his victories or accomplishments as from his gift to motivate, inspire, and influence lives in positive and enduring ways.

Rarely does a man pass through this world whose very presence impacts the way masses of people think and behave. "Coach Bryant was such a man," stated Dr. Gaylon McCollough, who played center for Alabama in the early 1960s. "He exemplified the true meaning of the word hero."

During his lifetime Bryant-watchers were everywhere. Bryant's disciples—and not just his players and associates but those who believed in him and respected him—abound, especially in Tuscaloosa.

ALABAMA

"THE BEAR"
COACH PAUL W. BRYANT'S
CAREER COACHING RECORD (1945–1982)

Year	School	W	L	T
1945	Maryland	6	2	1
1946	Kentucky	7	3	0
1947	Kentucky	8	3	0
1948	Kentucky	5	3	2
1949	Kentucky	9	3	0
1950	Kentucky	11	1	0
1951	Kentucky	8	4	0
1952	Kentucky	5	4	2
1953	Kentucky	7	2	1
1954	Texas A&M	1	9	0
1955	Texas A&M	7	2	1
1956	Texas A&M	9	0	1
1957	Texas A&M	8	3	0
1958	Alabama	5	4	1
1959	Alabama	7	2	2
1960	Alabama	8	1	2
1961	Alabama	11	0	0
1962	Alabama	10	1	0
1963	Alabama	9	2	0
1964	Alabama	10	1	0
1965	Alabama	9	1	1
1966	Alabama	11	0	0

continued

1967	Alabama	8	2	1
1968	Alabama	8	3	0
1969	Alabama	6	5	0
1970	Alabama	6	5	1
1971	Alabama	11	1	0
1972	Alabama	10	2	0
1973	Alabama	11	1	0
1974	Alabama	11	1	0
1975	Alabama	11	1	0
1976	Alabama	9	3	0
1977	Alabama	11	1	0
1978	Alabama	11	1	0
1979	Alabama	12	0	0
1980	Alabama	10	2	0
1981	Alabama	9	2	1
1982	Alabama	8	4	0
Career Record		**323**	**85**	**17**

"The first season without Coach Bryant, a lot of people told me that emotionally they couldn't stand to go to the games because he wasn't there," stated Wayne Atcheson, sports information director at the time. "Some said they came and had to leave early because emotionally they couldn't take it. It's hard for people to imagine what it was like here in 1983, especially those not familiar with Alabama football."

That made coaching football at Alabama for those who followed a bear of a job because, even if you won a lot of football games, in some people's minds you've still got to measure up to the man, and that is a lot harder than beating Auburn, Tennessee, and the other teams on the schedule.

"Coach Bryant had more influence on me and my family than my dad and my mom," said Clem Gryska, who coached with Bryant beginning with Alabama's first national championship team in 1961.

"When Coach Bryant died, there were a lot of people who felt that the University of Alabama could never be as successful again, and that no one could come in here and be nearly as successful," stated Bert Bank, who had sponsored and been affiliated with the radio broadcasting of UA football games since 1952. "There were followers of Bryant who were not nearly as bitter about losing a game when he coached as they were when those who followed him lost a game, which in my judgment is not the proper way to feel. But that's the way it was."

Bryant played football at Alabama from 1933 through 1935 on Crimson Tide teams that went 23–3–2, won back-to-back Southeastern Conference championships the first two years, and in his junior season beat Stanford in the Rose Bowl. Bryant played right end with blocking his primary responsibility. He was good, but not a star like fellow receiver Don Hutson, an All-American who set pass-catching records warranting future selection to the NCAA's all-time team. In fact, Bryant became known as "the other end," one of the few times in his life that he was overshadowed by anybody.

Bryant stayed four more years at his alma mater and assisted his mentor, head coach Frank Thomas, with Crimson Tide teams that won 73 percent of their contests. Winning being a well-entrenched habit by then, Bryant was prepared and ready to take over his own program.

CHAMPIONSHIPS UNDER BRYANT

National Championships (6)
1961, 1964, 1965, 1973, 1978, 1979

SEC Championships (14)
1950, 1961, 1964, 1965, 1966, 1971, 1972, 1973, 1974, 1975, 1977, 1978, 1979, 1981

National Coach of the Year (3)
1961, 1971, 1973

SEC Coach of the Year (10)
1950, 1961, 1964, 1965, 1971, 1973,1974, 1977, 1979, 1981

His first opportunity came in 1945 at Maryland, where he took over a Terrapin team that had won only one game the year before and guided it to a 6–2–1 record. The following year he went to Kentucky, where he stayed for eight years and won more than 70 percent of his games, the school's only SEC championship, and snapped Oklahoma's 31-game winning streak by upsetting the Sooners in the 1950 Sugar Bowl.

The next stop was Texas A&M, where the Bryant legend, if it didn't begin there, flourished. In 1954, not pleased with the quality and conditioning of the Aggies players that he inherited and lacking patience to wait for them to come around, Bryant took two busloads of football players to Junction, Texas, where he shaped them up his way.

In the midst of a drought and what some said was the hottest summer they could remember, Bryant drove the Aggies relentlessly. Many shipped out, overwhelmed by Bryant's boot-camp regimentation, which was essentially football, football, and more football, with time off only to eat and sleep.

"I don't know how they stood it. It was the most grueling thing I've ever seen," Joe Beck, the manager of the Junction Chamber of Commerce told former *Tuscaloosa News* sports editor Billy Mitchell in 1985. "I was amazed by the fact that the dropout rate was only 70 percent."

More than 100 players were on two buses that left for Junction, with only one bus, half-filled, needed to take home those who endured. Only eight Junction survivors graduated two years later. One of those was Gene Stallings, who would later assist Bryant, beat him in the 1968 Cotton Bowl, and—two coaches removed—follow him as the head coach at Alabama.

"I remember everything about that trip," recalled Stallings in his office in February 1992. "We had our first spring practice with Coach Bryant. Then we showed up in the fall and were told we were going somewhere and to bring clothes, a pillow, and our toothbrush. We had no idea where we were going, or the purpose of the trip.

"We go to Junction, Texas, where an old adjunct campus of Texas A&M was located. The facilities were not very good, not as good as Coach Bryant thought they would be. We lived in Quonset huts. It was just intense football, lunch, practice, dinner, meetings, and then to bed. To some people it wasn't worth it. It just so happened that it was to me."

"That trip to Junction created a mystique about Coach Bryant and those players that still lives today," John David Crow, who later went on to win the Heisman Trophy and coach with Bryant, told Mitchell. "There's no doubt about what that trip did for Coach Bryant's reputation. The whole world knew how tough he was then."

Playing with a depleted squad, Bryant suffered his only losing season as a coach, his first Aggies team finishing 1–9. A year later Bryant's no-nonsense methods began to pay off. Texas A&M turned around and lost only two games, proving Bryant right. In 1956 Bryant had his first undefeated season, nine wins with only a tie marring an otherwise perfect year. An 8–3 ledger followed.

Meanwhile, back at Alabama things were not going well. The Crimson Tide had suffered through consecutive 2–7–1 seasons and had won a total of four games the previous three years. Dr. Frank Rose knew of Bryant, since Rose had been president of Transylvania College in Lexington, when Bryant was guiding the Kentucky Wildcats to winning seasons. He also knew of Bryant's Alabama background and pursued him.

Rose offered Bryant $25,000, a car, and a home, but Bryant refused to take more than what the school's deans were then making. He accepted $18,000 and another $12,000 for his television show, and returned to Tuscaloosa in 1958. The deal would pay dividends millions of times over, considering how the University, city, and state benefited from Bryant's direct and indirect influence.

"It was like when you were out in the field and you heard your mama calling you to dinner," Bryant said in accepting Rose's offer enabling him to return to his alma mater. "Mama called."

That is a familiar phrase to Alabama football fans, and in retrospect has perhaps been a lot more helpful to UA football than even "Roll, Tide, Roll!"

And the rest, as they say, is history.

Bryant coached his last game December 29, 1982, in the Liberty Bowl in Memphis, Tennessee. He beat Illinois 21–15, marking the end of a long and glorious career. Football, more specifically winning football, had been his life. It's like his colleague, Darrel Royal, once said, "Coach Bryant is just tougher than the rest of us."

As Bryant was nearing the end of his career, he once said, "If I quit coaching, I'll croak in a week."

Bryant proved himself nearly as good a prophet as he was a coach, dying on January 26, 1983, at the age of 69, 28 days after coaching his last game. Bryant died in Tuscaloosa's

BOWL GAMES UNDER BRYANT

29 Bowl Appearances
24 Consecutive Bowl Trips

8 Sugar Bowls
5 Orange Bowls
4 Cotton Bowls
4 Liberty Bowls
2 Bluebonnet Bowls
1 Gator Bowl

ALABAMA

Bear Bryant is carried off the field by his players after a victory.

Druid City Hospital at 1:20 PM. Word spread fast, and the city, state, and nation responded to the death of a sports figure in a way unseen since baseball immortal Babe Ruth passed away 35 years earlier. Sports figures and dignitaries came to Tuscaloosa from around the country. The funeral procession drew throngs of onlookers on the overpass all along Interstate

59 from Tuscaloosa to Birmingham, with one banner reading, "God Needs a Good Offensive Coordinator."

More than 15,000 people inside and outside the gates gathered at Elmwood Cemetery in Birmingham, Bryant's final resting place. Bryant is buried at Block 30, Lot 57-126. A plain, ordinary stone rests above the plot of ground where many believe an extraordinary man lies. On it is simply engraved:

PAUL WILLIAM BRYANT, SR.

SEPTEMBER 11, 1913

JANUARY 26, 1983

Although the grave marker is very nondescript, Bryant's legacy will live forever in the minds and hearts of his fans and the people he affected, particularly in Tuscaloosa, where numerous things are named after him. There's Bryant-Denny Stadium, Bryant Hall, the Bryant Conference Center. Included in the conference center is the Bryant Museum. A portion of 10th Street that runs through downtown and the University section was renamed Bryant Drive. Fittingly, it passes the stadium, conference center, the museum, and the Alabama athletic complex that contains the football building and practice fields, where his famous tower again stands.

Several years later, other things were named after the gone but still loved coach, including Bryant Drive Apartments, Bryant Bank, Bryant High School, and the Bryant Bridge. Of course, Bryant's statue stands in front of the stadium co-named after him as a part of the Walk of Champions. There's another Bryant statue that still stands in front of Legion Field in Birmingham, and a head and shoulder bust of Bryant greets visitors entering the museum named for him.

There's also the Bryant Alumni-Athlete Award given by the UA Alumni Association to a former Alabama athlete whose accomplishments have been outstanding, based on character, contributions to society, professional achievements, and service; the Bryant Student-Athlete Award given to a Crimson Tide athlete who excels in the classroom, in athletics, and in the community; and the Bryant-Jordan Student-Athlete Scholarship that is named for Bryant and Auburn coach Shug Jordan and is presented to an outstanding high school student-athlete in the state.

Nationally, there's the Bear Bryant Award, given annually by the Football Writers Association of America to the nation's top Division I-A football coach. There was also a very mediocre movie entitled *The Bear*, starring Gary Busey, best known for his role as rock-and-roller Buddy Holly. Unfortunately the film did not do justice to Bryant, a man who on the contrary demanded excellence from himself and those who worked for him. Only John Wayne, "the Duke," an actor in his field on a par with the Bear in his field, could have pulled it off satisfactorily. And recently, there was a play on statewide tour called *Bear Country*, with Rodney Clark portraying the famed coach, which had a long run in Tuscaloosa and garnered praise from Bryant's former players, including athletics director Mal Moore.

He's been gone for almost 30 years now, but clearly 'Bama fans still love the Bear.

NICK SABAN

When Mike Shula was let go, Alabama was looking for a highly successful, big-name coach, and they got one in Nick Saban, who left his job as head coach of the NFL's Miami Dolphins to coach the Crimson Tide. Athletics director Mal Moore immediately targeted Saban, a hard-nosed, no-nonsense coach who through the years had gained a national reputation as a strong leader, tactician, recruiter, visionary, motivator, disciplinarian, and organizer who had a driving and uncompromising commitment to achieving excellence in every phase of the football program. Saban's attraction stemmed from his long-time sustained success at the college level, where he never experienced a losing season and produced a 91–42–1 record that included a five-year run at LSU (48–16) that resulted in two SEC championships, three SEC Western Division championships, and the NCAA championship. In 2003 Saban was the AP National Coach of the Year, won the Paul W. "Bear" Bryant National Coach of the Year Award, and the Football Writers Association of America Eddie Robinson Coach of the Year Award.

Moore delivered on his stated intention of "hiring a coach with a proven track record of championship success" and picked a high-profile coach who could raise eyebrows, command respect, win, and deal with the intense pressure that comes with heading a program that is scrutinized on an almost daily basis by university decision-makers, the media, and a football-crazed fan base.

From the moment he stepped off the airplane at Tuscaloosa Regional Airport through his official announcement as the

University of Alabama's next head football coach the next day, Saban was treated like a rock star and hailed by many as "St. Nick," the savior who would finally return the Crimson Tide to glory. Some in the media called the hiring an historic benchmark and went so far as to say that Saban was the most important football coaching hire since Bear Bryant. Immediately billboards went up and T-shirts were printed with phrases such as "I Love Nick" and "the Sabanator." The *Tuscaloosa News*, a morning paper, even published a special afternoon edition with a bold front-page headline proclaiming "Saban Time!"

Saban's contract was for $4 million a year and $30 million with incentives over eight years, making him the highest paid coach in the nation. The expectation was clear. Saban better win big and win fast.

Fifty-five years old at the time, Saban understood the charge and accepted the challenge of bringing championship football and top-tier bowls back to Alabama. When he was introduced to the media, he said, "I can tell you, I have even higher expectations for what we want to accomplish. I want to win every game.… I want the best football team and the best football program in the SEC.… I want to be a champion in everything that we do.

"We want to be a big, physical, aggressive football team that is relentless in the competitive spirit.… What I would like is for every football team that we play to say, 'I hate playing against these guys. I hate playing them, their effort, their toughness, their relentless resiliency on every play…their competing for

60 minutes. I can't handle it.' That's the kind of football team we want."

Saban generated even more excitement by stating that his expectation was for the Crimson Tide to not only return to playing championship football, but to dominate opponents—specifically Auburn.

Saban had a plan to restore the glitter to a program oozing with tradition, but that in recent years had fallen from the ranks of the elite. He fostered a sense of ownership among the Alabama Nation by quickly rallying people to support his "process," which emphasized that everyone interested in Alabama football be positive and come together to "create an atmosphere and environment where Alabama football can reach its goals." His first A-Day game, a controlled scrimmage that concludes spring practice, drew a national record–setting crowd of 92,138.

There is no question that Saban lived up to the hype and the expectations. In 2007, Saban's first season, the Tide finished 7–6, including a 30–24 victory over Colorado in the Independence Bowl. The record was later adjusted to 2–6 (1–4 SEC) when five wins were vacated because of NCAA infractions committed under the previous administration. The following year was when the Saban hire began to pay dividends. The Crimson Tide went 12–2 and won the SEC Western Division championship with an 8–0 mark. The Crimson Tide dropped its last two contests, however, falling to Florida 31–20 in the SEC Championship Game and then going belly-up against Utah 31–17 in the Sugar Bowl. No matter, it became clear that 'Bama was on the way back to where its followers believed it rightfully belonged.

Saban hit the jackpot in 2009 when 'Bama won the national championship and Mark Ingram won the school's first Heisman Trophy. Everything was again hunky-dory among the 'Bama Nation. Saban's statue joined the other UA national championship–winning coaches on the Walk of Champions entering Bryant-Denny Stadium. Although Alabama fans want and expect the Tide to win the national championship every year, the realists among the group understand that this is not possible. Twenty-ten was a pretty good follow-up year, with UA going 10–3, topped off by a 49–7 drubbing of Michigan State in the Capital One Bowl. In 2011, with Heisman Trophy finalist Trent Richardson leading the way, 'Bama played its way back into the BCS National Championship Game. An 11–1 Tide team got the game it wanted, a rematch against top-ranked, undefeated, untied, and undisputed No. 1 LSU, the team that gave UA its only blemish when it eked out a 9–6 win in overtime in Tuscaloosa on November 5. Saban hit the jackpot again, becoming the first coach to win three BCS National Championships when the Crimson Tide slapped LSU silly to win Alabama's 14th national championship.

In doing so, Saban had put together a team to his liking, one that was resilient, tough, relentless, and had a competitive spirit, just as he said he wanted when he was hired a few years earlier.

Perhaps more important, Saban's 48 wins in the last four years at Alabama, including two national championships in the last three years, has finally enabled Tide fans to enjoy the same sort of success that it had during the glory days of Paul "Bear" Bryant. Clearly, with Saban's quick and dramatic success at the Capstone, coupled with his ability to continue to bring in nationally top-ranked recruiting classes, 'Bama fans have reason to believe that another Bryant-like dynasty is underway. That's also because the competitive fires in Saban's belly are burning as hot as ever.

Think success has made Saban complacent? Then think again. With about three minutes remaining in the national championship game against LSU and the Tide having already salted the game away with a commanding 21-point lead, Saban almost blew a fuse on the sideline when a 'Bama player jumped offside while LSU was lined up to punt. It was Alabama's only penalty of the game, but Saban couldn't stop coaching. It's just not in his nature.

"A guy jumps offside with three minutes to go in the game and you still coach your team like it's the first game of the season," he explained after the game to the media who wondered why he was so upset. As if the rest of the world could understand his obsession for perfection.

Bryant coached in an era when things were much different. Everything is on a much grander scale now. The stadium is much larger, A-Day game and regular season game day atmosphere 10 times what it used to be, and ESPN and social media hyping college football in a way that Bryant could never have imagined. Bryant was the dominant college football coach of the 1960s and 1970s, for sure. Saban is, if he's not already there, fast becoming the dominant college football coach of this era.

Although Saban's wide-brimmed straw practice hat is not as popular as Bryant's houndstooth hat, it is a familiar site on the heads of many 'Bama faithful on game day. 'Bama fans love Nick Saban—a lot!

WALLACE WADE

Wallace Wade is considered one of the great early college football coaches. He is credited with bringing respect and prestige to southern football. After arriving at Alabama in 1923, Wade quickly built a powerhouse program, compiling a 61–13 record, winning the school's first four conference championships, three Rose Bowl games, UA's first three national championships, and putting Alabama on the football map. In 1925 the Crimson Tide outscored its opponents 277–7 and went undefeated (9–0). Regardless, compared to other parts of the country, southern football was considered mediocre.

After the 1925 season, Alabama was a heavy underdog when it played Washington in the Rose Bowl, but the Crimson Tide upset the Huskies 20–19. The win erased the image of southern football as being inferior and is therefore considered the most important game in southern football history.

In 1926 Wade guided Alabama to its second national championship and a 7–7 tie against Stanford in the Rose Bowl. He won his third national title in 1930 when UA outscored its nine regular season opponents 247–13 en route to blanking Washington State 24–0 in the 1931 Rose Bowl. The 1926 and 1927 Rose Bowl victories raised aspirations for Alabama football, triggering fund-raising efforts sufficient to build Denny Stadium.

Wallace Wade won three national championships in eight seasons as head coach at Alabama, then left for Duke, where the Blue Devils' football stadium is named in his honor.

After turning Alabama into a football power, Wade went to Duke in 1931, where his 1938 team was unbeaten during the regular season and didn't surrender a single point. In 16 seasons in Durham, Wade compiled a 110–36–7 record and played in the 1939 and 1942 Rose Bowl games. Having played in the 1916 Rose Bowl as a member of the Brown University team, Wade has the distinction of being the first person to both play and coach in the Rose Bowl. Considered one of the greatest coaches in history, Wade was inducted into the College Football Hall of Fame and the Alabama Sports Hall of Fame.

Alabama honored Wade by naming a street that runs alongside Bryant-Denny Stadium Wallace Wade Drive. Wade died on October 6, 1986, at the age of 94 in Durham, North Carolina.

FRANK THOMAS

When Wallace Wade went to Duke, Frank Thomas replaced him as head coach, and the Crimson Tide kept right on rolling. From 1931 to 1946, Thomas-coached Alabama teams won 115 games, lost 24, and tied 7, while winning four SEC championships and two national championships.

Only 32 years old when he was hired, Thomas had the burden of taking over a team that had won the national championship the year before but had graduated 10 of its 11 starters. Retooling with different players, Thomas won nine of 10 games his first year. His team scored 360 points while giving up only 51.

Frank Thomas, shown here with All-Americans Harry Gilmer (52) and Vaughn Mancha (41), won a pair of national titles at Alabama, in 1934 and 1941.

Thomas followed with 8–2 and 7–1–1 seasons, the latter in 1933 when Thomas coached the Tide to the first championship in the newly formed Southeastern Conference. The following year, Thomas trumped that with not only another conference championship, but the national championship when 'Bama beat Stanford 29–13 in the Rose Bowl.

After playing on the national championship team, Bear Bryant joined Thomas' staff as a graduate assistant coach. Bryant played for Thomas, who had played quarterback for legendary coach Knute Rockne at Notre Dame, where he roomed with All-American George Gipp.

Thomas won another national title in 1941, with the icing on the cake being a 29–21 victory over Texas A&M in the Cotton Bowl. World War II cancelled the 1943 football season at UA. In 1944, despite having a freshman-dominated team supported by players declared unfit for military duty, Thomas guided the group known as the "War Babies" to a 5–2–2 record and an invitation to the Sugar Bowl, where 'Bama came up short against Duke, 29–26. In 1945 Alabama was unbeaten and rolled over Southern Cal in the Rose Bowl, 34–14, to finish No. 2 in the nation.

In 1946 Thomas, only 48 years old but suffering from health problems, retired. At Alabama Thomas' .8116 career winning percentage trails only Wade (.8117) and Bryant (.8240). Despite a relatively short coaching career, Thomas' accomplishments warranted his enshrinement into the College Football Hall of Fame in 1951. Like Wade, Thomas has a street named after him near Bryant-Denny Stadium. Thomas died in 1954.

GENE STALLINGS

Gene Stallings earned a scholarship to Texas A&M, where he first came in contact with a hard-nosed football coach named Bear Bryant. One of the famed "Junction Boys," Stallings first earned Bryant's respect by sticking out that rugged preseason training camp in 1954 that weeded out so many others. The unexpected jolt of Bryant-style training stuck in Stallings' memory. "We weren't there weeks, it was just days," Stallings is quoted in an old Alabama football media guide in reference to the grueling regimen that was made into a movie. "Ten days. Been any longer and there wouldn't have been anybody left. We went out there in two buses and came back in one."

Toughened up for the task, Stallings played three years for Bryant, earning All–Southwest Conference recognition as a junior. The following year, as a senior tri-captain, he helped lead the Aggies to an undefeated (9–0–1) SWC championship en route to a No. 5 finish in both wire service polls.

Stallings impressed Bryant because Bryant kept providing opportunities for the then young man. Upon graduation, Stallings remained at Texas A&M as a graduate assistant coach. A year later Bryant took Stallings with him to Alabama. As Bryant's star rose across the nation, there was young Stallings by his side learning from the master.

Stallings spent seven years as an assistant at Alabama. He got a firsthand feel for building a winner from the ground up, as the 2–7–1 Crimson Tide team that Bryant inherited went on to win 60 of 76 games and two national championships while Stallings was there. In 1965, at the age of 29, Stallings

Gene Stallings, one of the "Junction Boys" who played for Bear Bryant at Texas A&M, guided the Crimson Tide to the 1992 national championship.

returned to Texas A&M as head coach. Three years later, he found himself across the field from Bryant in the Cotton Bowl.

Stallings looked forward to playing against Bryant and Alabama. He considered it an opportunity for his players to see and meet the man that they had heard so much about. "I always told my players about Coach Bryant whenever I could," Stallings related. "I wanted my players to be exposed to Coach Bryant."

Stallings' Aggies beat Alabama 20–16. Despite losing, pictures show Bryant, who hated to lose but was proud of his protégé, picking up a smiling Stallings.

After that, things soured at Texas A&M, and Stallings was let go. He teamed up with Tom Landry in the NFL. After being around Bryant for 12 years, Stallings spent 14 years with another legend at Dallas, where winning also became a habit. He was a part of an organization that came to be known as "America's Team," the Cowboys making the playoffs 12 times, with seven division titles, three conference championships, and one Super Bowl victory while Stallings was an assistant.

Stallings learned from two of the giants in coaching, trying to pick up what he identified as the particular strengths of each. "Coach Bryant was probably into people a little more, and Coach Landry into strategy a little more," he explained.

Stallings was given a second chance at being a head coach, this time with the NFL's St. Louis Cardinals. Again things didn't work out. When Alabama called, Stallings said it was "like a dream come true."

People said that Stallings looked like Bear Bryant, talked like Bear Bryant, and did things the way that Bear Bryant used to do. When he heard that, Stallings back then quipped in his down-home drawl, "Yeah, that's what they say. Now, if I could only win like him."

Alabama's bringing Stallings on board, like a snap of the fingers, united the Crimson Tide family, which had been in constant turmoil throughout the Billy Curry era.

"Gene Stallings is a very special person. He will earn the respect of the alumni and fans of the University, and he'll do it quickly," former Crimson Tide and Green Bay Packers quarterback Bart Starr told a group of reporters following the introductory press conference when Stallings was hired. "When he talks about commitment, you can just go and take that to the bank."

Former 'Bama and Miami Dolphin defensive lineman Bob Baumhower is quoted in the 1990 Alabama football media guide: "[Coach Stallings] has learned from the best ever in Coach Bryant and Coach Landry. He knows what this program means to the fans of Tuscaloosa and Alabama. He gives me a real good feeling."

Stallings must have also given then St. Louis Cardinals running back Ron Woolfey a good feeling because Woolfey, who played for Stallings with the Phoenix Cardinals, is quoted in the guide as saying, "If I could go back and get my master's degree, I'd go to Alabama just so I could play for Coach Stallings again. I couldn't give him a higher recommendation. He's such a natural for Alabama. He could win a national championship in three or four years. He'll be a mega-force in the college ranks where he can mold and shape young men."

And Landry himself added, "[Coach Stallings] worked for Bear Bryant, played for Bear Bryant, and he is a lot like Bear Bryant. He's a good, solid, fundamental coach. He knows the game very well, teaches it very well, and expects nothing but the best from the people he coaches. I don't know a better person. He's an exceptional person. He's straight and he's honest. If I had to go to war, he's the one I'd want with me. If I was the parent of an 18-year-old son, he'd be the type of person that I'd want my son to play for."

With ringing endorsements like that, it's no wonder the most immediate impact the hiring of Stallings had, as expected, was in recruiting, and the results soon became evident. Stallings became the third Crimson Tide coach in three years, and easily the most respected and best-liked of Bear Bryant's successors. At Stallings' press conference, the mood was a combination of nostalgia, satisfaction, enthusiasm, and, yes, celebration.

Stallings was a favorite of Bryant's, and after 25 years, he had come back. Among all the hugging and backslapping, the occasion—rather than your typical coach-meets-the-media gathering—took on a festive atmosphere, an emotional homecoming of former teammates, players, and old friends who came to welcome home a member of their family.

And, apparently among the happiest of the happy was Paul Bryant Jr., who was a young boy when Stallings was an assistant to his father. Paul Jr., called "Cub" by some of the players back in the day, told Stallings, "This is what Papa would have wanted."

After losing his first three games, Stallings rebounded to go 7–5 in his first season at the Capstone. Then bang, just like that, 'Bama football was back, as Stallings and the Crimson won 11 of 12 games in 1991, including a victory over Colorado in the Blockbuster Bowl. In 1992 Stalling took the Tide to its 12th national championship. In 1993, however, Alabama went 9–3–1 on the field, but because of NCAA violations that occurred under Stallings' watch, had to forfeit eight wins and a tie to officially finish with a 1–12 record. Regardless, some Alabama people more or less simply disregard the ruling.

"[The forfeit losses] are not what [any Alabama fan] thinks," stated Kirk McNair, editor of *'Bama Magazine*. "I was there and watched them win all the games on the field. Everybody thinks that Gene Stallings won 70 games in seven years, and I do too." Tommy Brooker, who played on the Crimson Tide's 1961 national championship team, feels exactly the same way. "I was there and saw all the victories, so the NCAA record book doesn't mean anything to me," he stated.

Stallings is loved by 'Bama fans—not just because he reminded people of Byrant—but because he restored consistent winning to a program that had been traditionally accustomed to winning.

6

TRADITIONS WE LOVE

WINNING AS MANY CHAMPIONSHIPS AND BOWL GAMES AS WE CAN

14 National Championships (the Most in the Nation)

22 Southeastern Conference Championships (the Most in the SEC)

59 Bowl Games (the Most in the Nation)

34 Bowl Wins

102 First-Team All-Americans

THE WALK OF CHAMPIONS

This is a relatively new tradition, but let's start here because no other school in the country has won as many national championships in football, so the name is fitting for a school that has won 14 national championships—and counting. When you walk from University Boulevard toward the north end zone of Bryant-Denny Stadium, you will pass the Walk of Champions Plaza, where nine-foot tall, 2,000-pound bronze statues of

Wallace Wade, Frank Thomas, Paul "Bear" Bryant, Gene Stallings, and Nick Saban—the five national championship–winning coaches—grace the entrance to the stadium. For home games, the coaches and players are dropped off in front of the Champions Plaza and as a group walk to the stadium as thousands of adoring fans applaud their every step and reach out to slap their hands. On game days the plaza is packed, with people milling around and taking pictures in front of the statues.

GAME DAY and FOOTBALL WEEKENDS

The 'Bama Nation loves football weekends, especially game day. Beginning on Thursday, as many as 3,000 RVs and motor homes start to roll into town. For many games, as many as 125,000 people pour into Tuscaloosa, even though the stadium only holds 101,821. No matter, the game aside, many travel hundreds of miles just to partake in the atmosphere.

On Friday as many as 1,000 pop-up tents fill the Quad, a quarter-mile, well-kept grassy stretch that runs along University Boulevard in the middle of the campus. It is one of several choice areas in Tuscaloosa where people tailgate. They string lights, get out lawn chairs, carpets, full-size couches, large flat-screen televisions, and anything that is Alabama and Crimson and White in preparation for what will be a long weekend of tailgating and partying with family and friends. The area is family-friendly, with concessions, carnival-like games, and activities for all ages adding to the hoopla.

When the grilling begins, the smell of barbecue, fried chicken, and Boston butts is everywhere. Some groups have catered food that's fit for a wedding. The A-Club tent has former

ALABAMA'S RECORD BY DECADE

Decade	Record	Pct.
1890s	11–13–0	.458
1900s	45–23–7	.647
1910s	50–24–4	.667
1920s	72–21–6	.758
1930s	79–11–5	.858
1940s	66–23–4	.731
1950s	50–48–10	.509
1960s	90–16–4	.836
1970s	103–16–1	.863
1980s	85–33–2	.713
1990s*	83–40–0	.675
2000s†	57–48–0	.538

*Reflects 1993 forfeits (actual record was 91–31–1, .744
†Reflects 21 vacated victories from the span of 2005 through 2007 (actual record was 79–48–0, .622)

Alabama players meeting and greeting people and signing autographs. The University Supply Store tent is selling anything Alabama. It doesn't take long for the Quad to start jumping. It's an experience. For the big games, Homecoming, or when the ESPN *GameDay* crew is broadcasting on the Quad in front of Denny Chimes or on the Walk of Champions Plaza, everything is over the top.

When No. 1–ranked LSU came to town for "the Game of the Century" in 2011, an estimated 200,000 football fans descended on Tuscaloosa, with plans made to accommodate 40,000 people who had no chance of getting a ticket but just wanted to go to the Quad to be where the action was. Every police officer in the county was on duty, plus another 100 who were called in from elsewhere to maintain order over what was described that day as the most populated square mile in the Southeast. For a regular season game, the atmosphere was as close to a big-time bowl game as you could get.

Gene Hallman, president and CEO of the Birmingham-based Bruno Event Team that orchestrates the experience, said that "Green Bay is considered the best tailgate experience in professional football, and Green Bay pales in comparison to what we have here."

For those who enjoy being around people, having fun, and watching football played at its best, game day in Tuscaloosa—the home of the famed Crimson Tide—is the place to be.

At Bryant-Denny Stadium, just before kickoff, the stadium announcer bellows, *"This is Al-a-Bam-a Football!"* And the fans go crazy. As Alabama athletics director Mal Moore likes to say, when people start screaming "Roll Tide!" it sends a tingle down your spine. For Tide lovers, it doesn't get any better than that. Maybe a fan interviewed on television best explained the phenomena that is Alabama football when he stated, "Even with the recession and the economy as bad as it is and, even if people didn't have jobs, they'd still be at the stadium." And if they didn't have a ticket, they'd be hanging around the Quad and the stadium, soaking up the atmosphere.

Football in the South is big, but especially so at Alabama. 'Bama fans think a football weekend and the game-day experience at the University of Alabama is the best in the country.

THE A-DAY GAME

In Nick Saban's first year, 2007, a national record–setting crowd of 92,138 showed up to watch the A-Day game, which is a scrimmage that concludes spring practice. Where else in the country will a *scrimmage* attract that many people? Seriously, many Division I schools don't draw close to that for a regular season game!

But this is Alabama. If Bear Bryant were alive, he probably wouldn't believe it, but A-Day weekend at the University of Alabama and in the city of Tuscaloosa has grown so that the atmosphere surrounding it now is similar to that of Crimson Tide home games during the season, with all the belles and whistles associated with big-time southern football. Just like what you would see on a typical Saturday fall football afternoon in T-Town.

The event, which drew a couple thousand people when Clem Gryska played in the late 1940s and around 15,000 for many of the years when Bear Bryant coached, now draws 75,000-plus annually. A-Day has become the eighth home game of the year. "We are operating A-Day now like a regular fall game," Gina Johnson, associate vice president for auxiliary services told the *Tuscaloosa News*.

The growth of A-Day is just a part of football fever that has reached new heights in Tuscaloosa.

Saban said that the fan support "sends a message to everyone that we're recruiting—that being that there's a lot of enthusiasm and support for what's happening here now. That's what makes this place special."

Alabama alumni and fans think the A-Day Game, Alabama's intra-squad scrimmage at the end of spring practice, is the best in the country.

THE BRYANT MUSEUM

Across from the athletics complex that includes the football building, basketball arena, and baseball stadium is the Paul W. Bryant Museum. The museum opened on October 8, 1988, and, according to Director Ken Gaddy, has approximately 500,000 photographs on file; 6,000 books in a small library; 7,000 videos; and traditional collectibles such as game balls, player jerseys, media guides, game programs, and tickets from

NCAA TEAM STATISTICAL CHAMPIONS

SCORING DEFENSE

Year	Average
1961	2.2 ppg
1966	3.7 ppg
1975	6.0 ppg
1979	5.3 ppg
2005	10.7 ppg
2011	8.15 ppg

RUSH DEFENSE

Year	Average
1945	33.9 ypg
1992	55.0 ypg
2011	71.1 ypg

PASS DEFENSE

Year	Average
1953	45.6 ypg
1959	45.7 ypg
1990	82.47 ypg
2004	113.1 ypg
2011	111.5 ypg

TOTAL DEFENSE

Year	Average
1938	77.9 ypg
1945	109.9 ypg
1961	132.6 ypg
1992	194.1 ypg
2011	191.2 ypg

ALABAMA

long-ago games. It attracts more than 40,000 visitors a year and is particularly busy on game days. On A-Day or some game days, as many as 5,000 people pass through the museum.

The museum has a number of exhibits, which, like other things, change from time to time. Some fans visit the museum every time they come to town for a game.

"We collect things to record and preserve history and at the same time make things accessible to the public," explained Gaddy, who added that everything is donated.

A visitor walking from the lobby into the Museum will be greeted, if you will, by a large head-and-shoulder bust of Bryant in front of the Hall of Honor, a lighted display of team portraits of all the teams he coached. On the other side of the display is a small theater that shows a video about Bryant, narrated by legendary sportscaster Keith Jackson, which runs continuously.

Turning left in a circular route around the museum, a visitor will see various displays of Crimson Tide tradition through time, beginning with the 1892 team through the present. Included is a replica of Bryant's office, including his desk, couch, and a few personal items. A crystal replica of Bryant's famed houndstooth hat sits in a display case. Each Alabama coach has a display that shows highlights from his era. Along with the Nick Saban display is a 4′ replica of the Saban statue that is included in the Walk of Champions entrance to Bryant-Denny Stadium. And there is so much more that some visitors spend hours in the museum and others come back repeatedly.

Crystal replica of Bear Bryant's houndstooth hat that can be seen in the Bryant Museum

Upon completion of the circle many people stop in the gift shop that is on the left that sells a variety of Alabama clothing and souvenirs. The last thing a visitor sees is a large Daniel Moore portrait of Cornelius Bennett smashing Notre Dame quarterback Steve Beuerlein into the Legion Field turf in 1986. Along with the bust of Bryant, it is a popular spot for pictures.

The 25th anniversary of the opening of the museum will be celebrated in 2013. It will take place within a month of what would have been Bryant's 100th birthday, which will be celebrated on September 11.

THE "RAMMER JAMMER" CHEER

When a victory looks eminent, Alabama fans, led by the Million Dollar Band, love to taunt their opponent with the "Rammer Jammer" cheer. Calling out the nickname of the team that the Tide just beat—for example, Tennessee—the crowd yells:

> *Hey, Vols!*
> *Hey, Vols!*
> *Hey, Vols!*
> *We-just-beat-the-hell-out-of-you!*
> *Rammer Jammer, Yellowhammer, give 'em hell, Alabama!*

The cheer is chanted twice following a win. However, when the opponent is Auburn, the chant is even more direct. Fans scream:

> *Hey, Auburn!*
> *Hey, Auburn!*
> *Hey, Auburn!*
> *We-just-beat-the-hell-out-of-you!*
> *Rammer Jammer, Yellowhammer, give 'em hell, Alabama!*

The Rammer Jammer cheer is very popular but at times has been a controversial cheer, so much so that on a couple of occasions for a short period of time it was banned due to the use of the word *hell* and because its mocking nature was considered unsportsmanlike.

In a vote taken during 2005 Homecoming, students were polled on whether they wanted to keep the cheer or ban it again. In an overwhelming show of approval for the chant, 98 percent of the students polled voted to keep the cheer.

"Rammer Jammer" comes from the name of the student newspaper the *Rammer Jammer*, which dates back to the 1930s, and "Yellowhammer" comes from the state bird.

It was also played before games until the early 2000s with the cheer modified to: "We're-*gonna*-beat-the-hell-out-of-you!" When the chant was officially reinstated, it was allowed only at the end of games.

DENNY CHIMES AND THE UNIVERSITY OF ALABAMA'S BELL TOWER

Denny Chimes is a campus landmark that is located on the south side of the Quad along University Boulevard. It was dedicated in 1929 to honor George H. Denny, who served as president of the University from 1912 to 1936.

Beginning in the 1940s, Crimson Tide football captains have had their hand and foot impressions made in the cement at the base of the structure. The ceremony takes place in the spring prior to the A-Day game.

Denny Chimes is another popular spot for visitors to take pictures.

BEAR BRYANT'S HOUNDSTOOTH HAT

The late football coach Paul "Bear" Bryant frequently wore a houndstooth hat. Because of the success and fame of the legendary coach, the hat and black-and-white, houndstooth checkerboard design became very popular, and thousands of fans still wear a houndstooth hat on game day in honor of their iconic coach. The houndstooth design is also commonly seen on dresses, skirts, scarves, and purses, among other things.

According to Bryant Museum director Ken Gaddy, Bryant began wearing his trademark houndstooth hat in 1966 when New York Jets owner Sonny Werblin sent him one. Bryant and Werblin had become friends, even though Werblin failed in his attempt to lure Bryant away from Alabama to coach the Jets. When Werblin noticed that Bryant wore the houndstooth hat on the field during Alabama games, he continued to send Bryant houndstooth hats, and Bryant continued to wear them.

Now thousands of 'Bama fans wear them.

NICK SABAN'S PRACTICE STRAW HAT

Because of his almost immediate and dramatic success and his popularity, the straw hat that Nick Saban wears at practice is another piece of headwear commonly seen on game day.

Saban's straw practice hat is not as popular as Bryant's houndstooth hat but is a popular piece of headwear seen on fans on game day.

BRYANT-DENNY STADIUM

Bryant-Denny Stadium is one of the most famous football stadiums in the country. Through the years, the sustained success of Alabama football has required that the stadium be periodically expanded to accommodate the Crimson Tide's huge and rabid fan base. It was constructed in 1929 to seat 12,000, but was enlarged in 1946 to seat 31,000. Further expansions occurred in 1961 (43,000), 1966 (59,000), 1988 (70,123), 1998 (83,818), 2006 (92,138), and again in 2010 to its current capacity of 101,821, making it the fifth largest on-campus stadium in the country. If Saban keeps winning like he is now, look for more expansion in the near future.

The first game played in what was then called Denny Stadium was on September 28, 1929, with the Crimson Tide overwhelming Mississippi College 55–0. In 1975, while he was still coaching, Bryant's name was added to the stadium.

The atmosphere at an Alabama football game in Bryant-Denny Stadium is as good as it gets. Prior to the team running out of the tunnel, the crowd roars its approval as the huge video screens show highlights of past games, reaching a crescendo when a picture of Bear Bryant appears, and in his gruff voice, bellows, "I ain't nothing but a winner." Then: *"This is Al-a-Bam-a Football!"*

Not Auburn football, or Tennessee football, but *Al-a-Bam-a football*, and there's a difference!

Alabama enjoys an impressive 217–46–3 record when playing in Tuscaloosa. More than 10 million fans have witnessed the

TOP 5 TACKLES *IN A* SEASON

1. **Woodrow Lowe** | 134 | 1973
2. **DeMeco Ryans** | 126 | 2003
3. **Wayne Davis** | 125 | 1985
4t. **Thomas Boyd** | 120 | 1980
    Mike Hall | 120 | 1968

Crimson Tide play in 145 games in Bryant-Denny Stadium in the last 21 years.

THE MILLION DOLLAR BAND

The Million Dollar band, an integral part of the athletic atmosphere of the University of Alabama, entertains and energizes fans during pregame and halftime festivities. Originally organized in 1913–1914, 82 years after the University was founded, the 14-member, all-male band was simply called the University Band. It made its first appearance at a UA football game that season. In 1917 another band, the ROTC Band, was formed. The two bands combined in 1923 and included 65 marching members.

There are many stories about how the band got its current name. One such story has it that an Army colonel was visiting the Alabama campus, heard the band playing, and remarked, "This band is worth a million dollars to our troops' morale." Another has it that in 1922 during a football game against Georgia Tech in Atlanta, the band outperformed the 88-member Yellow Jacket Band, with someone saying, "The band played like a million dollars." Another version is, that same year it took a successful fund-raising effort to financially support the band's trip to Atlanta, with the effort resulting in the band being called the Million Dollar Band. No matter, the Million Dollar Band has become a long-standing tradition at Alabama football games. Today it numbers almost 330 students and is the largest single organization on campus. The Million Dollar Band plays during Homecoming and at other pep rallies as well as at the Quad before games, always bringing additional excitement to the Alabama football environment.

BIG AL

The University of Alabama's nickname is the Crimson Tide, but its mascot is an elephant named Big Al. What does Big Al have to do with the Crimson Tide and how did the elephant mascot come about?

TOP 5 TACKLES IN A CAREER

1. **Wayne Davis** | 327 | 1983–1986
2. **Thomas Boyd** | 324 | 1979–1982
3. **Woodrow Lowe** | 315 | 1972–1975
4. **DeMeco Ryans** | 309 | 2002–2005
5. **Roman Harper** | 307 | 2002–2005

ALABAMA

History has it that the elephant came about in a couple of different ways. One story credits the elephant association to the Rosenberger Trucking Company located in Birmingham. J.D. Rosenberger, the owner of the company, had a son who attended the University of Alabama. In 1929, when the undefeated Crimson Tide traveled to California for the Rose Bowl game, Rosenberger provided the team with "good luck" luggage tags that had the company's trademark red elephant standing on a trunk. The Alabama football team had a lot of big players that season. When the players arrived in Pasadena, reporters, including famed syndicated columnist Grantland Rice, associated their large size with the elephants depicted on the luggage tags.

Another story is that on October 4, 1930, a mild earthquake caused a tremble during the Alabama-Mississippi game. That, along with the size of the Alabama players, caused *Atlanta Journal* sportswriter Everett Strupper to write, "At the end of the quarter, the earth started to tremble, there was a distant rumble that continued to grow. Some excited fan in the stands bellowed, 'Hold your horses, the elephants are coming,' and out stomped the Alabama varsity. It was the first time that I had seen it, and the size of the entire 11 nearly knocked me cold, men that I had seen play last year looking like they had nearly doubled in size."

Some sportswriters picked up on it and, with the school colors crimson and white, started to refer to Alabama as the "Red Elephants." Both stories partially attribute the elephant association to the physical size of the Alabama teams of that era. The 1930 team shut out eight of 10 opponents, allowing a total of only 13 points all season. The "Red Elephants" rolled up

His face has changed over the years, but Alabama's "Big Al" remains among the most-recognizable and beloved mascots in college football.

271 points that season, including 24 against Washington State in the Rose Bowl, while holding the Cougars scoreless.

Although the elephant has been associated with Alabama since the 1930s, it wasn't until 1979 that it officially became the school mascot. Children's books have been written about "Big Al."

THE CRIMSON TIDE NAME

Why do Alabama fans love their nickname? Because it's unique! It's part of the Alabama brand. When people around the country hear the name *Crimson Tide*, it resonates because everyone knows it's Alabama.

When Alabama started playing football, like most other schools, the team didn't have a nickname. The team was just called "the varsity." At other times, the team was just referred to as the "Crimson White" because it was a common practice back then for schools to designate their teams by school colors.

In the early years, before they were described as the Red Elephants because they had big players, paradoxically some writers tagged the team "the Thin Red Line" because the players were smaller than most of their opponents.

According to the 2011 Alabama media guide, *Birmingham Age-Herald* sports editor Hugh Roberts referred to Alabama as the Crimson Tide when, in 1907, in a game played in rain-drenched, reddish-looking muddy conditions, Alabama's Thin Red Line battled to a 6–6 deadlock against heavily favored Auburn. Other writers picked up on it, and Alabama became the Crimson Tide.

"ALABAMA ALMA MATER"

Alabama, listen, Mother,
To our vows of love,
To thyself and to each other,
Faithful friends we'll prove.

Faithful, loyal, firm and true,
Heart bound to heart will beat.
Year by year, the ages through
Until in Heaven we meet.

College days are swiftly fleeting,
Soon we'll leave their halls
Ne'er to join another meeting
'Neath their hallowed walls.

Faithful, loyal, firm, and true,
Heart bound to heart will beat.
Year by year, the ages through
Until in Heaven we meet.

So, farewell, dear Alma Mater
May thy name, we pray,
Be rev'renced ever, pure and stainless
As it is today.

Faithful, loyal, firm and true,
Heart bound to heart will beat.
Year by year, the ages through
Until in Heaven we meet.

The "Alabama Alma Mater," written around the turn of the 20th century, is set to the tune of "Annie Lisle," a ballad written in the 1850s. Helen Vickers is generally credited for the words.

"YEA, ALABAMA"

"Yea, Alabama" is Alabama's fight song. In 1926 *Rammer Jammer*, the student newspaper, conducted a contest to come up with a fight song. Original reports state that Ethelred Lundy "Epp" Sykes, an engineering student, composed the winning entry, "Yeah, Alabama." It was adopted after the Crimson Tide defeated Washington in the 1926 Rose Bowl. In football games, after Alabama scores, the chorus to the song is played by the Million Dollar Band. "Yea, Alabama" was also used as the theme music for *The Bear Bryant Show.*

The fight song, as played today, has been shortened to begin with the words "Yea, Alabama." Here is the fight song as it was printed in the *2011 Alabama Football Media Guide*:

> *Yea, Alabama! Drown 'em, Tide!*
> *Every 'Bama man's behind you,*
> *Hit your stride.*
> *Go teach the Bulldogs to behave,*
> *Send the Yellow Jackets*
> *to a watery grave.*
> *And if a man starts to weaken,*
> *That's a shame!*
> *For 'Bama's pluck and grit have*
> *Writ her name in Crimson flame.*
> *Fight on, fight on, fight on, men!*

Remember the Rose Bowl,
we'll win then.
So roll on to victory,
Hit your stride,
You're Dixie's football pride,
Crimson Tide, Roll Tide, Roll Tide!!

THE HOMECOMING BONFIRE

During Homecoming weekend, along with all the other pageantry that goes on, there is a pep rally on the Quad that ends with the lighting of the bonfire. Sometimes a fireworks show follows. It is a family-fun atmosphere.

SWEET HOME ALABAMA—ROLL, TIDE, ROLL!

The Million Dollar Band at Alabama football games periodically plays "Sweet Home Alabama," a song by southern rock group Lynyrd Skynyrd. It is a favorite among Crimson Tide fans who insert the school's battle cry, "Roll, Tide, Roll!" in the lyrics after the chorus "Sweet Home Alabama."

'Bama fans love to include "Roll, Tide, Roll!" They do it in unison as if it fits right into the song.

Incidentally, former Alabama star running back Shaun Alexander, when he played for the Seattle Seahawks, had the song played after he scored a touchdown at each Seattle game. That inspired "Dustin Blatnik and the 12th Man Band" to record the 2005 parody song "Sweet Shaun Alexander," a tribute to Alexander's record-setting season when he spearheaded the Seahawks run to Super Bowl XL.

VICTORY CIGAR
WHEN ALABAMA BEATS TENNESSEE

The late Jim Goostree was a beloved, longtime trainer at the University of Alabama. A graduate of the University of Tennessee, Goostree in the 1950s began purchasing and passing out cigars to the team and coaches following victories over Tennessee. The tradition of lighting up a cigar after beating Tennessee continued until 2005, when the NCAA found out about it and banned the practice.

Coach Dennis Franchione joins players with a victory cigar, a former Alabama tradition after a win over Tennessee. The tradition has been discontinued due to an NCAA ruling.

PLAIN UNIFORMS

Many schools change their uniforms periodically, depending upon what the fashion or trend is at the time. Not Alabama. Like the New York Yankees, with their trademark pinstripes, and Penn State, with its blue-and-white vanilla uniforms, Alabama has for the most part stayed with its traditional plain uniforms and red helmet with a white number. It's the Alabama brand. The uniforms are a reminder of championships won years ago and serve as another link to the Crimson Tide's glorious history of football success.

NICK'S KIDS

Nick Saban has been a very successful head football coach. Besides his main focus of winning as many games and championships as he can, he and his wife, Terry, have made it a priority to give back to the communities in which they have lived. In the mid-1990s, when he was the head coach at Michigan State, the Sabans founded Nick's Kids, a charitable foundation that they have continued to this day, with which they have made it a point to help the less fortunate and those in need.

The mission statement of Nick's Kids is, "To work together in the spirit of faith and giving in our community. To promote and support children, family, teacher, and student causes. It's All About the Kids!"

Nick's Kids made a significant contribution in a variety of ways in helping after tornadoes devastated the city of Tuscaloosa in the spring of 2011.

According to its website, donations distributed by Nick and Terry Saban and through the Nick's Kids Fund to the University of Alabama through the end of 2011 totaled $2,194,360, with the Sabans personally donating $520,000 to the University of Alabama.

This is a tradition of giving back that the Sabans brought with them when they came to Tuscaloosa in January 2007.

THE "FAIL ROOM"

The visitors locker room at Bryant-Denny Stadium is named "the Fail Room." No joke. It's named after James Fail, an Alabama donor.

How apropos, as the visiting teams fail almost every time they come to Alabama to play the Crimson Tide. 'Bama has a 217–46–3 all-time record in Tuscaloosa.

7

STORIES WE LOVE

ANY BEAR BRYANT STORIES

People love to tell them, and retell them. They never get old.

Steadman Shealy was a wishbone quarterback on Alabama's national championship teams in 1978 and 1979, and as a senior was the starting QB on a team that went 12–0. He earned SEC MVP and Academic All-America honors and played on Crimson Tide teams that won 34 of 36 games. He reiterated the commonly told story of how Bryant tried to teach his players about responding to adversity. "Coach Bryant would say, 'Suppose that you just found out that you were fired from your job, your bank account was overdrawn, and your wife just ran off with some other guy and took everything you owned. What are you going to do, quit or do whatever it takes?'"

Shealy, who became an attorney, said Bryant, who frequently preached about the importance of overcoming adversity, "taught us about life." Shealy also related how he experienced adversity as a freshman football player at Alabama:

> I was as down and out as you can get. I didn't play and I
> didn't travel. I was a tackling dummy. I was getting killed

daily. It seemed like a big waste of time. I wondered if there was a place for me at Alabama. When I went to speak to church groups, kids would ask if I played for Alabama. I said, "No, I just practice with them."

When I finally got in a game, it didn't get any better. The first time I played was at Nebraska, and I got in for three plays and lost 14 yards. Running off the field, I'm thinking, *Where can I transfer?*

The next day I was told to report to practice. That's not important, because everybody has to practice. But when you're the only one, it's important. The following week, I pitched the ball to Major Ogilvie, who scored on a 37-yard run, but I was knocked unconscious on the play. That's how my career started.

Jerry Duncan was an offensive lineman on Alabama's national championship teams of 1964 and 1965, on the unbeaten team of 1966, and later for many years was a sideline reporter for Alabama games. He related that, when he was a graduate assistant coach, one of his jobs was to go and get whichever player Bryant wanted to insert in the game. "Once he asked me to get Ron Durby, a lineman who had graduated four years earlier." Duncan said that he went looking for Durby on the sideline, knowing full well that Durby was nowhere near Tuscaloosa.

"I didn't feel that bad, though, because several years later I heard Coach Bryant sent Sylvester Croom looking for Kenny Stabler 10 years after Stabler had graduated, and Sylvester went looking for him too."

Duncan also related when Bryant was asked by an out-of-town reporter which coach he feared the most. After hemming and

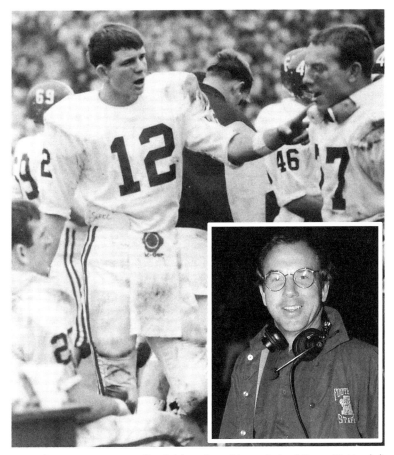

'Bama lineman Jerry Duncan (67, right) confers with quarterback Kenny Stabler (12) on the sideline during a game. A popular player, Duncan was equally loved as a reporter for Crimson Tide football radio broadcasts.

hawing, he replied, "Old Logan, I guess." Surprised, since he expected Bryant to say Texas' Darrell Royal or Notre Dame's Ara Parseghian, whose teams had given Bryant trouble, the reporter asked, "Who's Old Logan?" Bryant said, "He's the undertaker in Tuscaloosa. If I see him coming to practice, I'm going to get nervous."

Kenny Stabler had recently quarterbacked the Crimson Tide to an undefeated season in 1966 and won the MVP Award for his performance in the 34–7 win over Nebraska in the Sugar Bowl. A few months later, however, Stabler ran into academic problems. After passing summer school courses to regain his eligibility, he had to ask Bryant for permission to rejoin the team. Bryant told Stabler, "You don't deserve to be on the team."

Bryant later relented, but Stabler was given a brown jersey, designating his place on the fifth-team. "Here I was, a hotshot MVP in the Sugar Bowl going into my senior year, and I got a brown jersey," Stabler recalled. "Coach Bryant had a name for that team, and it had something to do with the color of the jersey. I didn't start until the third game of the season. Coach Bryant sent me a message, and I got the message. If it were not for that discipline, I don't know where I would be now."

Beside Namath and Stabler, there are numerous other players Bryant punished but salvaged with his tough-love philosophy, including Rich Wingo, who played on Tide teams that went 31–5, won three conference championships and in 1978 the national championship. As a junior, after receiving preseason All-America nominations, Bryant kicked Wingo off the team for not hustling in practice.

"I waited until practice was over, and I went to see Coach Bryant, and Coach Bryant told me, 'You're satisfied. You're content. I don't want you on my team. I want people who are committed.'

"I asked Coach Bryant for a second chance, and he told me he would think about it and that I should see him at 9:00 AM the next morning. He let me back on the team. I think he got my attention. I went from contentment to commitment in 12 hours. I've carried that message with me to this day. It's funny now, but let me tell you, it was serious then."

Wingo said that the previous year, in 1976, Bryant got the team's attention following a lackluster 24–8 win over Southern Mississippi when he announced a 6:00 AM Sunday morning scrimmage. "It was a nonstop bloodbath for two hours with the best against the best and the rest against the rest," related Wingo. "Then he said, 'Okay, you Christians go to church. The rest of you stay here and practice. I think he converted the whole football team that day," laughed Wingo.

John Hannah, a two-time All-American, 10-time All-Pro, and a College and Pro Football Hall of Famer who is considered by many the best offensive lineman to ever play the game, recalled a practice session after Alabama came from behind to beat Tennessee. "We had what Coach Bryant called a 'gut-check.' The next morning he said, 'Now, boys, you learned a valuable lesson yesterday. You pushed yourself until you thought that you were going to die, but the human body is a wonderful thing. It will pass out before you die.'"

Jeremiah Castille was an All-America defensive back who played on the 1979 national championship team before embarking on a six-year pro career. He praised Bryant as the greatest college football coach of all-time. "When I was an 18-year-old freshman, he called me into his office and told me how much he believed in me, that I could play that first year. He changed my entire outlook, from being unsure to being confident. After he got finished with me, I thought that I could run through a brick wall," Castille said.

"During games, even though I was only 170 pounds, I wasn't afraid of the opposing players. I was afraid of that man on the sideline."

The 1982 Liberty Bowl was Castille's last game as a player, and Bryant's last game as a coach. Castille intercepted three passes in the Crimson Tide's 21–15 victory over Illinois, which sent Bryant out the winner he was.

"After the game, it dawned on me that I should thank Coach Bryant for all that he had done for me," related Castille, a 2004 recipient of the Paul "Bear" Bryant Alumni Award. "So I stood up before the team and said that I had come here as an 18-year-old kid, and that I'm leaving as a 22-year-old man. I told Coach Bryant, 'That's what you have done for me—you've helped make me a man.'"

Castille's relationship with his famous coach was such that Castille was chosen to be a pallbearer at Bryant's funeral.

Kareem McNeal was a member of the 1992 national championship team. After winning the starting right tackle position as a junior, McNeal was in an accident that left him paralyzed from the waist down and wheelchair-bound. He told this story as part of the *Crimson Classic* series produced by the Bryant Museum that was broadcast on WUVA. Following months of intensive rehabilitation, McNeal said Coach Stallings asked him to walk into the locker room to speak to the Crimson Tide team prior to the 1996 Iron Bowl game. With the assistance of braces, McNeal walked into the locker room. He said he told the team, "The doctors said that I would never be able to walk again, but here I am walking, even if it is with braces. I told the team, 'If I can walk again, you can beat Auburn.'"

And the Crimson Tide did just that, defeating the Tigers in a thriller, 24–23. After the game Stallings called McNeal back into the locker room and presented him with the game ball. Stallings told McNeal, "I'm giving you the game ball because, as much as anything else, I think your inspiration helped us beat Auburn." McNeal said he didn't think many people knew that story, so he told the commentator, "I'm telling it now." Showing his continued determination, McNeal went on to earn his undergraduate degree in human performance in 1996 and his master's degree in 1999. He teaches weight training, personal health, and stress management at Shelton State Community College.

THE JUNCTION STORIES NEVER GET OLD

Bobby Skelton, the second quarterback to play for Bryant at Alabama said, "What we went through was just as bad as Junction. The only difference was we were on campus, and they were off-campus. Our dorms didn't have air-conditioning, and it was just as hot as those Quonset huts. We had 150 players, and they were dropping like flies, with 40 or 50 leaving that first night. We learned a lot real quick."

Skelton said that in 1960, when Alabama trailed Georgia Tech by 15 at the half, the Tide players dreaded going into the locker room because they were expecting a real chewing out from Bryant. Instead Skelton said Bryant shocked them when he calmly said, "Great. Now we've got them right where I want them."

The Crimson Tide came back in the second half to beat the Engineers 16–15, with Skelton replacing the injured Pat Trammell, throwing a touchdown pass to Norbie Ronsonet for 'Bama's first score.

Skelton thought the Georgia Tech win was "the turning point, the game that brought Alabama back and got us on our way to winning more national championships."

College Hall of Famer Billy Neighbors, a co-captain of Bryant's first national championship team and a member of Alabama's 1960s All-Decade and All-Century Teams, said that he had never heard of Bear Bryant before he became Alabama's coach. "But it didn't take me long to figure out who he was," stated Neighbors, who arrived at the Capstone a year before Bryant returned to his alma mater. "The first thing he said to me was, 'You've got to lose weight. Then he sent me a letter that said that I had to come back at 220 pounds and be able to run a six-minute mile. I came back at 217 and ran a 5:55 mile.

"Coach Bryant used all kinds of ways to motivate us, and one of them was fear—fear of dying. There were 118 freshmen [football players] when I came here, and two and a half years later there were only eight of us left. Coach Bryant worked us to death. It was Junction, but Junction here…Coach Bryant would cuss at the [assistant] coaches too. He'd cuss them out,

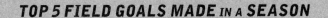
TOP 5 FIELD GOALS MADE *IN A* SEASON

1. **Leigh Tiffin** | 30 | 2009
2. **Leigh Tiffin** | 25 | 2007
3. **Philip Doyle** | 24 | 1990
4t. **Philip Doyle** | 22 | 1989
    Michael Proctor | 22 | 1993

ALABAMA

and then he'd cuss us out. After a while we realized they were in the same boat as us....

"I didn't have too many conversations with Coach Bryant all the while I was here, to tell you the truth," said Neighbors. "Whenever I saw him coming, I went the other way."

Butch Wilson also played on the 1961 national championship team. He said that when he was with the Baltimore Colts, veterans like Johnny Unitas and Raymond Berry would pull him aside and say, "Tell us what Coach Bryant was really like. Did he really put all you guys in that pit?"

The pit legend, in fact, was what motivated Neighbors to commit to Alabama. "I read in *Sports Illustrated* about this new coach who was coming to Alabama—Coach Bryant— and how he would dig this pit and put players in it, and they would fight to see who was going to come out of it. I figured I'd been fighting all my life, and all I had to do to play was win a damn fight."

ALABAMA

FIVE ALABAMA QBS WHO PLAYED IN THE SUPER BOWL

1. **Bart Starr**

2. **Joe Namath**

3. **Kenny Stabler**

4. **Jeff Rutledge**

5. **Bobby Jackson**

(Many people forget Jackson, Bryant's first QB at Alabama, who played safety for the 1960 Philadelphia Eagles.)

Neighbors' teammate on the 1961 national championship team as well as on the 1960s All-Decade Team, Darwin Holt, said, "Coach Bryant had told his first group of players that Alabama would win the national championship when they were seniors. That's what I wanted to hear. Coach Bryant may have gotten a little softer when he got older, but when I played for him, he was tough as nails. I was not on the Junction team at Texas A&M, but location had nothing to do with it." Holt, a Texas native, had at first signed with the Aggies. "Coach Bryant wasn't going to change his methods just because he wasn't out in the desert. It wasn't always a happy family, because we were working so hard. We were tired. We were putting in 40 hours a week with football. I could have been out in the coal fields and been better off."

Bob Baumhower, a two-time All-American who went on to a nine-year career in the NFL, where he became part of the Miami Dolphins' "Killer Bs" defense, said that he remembered his first practice with the Dolphins. "I remember it like it was yesterday," he said. "Someone blew the whistle and said that practice was over. I hadn't even broken a sweat. I said to myself, 'After playing at Alabama, I'm gonna love this place.'"

Tim Davis, a kicker on Tide teams from 1961 through 1963, related that the 7–6 loss to Georgia Tech in 1962 was the "worst thing that happened to me while playing football at Alabama. We were No. 1 in the nation. At the end of the game, we were down on their 14-yard line, and we threw a pass that got intercepted. That was very frustrating for me because I never got a chance to kick a field goal that would have won the game.

"I remember that the intensity of that game was unbelievable. That was the most hostile environment I ever played in. We were bombarded by whisky bottles. Two years later, when we went back to Georgia Tech, Coach Bryant wore a helmet on the field. That was his response to that game."

Homer Smith, the late offensive guru who coached at Alabama under Bill Curry and Gene Stallings, said that he better understood the Bear when, at a Coach of the Year Awards banquet, Bryant asked everyone associated with him and his program to stand, and then Bryant sat down. "We're there clapping for his assistants," Smith explained. "Not everyone would have done that."

Earlier in his career, when he was the head coach at Army, Smith said that Bryant called him to recommend Ronnie Joe Barnes, who had been a second-team defensive end at Alabama, for a position on his staff. "Bear Bryant, the famous coach, called me to recommend a second-team player. Not everyone would have done that, either," Smith said. "Based on that call, I hired him.'"

Alabama athletics director Mal Moore, who has been at Alabama for more than 50 years and is the only person to be a part of nine national championships, 14 SEC championships, and 28 bowl teams, likes to tell Bear Bryant stories. Here are a few:

When he was offensive coordinator, Moore told about a time when Bryant wanted him to run a reverse, but the play lost yardage, and Bryant said, "I meant run it the other way."

Moore told a similar story when he served as offensive coordinator under Stallings. Stallings suggested running a draw play, and the opposing team stuffed it. Stallings said, "Well, you got to block somebody."

Moore told how Bryant, following a speech, once prefaced a question-and-answer session. "When Coach Bryant said that he would answer questions, immediately 15 hands went up," Moore said. "Then Coach Bryant said, 'Now don't go asking any dumb-ass questions,' and suddenly all at once 15 hands went down."

Everyone knows Bear Bryant was a tough coach and everyone seems to have a story reinforcing that hard-nosed image. Jackie Sherrill, who played several different positions for Alabama's national championship teams in 1964 and 1965, said that he came to Alabama "with 67 other freshmen football players, and of that group only six others were seniors four years later. Paul Crane, Steve Sloan, Steve Bowman, Tim Bates, David Ray, and Lynwood Strickland. That's a good group of guys."

Longtime assistant coach Clem Gryska expressed his appreciation for his head coach by saying, "Coach Bryant had more influence on me and my family than my dad and my mom. I spent more time with Coach Bryant than I did with my parents."

Joe Kines also had two coaching stints at Alabama, working for Ray Perkins and later for Mike Shula. He finished up his career as an assistant at Texas A&M. He said, "Coach Bryant's footsteps are still all over the Texas A&M campus. The 'Junction Boys' tell the same stories as the guys who played here in the 1960s. It's the same thing, just the names change."

Speaking to the Tuscaloosa Quarterback Club, Chris Stewart, the sideline reporter for radio coverage of Alabama football games and the television host of *The Nick Saban Show*, told what he said was his favorite Kenny Stabler joke. Stewart led off by saying, "Now I don't know if it's true or not, and I'm not going to ask Kenny because I want to keep on telling it, but someone told me that one night Kenny Stabler was sitting at the bar and it was getting near the 2:30 closing time. The manager flicked the lights indicating last call. Snake picks up his glass, finishes up his drink, and then throws the glass across the room and watches it smash against the wall. The bartender asks Kenny, 'Why did you do that?'

"Snake responds, 'I was just throwing the thing out of bounds to stop the clock.'"

Roger Shultz, who played in the 1980s for Bill Curry, is always good for a story. He recalled that, when he was being recruited, his father Ken, a big 'Bama fan, told him, "It's your decision."

Shultz said that when he returned from Columbus, Ohio, his father asked him how it went. "I told him I wanted to be a Buckeye. My dad then said, 'Go to your room. You're not old enough to make a decision like that.' So that's how I ended up at Alabama."

There are a lot of true stories about Alabama football that get passed around from person to person and generation to generation, and there are a lot of legends and tales relative to the famed football program, like the Bear Bryant pit story, and sometimes it's hard to tell which are fact and which are fiction. One such story is that, prior to curfew, Lee Roy Jordon punched out Joe Namath and took him back to the dormitory after the quarterback refused to leave The Jungle Club, a popular nightspot in T-Town back in the day. "That's not true," stated Jordan. "That never happened. Joe was the starting quarterback my senior year, and I think if I told Joe to leave, Joe would have left."

Doesn't matter. People like to tell and retell the stories, true or not.

ACKNOWLEDGMENTS

THANKS TO THE PEOPLE at Triumph Books for offering me the opportunity to write this book. The author appreciates all who participated in this project by sharing their thoughts, information, feelings, and opinions. Special thanks to the Paul W. Bryant Museum and the *Northport Gazette* for providing courtesy photographs and granting permission to publish them. Their contributions added greatly to the book.

I
HATE
AUBURN

DONALD F. STAFFO

TRIUMPH
BOOKS

CONTENTS

Introduction: I Hate Auburn v

1. **Games We Hate** *1*

2. **Traditions We Hate** *33*

3. **Players We Hate** *47*

4. **Coaches We Hate** *62*

5. **Other Games We Hate** *77*

About the Author *98*

INTRODUCTION
I HATE AUBURN

DAVID HOUSEL GREW UP in Gordo, less than a half hour from Tuscaloosa. But make no mistake about it, he is an Auburn man through and through. He bleeds orange and blue. "I grew up in an Auburn family and in an Auburn environment, and my only dream was to go to Auburn and be the sports editor of the college newspaper [the *Plainsman*]," said Housel. "My dream was to go to Auburn and become a part of it."

That he certainly did, as following graduation from college, Housel spent nine months as the news editor of the *Huntsville News*, before returning to his alma mater. He worked there for almost 40 years, first as an employee in the ticket office, then an instructor in the journalism department, and after that a member of the sports information department, where he rose to become its director in 1981. In 1985 Housel was made an assistant athletics director and in 1994 was tapped to be Auburn's 13th athletics director. In his 10 years as AD, Auburn won eight national championships, 30 SEC titles, and had 143 teams advance to postseason play.

Having spent almost all his working career at Auburn, Housel, a self-described "ultimate Auburn man," said that he in fact

has lived his dream. "One of the highlights of my life was in 2001 when I was riding in the front car leading the Auburn football team into Tuscaloosa [when the Tigers played their first football game in T-town since 1901], and riding down Greensboro Avenue and University Boulevard, where I was made fun of as a child."

Years earlier, Housel, then the sports information director at Auburn, said that some people live vicariously through the athletic accomplishments of 19- and 20-year-old kids. "I think too many people on both sides internalize the outcome of this game and how they feel about themselves in relationship to other people, and that is unfortunate," he told the Tuscaloosa Quarterback Club in the week leading up to the Iron Bowl.

"To some people the game is too important. The measure of a person's character and success as a human being is not measured by the outcome of a football game. A lot of people like to stir things up this time of year, and there are a lot of rumors being started by fans of both schools."

Housel explained that although a lot of people don't realize it, the athletics departments of both schools respect each other. "When it comes to issues confronting college football today, Auburn and Alabama stand together. We walk arm-in-arm and shoulder-to-shoulder because we come from the same background and stand for the same things. On NCAA matters, we usually vote the same way."

Housel said that Auburn fans "abhorred Bear Bryant. They abhorred him because they feared him. They feared him because he was winning."

Housel said that Auburn coach Pat Dye, a former assistant at Alabama under Bryant, helped change how Auburn felt about itself. "Coach Dye helped Auburn people stop measuring our program by the Alabama program. He made us concentrate on the things we could do something about in our own program. He made Auburn people be concerned about Auburn, and not external forces over which we have no control.

"And another thing, and some Auburn people might not like to hear me say this, is that Coach Dye took away the fear Auburn had of Alabama. At one time Alabama may have intimidated us, but we're not afraid anymore. Alabama may win the game, but we're not scared anymore. One thing Alabama should know is that we're always coming after them, just like they're always coming after us. That's what makes this a great series. So remember this, if Alabama wins, we'll be back."

Housel, a 300-pounder, said that not many people know that Coach Bryant recruited him for Alabama. "He talked about me coming and being a part of Alabama's tradition. He almost had me sold on the idea, but my daddy didn't want me to come here and be Big Al for four years."

In 1996, when he was athletics director, Housel—who recalled several past Tide-Tigers games, including Auburn's victories in 1956 (34–7), 1957 (40–0), and 1958 (14–8)—said that he changed his mind about the rivalry. "I used to think the game was too divisive. I used to think it was one of [the state's] darkest hours. But I no longer feel that way. If you look at the guys on the field, they probably represent some of the very best this state has to offer in terms of young men striving toward common goals. If you appreciate the effort they put forth and

the specialness of the moment and spread it throughout the state, instead of looking at it as our worst moment, it should be our finest moment, no matter who wins. Unfortunately, the further away from the field you go, the worse the rivalry becomes."

In 1958 Dwight D. Eisenhower was president of the U.S.; Nikita Khrushchev was premier of the Soviet Union; *Sputnik* was in the news; the Beatles were an unknown singing group in England still called The Quarrymen; Elvis Presley was inducted into the U.S. Army; and another singer who would go on to become legendary, Michael Jackson, was born. Noteworthy things for sure, but down in Tuscaloosa, Alabama, something else happened that would have long-term significance on college football.

"Then Mama called, and the world has been fundamentally different ever since," Housel wrote in reference to Bear Bryant's being named the head football coach at the University of Alabama and his dominance of the Iron Bowl from the time he took over as the Crimson Tide's coach until his retirement in 1982.

Nineteen eighty-two also was a year after Pat Dye, a former Bryant assistant coach, became Auburn's head coach, and the pendulum was beginning to swing the War Eagles' way.

Scott Brown and Will Collier write about the conversation that Bryant and Dye had while Dye was waiting to be named Auburn coach. It went something like this: Bryant called his former assistant coach, who had just relinquished the head job at Wyoming to show how serious he was about taking over the Tigers, and bellowed, "You aren't going to take that job!"

"I am if it's offered," replied Dye.

"Well, you're not going to beat me," Bryant warned.

To which Dye responded, "Maybe not, but the one that follows you, I'm gonna beat like a stepson."

Dye did not go to Auburn to chase Alabama. He went there to push the program past Alabama. He said so when recruiting high school star running back Bo Jackson, who had grown up an Alabama fan. He pointedly told Jackson that with Bryant very close to retirement that Alabama's success was in the past, and that he and Auburn represented the future. He convinced Vincent "Bo" Jackson that if he hitched up with him, he could make that happen.

In Dye's first year, Auburn lost to Alabama 28–17, but in his second season he beat the Bear in the Iron Bowl 23–22 when Bo Jackson dove over the top for the winning touchdown that sent Bryant exiting the series on a losing note. Right then and there, people sensed the momentum shifting and that the tide was turning (pun intended).

Dye was not the only person who switched allegiances from one school to the other. There were others, including beloved Bill "Brother" Oliver, who played on three Alabama bowl teams, including the 1961 championship team, and later served as an assistant on 11 'Bama teams that went to bowls. After being the defensive coordinator who stymied Miami in the Sugar Bowl that enabled Gene Stallings and Alabama to win the 1992 national championship, Oliver left to accept the same position at Auburn. After doing so, Oliver was called a

traitor by many 'Bama fans for leaving the Tide for the Tigers, not once but twice. Asked why he left Alabama for, of all places, Auburn, Oliver said that he "wanted to set the record straight" and then clearly expressed his thoughts. He pointed out that he had hoped to close out his coaching career at his alma mater, but that things didn't work out as he had been led to believe that they would.

"I was told by two different people twice that I would be the next head coach at Alabama," Oliver stated. "I was told by [the athletics director] Hootie [Ingram], and then Hootie left. And [then head coach Gene] Stallings asked me to stay, and if I did that I would be the next head coach.

"I took him at his word and then he ended up staying on, and I stayed around three more years under those circumstances. Then nothing changed, nothing happened, and I never heard a word about it again."

Feeling misled and not wanting to wait any longer since he was in the twilight of his career, Oliver took the defensive coordinator's job at Auburn, much to the consternation of Alabama Nation. "When I went to Auburn, it was a business deal," Oliver explained. "Alabama fans didn't say anything the first time [when in 1966 he left to become a defensive backs coach on the Plains]."

Asked at the time how Auburn fans were accepting Oliver as the Tigers' new defensive coordinator, Housel quipped, "Brother is fitting in real well. When the defense shuts the opponent out, he fits in even better." In parting, Housel said, "Yeah, War Eagle, War Eagle now, and War Eagle forever!"

Oliver was named interim head coach at Auburn in 1998 after Terry Bowden abruptly resigned during the season. However, his stint as head coach was short-lived, as Tommy Tuberville was named the Tigers head coach in 1999.

When Pat Dye was introduced before he spoke to the Tuscaloosa Quarterback Club, he got a standing ovation. But that was not for the eight years he coached archrival Auburn. It was for the eight years from 1965 to 1973 that he was linebackers' coach on Bear Bryant's staff at Alabama.

Asked about his biggest wins, Dye said, "My most significant win was the 1982 [Iron Bowl] game in Birmingham, probably because Auburn went nine years without winning.

"One of the greatest football games that I've ever been involved in, we lost," he stated, noting Van Tiffin's last-second field goal in the 1985 Iron Bowl that beat the Tigers.

Dye noted that he always had respect for Alabama and he wanted Alabama people to have the same kind of respect for Auburn. "But I don't know if that's always been true," he said. "Alabama is big enough for two good teams, and that's the way that it should be."

Two good teams, fine, but in 2002 Housel, with a dramatically different take on the rivalry than he expressed years ago to the Tuscaloosa Quarterback Club, adamantly made it clear that that is okay only if Auburn is the dominant team. In a six-and-a-half minute radio address prior to the Iron Bowl, Housel does his very best to piss off the 'Bama Nation and warn them that the Tigers will take over the state, and that they

best get ready for it. Referencing wars and history to make his point, Housel—who has to be the most optimistic and ardent Auburn supporter ever—said:

> I want [the Alabama fans] to know what we're saying, what we're talking about, what we're thinking. They need to know, and when they find out they won't sleep good tonight, tomorrow night, or any night.
>
> We're coming after their butt. We're coming after them today, tomorrow, the day after tomorrow, and the day after that, and the day after that. We will not rest. We will not sleep. We will not be deterred until we reach our goal, and that goal is simple—to paint the state, the entire state—not North Alabama, not South Alabama, not East Alabama, not West Alabama, the entire state—orange and blue.
>
> We might not get them—the Alabama papas and mamas, but we'll get the sons and daughters. We're going to get the children, and we are getting them.…
>
> Birmingham used to be their bastion, their home ground, their turf, but we're winning the battle there. Look at the statistics. Statistics don't lie. Birmingham and Jefferson County students are coming to Auburn like never before.… We're winning the war.… Inch by inch, person by person, child by child, we're winning the war.… All we have to do is keep the faith and keep on fighting, every day in every way and in every arena. The future is ours. All we have to do is fight for it and take it.
>
> We're winning the war. That's what will keep them awake tonight.… We won't win all the battles, but we'll win the war. You can bank on it. We're going to win the war.…
>
> This is a call to arms—today, tomorrow, the day after that, and the day after that. We will fight until victory is

ours. As for today, Coach Jordan said it best: "Beat the hell out of the University of Alabama."... We may get knocked down, but we won't get knocked out. We will not be defeated—Never! It is not in our nature. It is not in our makeup. It is not in our heart and not in our soul.

Wow! If those statements don't rile up Alabama fans, nothing will. Those in 'Bama Nation who listened to or later heard that diatribe undoubtedly ratcheted up their hate for Auburn to new heights. And that was *before* Auburn beat Alabama six straight times!

In his introduction to the 2009 book, *Alabama-Auburn Rivalry Football Vault*, which he coauthored with Alabama alumnus Tommy Ford, Housel again changed his tune and demeanor considerably and tried to explain and put into perspective the heated and bitter intrastate rivalry that divides the state in ways people outside the state will never understand. Housel even admitted to hating Alabama during the years that Bear Bryant dominated the series and ruled college football, but clarified it by writing, "It was never really 'hate,' just something akin to hate, more envy and jealousy than true hate—to grudgingly admiring and then respecting and appreciating what Coach Bryant and Alabama had accomplished. I had put away childish things. I had become a man."

The thing is that most people obsessed by the Alabama-Auburn rivalry don't outgrow what Housel called "childish things." With some people, the hatred grows as they get older.

Housel, who also authored *Auburn University Football Vault: The Story of the Auburn Tigers 1892–2007*, reiterated that the

rivalry is best on the field, where the players compete ferociously against each other, but maintain a mutual respect and appreciation for each other and what they go through in preparing for this matchup. "They lay everything on the line, and then come together again in victory or defeat," wrote Housel, who then added, "If only the fans could have the same attitude."

Fat chance that is. Some Alabama fans would rather put a hot needle in their eye than acknowledge that "other" team, let alone consider them their equal. Housel knows this, pointing out that "family relationships, friendships, and business relationships have been broken forever because of this one day, this one supposed 'game.'"

Former Alabama linebacker Derrick Oden, the captain of the Tide's top-ranked defense when it won its 12th national championship in 1992, echoes pretty much what Housel said. "I was heavily recruited by Auburn. For the players, we just strapped on the helmet and played the game. We were excited when we shut them out 17–0 in 1992 in Pat Dye's final Iron Bowl. I have a lot of respect for their program and what Coach Dye did there. It was kind of bittersweet beating him.

"I played pro ball with several guys who played at Auburn. Among the players on both sides, there was a lot of respect [for the opposing players] and for the game. Over the years when you're removed from college football, we did a little fun stuff. Like if your school lost, then you had to wear the other school's jersey.

"It's the fans who [harbor] the hate. I listen to about as much talk radio as I can stomach."

Prior to the 2011 game, Alabama center William Vlachos said, "I think you've got two sides where people are just so passionate on whichever side they're on. It means a lot to everybody in this state, no matter whether you play on a team or you just watch it on TV. It's very important to a lot of people. It's obviously very important to us."

ALABAMA FANS HATE TO LOSE TO AUBURN IN ANYTHING

If Alabama and Auburn competed in Tiddlywinks, rest assured that each school would compete to win. Because the football rivalry between the two schools was so heated, in 1994 the student organizations of each school thought it would be a good idea to do something cooperative and promote a social cause, so they organized the Hunger Food Drive. Six weeks leading up to the Iron Bowl, bins are placed throughout both campuses for people to deposit nonperishable foods to be given to needy families.

A part of the hunger drive was that the top two donors got a chance to hit someone of their choosing in the face with a pie. In 2011 the two donors were Andres Mendieta and Candace Dunn. From a group of faculty, administrators, and other people, they picked Alabama offensive lineman Barrett Jones as the person they wanted to pie-face. Reluctant at first, Jones was a good sport and took a face full of pie for the cause. "I guess I wasn't thrilled about it at first, but I guess if it takes getting pied in the face to beat Auburn, I guess it's worth it," Jones told Chase Goodbread of the *Tuscaloosa News*. "It was an interesting experience. I've never been pied in the face before."

Twenty eleven marked the 18th year of the Hunger Food Drive. The passion from the Iron Bowl rivalry has been diverted at each school to raise more than 3 million pounds of food, which is distributed to people in need. Monetary donations are also accepted, with each dollar equaling two pounds of food. The food and money generated by the Alabama Beat Auburn Hunger Food Drive benefits the West Alabama Food Bank, while the food and money raised by the Auburn Beat Alabama Hunger Food Drive goes to the East Alabama Food Bank.

While the Crimson Tide is ahead in the Iron Bowl series, Auburn leads the food drive. Alabama had won three straight food drives from 2007 to 2009, but the War Eagles won in 2010. Alabama won in 2011 and now trails 10–8 in the annual competition. Except for four years, the winner of the Beat Hunger Food Drive has also been the winner of the Iron Bowl game.

In 2011 Alabama students and supporters collected 237,079 pounds of nonperishable food, while Auburn students and fans collected 134,102 pounds of food. UA has now collected a total of 1,687,874 pounds of food to AU's 1,577,866 since the food drive originated.

A commentator on the East Alabama Food Bank website wrote, "It just shows that no matter what other parts of the country may think of this state, when it comes to helping people, no one does it better than the state of Alabama."

Whereas hungry people throughout the state are the real winners in this competition, Alabama hates to lose to Auburn in anything.

Another way the two schools have collaborated for a good cause is the formation of the not-for-profit HEARTinDIXIE Foundation, a fund-raising effort to assist recovery from the devastating tornadoes that ravished Tuscaloosa and other parts of the state in the spring of 2011. Working with Unite|364, the foundation, which consists of players and supporters of both schools, hosted a three-day weekend in mid-August 2011 that included an alumni football game and golf, with the monies going to the Governor's Emergency Relief Fund.

Participants in the event included Gene Stallings, Ray Perkins, Lee Roy Jordan, Derrick Oden, Cornelius Bennett, and Bobby Humphrey from Alabama, and Pat Dye, Bo Jackson, Al Del Greco, Stan White, and Joe Cribbs from Auburn.

"People don't understand, it's a rivalry that we play one day a year," said Derrick Oden, a former University of Alabama and NFL linebacker. "But when the lights turn off and you walk off the field, you're friends with a lot of the guys who play on the other side.… This event allows us to come together and support a state that supports us year around. If you look across the landscape of Alabama, it's either orange and blue or it's crimson and white. We love this state, we love the people of this state that support us, and it's just our way of giving back."

Former Auburn and NFL kicker Al Del Greco agreed that the HEARTinDIXIE event provided a great opportunity to unite the people of Alabama. "When you talk about what happened here in April [the 2011 tornadoes that devastated Alabama], I think it's only natural that we, as former players, can show everybody that we can coexist together in the same state," he said. "We can live in the same state and we can all enjoy what

Alabama gives all of us. Then that one day of the year we can put on the pads and find out who the best football team is that particular year."

Many people, including some players, on both sides try to put some perspective into the rivalry, but this is what they're up against. During the 2010 SEC Media Days in Hoover, an Alabama fan wore a T-shirt with "I Hate Auburn" written in bold letters across the front. He obviously was stating his thoughts very clearly. Alabama coach Nick Saban either saw the T-shirt or was told about it. No matter, in trying to instill sanity into fans, his response was, "It's not personal. That is not really the way that we should respect the opponents that we have."

But we're just getting warmed up here. An Alabama fan on a chat-line writes what a lot of 'Bama fans feel: "I just hate Auburn because they're Auburn! That's enough of a reason right there. I also just hate Auburn because I can't think of anything else to hate them about!"

Roger Shultz, a four-year starting center for Alabama, who is always good for a quote, told this story: "I remember the first Iron Bowl that I went to in person. I was about 12 years old. I had a foam Alabama No. 1 finger and I was walking through the Auburn student section, and somebody ripped my finger off, and I've been giving Auburn the finger ever since."

JoeBama57, who hates Auburn and Tennessee equally, has put a little fun into the "I hate Auburn" theme by stringing together a folksy tune that includes the following lyrics:

Mama taught us to love everyone.

Mama tried to teach us right from wrong.

She said turn the other cheek and lend a hand to all you
meet.

She calls for love and peace and kindness if you can.

*But I Hate Auburn and Tennessee. I Hate Auburn and
Tennessee.*

I Hate Auburn and Tennessee. It comes naturally.

I was raised in Alabama…My first words were Roll Tide
and bowl bound.

Some Tide fans say they'll root for Auburn when they're
not against the Tide.

Well, I gave it a try, but now I cannot lie, the other team
becomes my favorite every time.

*Cause I Hate Auburn and Tennessee. I Hate Auburn and
Tennessee.*

I Hate Auburn and Tennessee. It comes naturally.

Of course, it's better if you listen to it.

1

GAMES WE HATE

ALABAMA DOESN'T LIKE to lose to anybody, especially Auburn! Tide fans hate all losses to Auburn. Following are the Iron Bowls that especially stick in the craw of 'Bama fans.

1972: AUBURN 17, ALABAMA 16

'Bama Nation hates this game more than any other because it's the game that Auburn fans love to throw in their faces. Auburn turned sure defeat into victory by blocking two straight punts and taking both of them back for touchdowns to come from 13 points down to win the game in its waning moments. The game is simply referred to as the "Punt, 'Bama, Punt!" game. Just mentioning it causes diehard 'Bama fans to cringe. Many still get angry when it is brought up.

This was a battle of two good teams. Alabama, coming off a national championship season, came into the game 10–0 and ranked No. 2 in the nation. An overachieving Auburn team, minus the graduated Heisman Trophy winner Pat Sullivan and consensus All-America receiver Terry Beasley, was 8–1.

The Tigers, despite their record, were a 16-point under-dog and performed like it. They were outplayed the whole

game. With its offense inept, Auburn was behind 16–0 in the fourth quarter. The Plainsmen finally managed to make a field goal to make it 16–3. Then, with the game winding down, Bill Newton blocked Greg Gantt's punt, and David Langner picked it up and ran 25 yards for a touchdown. The Tide was hardly over that miscue when, with 1:34 remaining, in an eerily similar "instant replay" of the disaster that had just occurred, Newton blocked another Gantt punt, and Langner again scooped the ball up and raced 20 yards into the end zone, enabling Auburn to pull out a 17–16 victory after Gardner Jett's extra point.

"It was by far the greatest thrill that I've had," stated Langner.

"Whoever said lighting doesn't strike twice in the same place was not at Birmingham's Legion Field that afternoon," writes AU football expert David Housel.

The Tigers actually blocked three kicks that day, the other being Roger Mitchell's second-quarter block of a Bill Davis extra-point attempt, which turned out to be the margin of victory.

The Crimson Tide had a chance at payback when, with less than 30 seconds left in the game, Auburn was forced to punt. However, with 'Bama sending everybody, David Beverly still managed to get off a 39-yard punt that forced the Crimson Tide to start on its own 27-yard line. Only seconds remained in the game, allowing Alabama time to run only two plays. Auburn hung on to pull off the upset. That Auburn team was tagged "the Amazins."

"I was so upset that I didn't think the sun was going to come up the next day," recalled H.B. Paul, a hardcore 'Bama fan who resides in Tuscaloosa.

"Punt, 'Bama, Punt" is perhaps the single most memorable game in AU history, claims Housel. When Alabama lines up to punt, Tigers fans who want to get under the skin of Tide fans only need to taunt them to punt, 'Bama, punt.

2010: AUBURN 28, ALABAMA 27

Unbeaten and No. 2–ranked Auburn (11–0) came to Tusca-loosa to play Alabama (9–2, 5–2), ranked No. 9, in the historic 75th Iron Bowl. The two teams hadn't been rated this high when they played each other since 1994. The Tigers, with star and Heisman-hopeful Cam Newton at quarterback, were favored. Playing at home, 'Bama bolted to a 24–0 lead and seemed like they were going to embarrass the War Eagles and ruin their dream season, only to see Auburn stage a dramatic comeback to overtake the Tide and hand UA its most deflating loss to its hated rival since the "Punt, 'Bama, Punt" game 38 years earlier.

The game started with Alabama completely dominating the Tigers. The Crimson Tide stormed out to a three-touchdown lead, scoring the first three times it had the ball, while chasing Newton behind the line of scrimmage and sacking him twice. After Mark Ingram tallied on a nine-yard run, Greg McElroy connected with Julio Jones on a 68-yard scoring strike and followed that with a 12-yard touchdown toss to Darius Hanks. Jeremy Shelley then booted a 20-yard field goal, and it looked like it was going to be a cakewalk for the underdog Tide.

Auburn wide receiver Terrell Zachery (81) eludes 'Bama DB DeMarcus Milliner for a 70-yard TD reception in the second half of the Tigers' 28–27 comeback win over the Tide on November 26, 2010, in Tuscaloosa. Photo courtesy of AP Images

As ESPN's Lee Corso is fond of saying, "Not so fast, my friend."

Alabama had a couple of chances to really put some nails in the coffin, but blew scoring opportunities deep in Tigers territory. Ingram was barreling toward a touchdown and stumbled just long enough for defensive end Antoine Carter to catch up with him and punch the ball out of Ingram's grasp into the end zone, where Demond Washington recovered the ball for a touchback.

Auburn linebacker Daren Bates said, "That's when we got our motivation on offense and defense. I think that's when things turned."

Alabama had another chance to extend its lead, but AU's Nick Fairley caused quarterback Greg McElroy to fumble at the Auburn 12-yard line. The two lost scoring opportunities would come back to bite Alabama.

Late in the first half, Newton hit Emory Blake with a 36-yard touchdown pass to make it 24–7. The comeback kicked in on the second play from scrimmage of the second half when Newton and Terrell Zachery teamed up on a 70-yard scoring pass to make it 24–14. Newton then scored on a one-yard run as the Tigers pulled to within 24–21. But Shelley kicked his second field goal to push 'Bama's lead to 27–21.

At the 11:55 mark, Newton tossed a seven-yard touchdown pass to Philip Lutzenkirchen to tie the game 27–27. Wes Byrum kicked what proved to be the game-winning extra point that saddled Alabama with a heartbreaking defeat and enabled Auburn to continue on its way to winning the SEC and beating Oregon 22–19 in the BCS National Championship Game on January 10, 2011.

The problem was that the Tide didn't finish, something they prided themselves on throughout the 2009 season when they won the national championship.

Newton completed 13 of 20 passes for 216 yards and three touchdowns. McElroy completed 27 of 37 passes for 377 yards

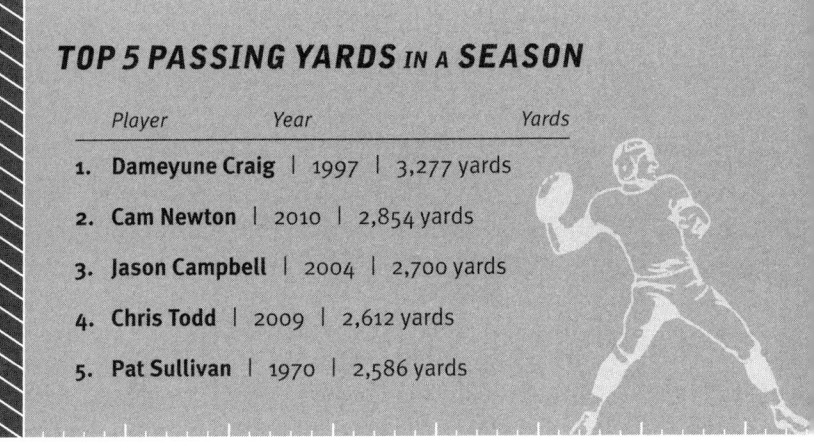

TOP 5 PASSING YARDS *IN A* SEASON

	Player	Year	Yards
1.	Dameyune Craig	1997	3,277 yards
2.	Cam Newton	2010	2,854 yards
3.	Jason Campbell	2004	2,700 yards
4.	Chris Todd	2009	2,612 yards
5.	Pat Sullivan	1970	2,586 yards

and two touchdowns, before departing late in the game with a concussion.

The way Alabama collapsed stunned the Crimson Tide and its fans, and was in some ways reminiscent of the "Punt, 'Bama, Punt" game when UA squandered a 16–3 lead in the final six minutes. The 1972 loss cost the then unbeaten No. 2–ranked Tide a chance at winning the national championship, while this setback helped its hated foe stay on track to win the national championship. That—helping the enemy—is just as bad to some 'Bama fans.

It's as former Auburn athletics director David Housel said: "The fear of losing is worse than the joy of winning. It's not enough to win, you want the other team to know that they got their ass beat."

The year before, Alabama came from two touchdowns back to beat Auburn in Jordan-Hare Stadium 26–21. To Auburn fans,

turnaround is fair play, but it's not to 'Bama fans when it comes to the Iron Bowl. 'Bama Nation wants to beat Auburn to a pulp every year! Younger Alabama fans, who weren't around or are too young to remember the 1972 Iron Bowl, hate this game more than "Punt, 'Bama, Punt!"

The victory, the largest come-from-behind win in the storied rivalry, enabled Auburn to close the gap in the series between the two schools to 40–34–1.

1997: AUBURN 18, ALABAMA 17

Mike DuBose won his first two games as Alabama's head coach, but then the Crimson Tide suffered through seven losses in its last nine games to finish the season 4–7. It was the worst season the school had experienced since 1957, the year before Bryant arrived to resurrect the downtrodden program.

It bears repeating. Any Alabama loss to Auburn hurts—a lot! It's just that some hurt even more, and the sting lingers long after. Like the two previous games noted, this game fits in that group. Alabama led 17–15 with under a minute to go in the game. Confronted with a third-and-long situation and not wanting to give the ball back to the Tigers if they didn't make it, Alabama elected to throw a screen pass to try and pick up the first down and then run out the clock.

The play, a swing pass from Freddie Kitchens to Ed Scissum, backfired with the Tide fumbling, Auburn recovering, and the Tigers winning the game 18–17 with a field goal. With 15 ticks on the clock remaining, the probable *W* changed to an *L*.

DuBose absorbed a lot of criticism when it was learned that he, as the head coach, did not only not call the play, but did not know what play was going to be run. Offensive coordinator Bruce Arians called the play.

"If I had been the head coach, I wouldn't admit that I didn't know what play was being called," adamantly stated Tommy Brooker, who played for the Crimson Tide and then the Kansas City Chiefs in the AFL. "The call was stupid, and I hate to lose a game on a stupid call. That's a big mistake, the difference between winning and losing the game."

The improbable victory sent Tigers fans into delirium and made 'Bama fans sick to their stomachs. Worse yet, Auburn marched on to play in the SEC Championship Game, something that upset Tide fans even more. The bitter loss brought to an end a totally unacceptable season, and everyone who bleeds Crimson and White was upset. DuBose was already on the hot seat, and losing to the hated War Eagles like that made the seat even hotter.

1989: AUBURN 30, ALABAMA 20

Former Alabama coach and athletics director Ray Perkins said, "It'll never happen." But it did. After waiting for six decades, Auburn finally got what they wanted, a chance to play Alabama at home at Jordan-Hare Stadium. Auburn coach Pat Dye called it the most emotional day in Auburn history.

With an off-week after beating Southern Mississippi, Alabama had two weeks to prepare for its "one-week-season." 'Bama coach Bill Curry, of course, had a history of problems with

Auburn, by this time failing to beat the Tigers in nine tries (including his seven years as Georgia Tech's head coach). Because of the controversy that came with the decision to play there, Curry said that this particular contest historically had to rank among the biggest in the annals of the Iron Bowl.

Curry called the rivalry the most intense in the country and said that there were good and bad points to that. "It is obsessive for almost everyone in the state," he said. "The players hear about it almost every day. As a child in this state, you are forced to choose sides. Now, there are some real ugly things about that because some sick minds use it to create a hatred situation, and that's disgusting."

Curry was referring to threatening letters and calls that he and some of his players had received. He indicated that he had contacted the FBI to make them aware of what could be a potentially dangerous situation.

Some of the former Alabama players, especially the older ones who played for Bear Bryant, scoffed at Curry for going to the FBI with the reported death threats, though Billy Neighbors, who played on 'Bama's 1961 national championship team, did say, "Every year before the Alabama-Auburn game, you get prank letters."

Curry, however, explained his motive to the media at his Monday press conference, even handing out material about his position on team security and fan conduct. He pointed out that people are breaking the law when they use the federal postal system and the telephone system to make threats. He wrote, "I want to ensure the families of all our players that

we consider it our sacred responsibility to protect these young men, and we are prepared to use every legal method to do so.... We will be prepared to protect our players every single minute that they are traveling to or from the stadium as well as during the game.

"When our players are threatened by those gutless wonders who find some perverse pleasure in making anonymous letters.... I will use every mechanism at my disposal, including the FBI, and prosecute them to the fullest extent of the law."

An editorial in the *Crimson White*, the student newspaper, stated in part, "Some people have assumed that the threats are related to the upcoming Iron Bowl and have wondered aloud if they came from Auburn fans or disgruntled Alabama supporters [who disliked Curry and wanted him out]. But the fact is we don't know, and these questions do not really matter. The important issue is that some people somewhere have completely lost sight of priorities and ethics."

All this, as if the Alabama-Auburn game needed any extra hype. And they say Ohio State–Michigan, Oklahoma-Texas, and Oklahoma-Nebraska compare to the Iron Bowl. No way.

The day all football fans in the state of Alabama wait for each year had arrived. It was 52°, partly sunny, hazy, with winds from the west at 7–10 mph. Good weather to play football. As it turned out, Auburn took the wind out of Alabama's sails, defeating the No. 2–ranked Crimson Tide 30–20. The loss relegated Alabama to SEC tri-champions, along with Auburn and Tennessee. That just rubbed salt into the wound. It also

ended any hopes for a national championship. Worse yet, it was Alabama's fourth straight loss to Auburn, and Curry's 10th overall and third straight since taking over the Tide.

More important, despite rumors of possible violence, the behavior of the fans of both schools was courteous and respectful. That was in part due to the Alabama-Auburn Better Relations Day, spearheaded by the efforts of UA Student Government Association president Lynn Yeldell and Auburn SGA president Scott Turnquist. Both worked hard and cooperatively to ensure, as the *Crimson White* said, "a civilized encounter during this year's especially sensitive game." Auburn proved to be a cordial host, except on the field.

As the coach of the Crimson Tide, this was Curry's third and final loss to Auburn, as he left to take the Kentucky job following the season. Curry wore his inability to beat Auburn like an albatross. On the other hand, to be fair, Curry never lost to Tennessee, the Tide's other hated rival, during his short tenure in Tuscaloosa.

Housel said beating Alabama at Jordan-Hare Stadium was perhaps the biggest and most emotional game in AU history. "Never had the War Eagle flown higher or the Tiger growled louder," was the way he put it.

Some still say that just to finally get Alabama to come to the Plains, in some ways, was the biggest victory in Auburn history. Don't think so? Well, here's the way Pat Dye described it, like a conquest of great magnitude: "I'm sure that [the atmosphere in the stadium] resembled what went on the night the

wall came down in Berlin. I mean, it was like [Auburn fans] had been freed, and let out of bondage, just having this game at Auburn." Clear enough?

1982: AUBURN 23, ALABAMA 22

Alabama fans hate every game they lose to Auburn, but they especially hate this game because it was Bear Bryant's last Iron Bowl, and he came up just short. Auburn edged the Crimson Tide 23–22. To have their esteemed leader bow out of the bitter series on this note left a bad taste in the mouths of 'Bama fans. Close, yes—very—but no cigar. They also hate this game because it snapped a nine-game Alabama winning streak.

In his second season coaching Auburn, Pat Dye became the first Bryant pupil to beat the teacher in 31 games over a span of 12 years.

1963: AUBURN 10, ALABAMA 8

The 1963 Iron Bowl was a matchup of two top 10 teams. Alabama was sporting a 7–1 record and ranked No. 6 in the country. Auburn was 8–1 and ranked No. 9. The Crimson Tide had already secured a berth in the Sugar Bowl. The Tigers were already ticketed for the Orange Bowl. Like all Iron Bowls, it was a hard-hitting, helmet-busting affair.

Auburn got on the scoreboard first on a field goal by Marvin "Woody" Woodall, the first time the Tigers had a lead over Alabama in five years. Mailon Kent then fired a pass to Auburn All-American Tucker Frederickson to extend the advantage to 10–0.

Auburn fans tear down the goal posts in the south end of Legion Field on November 27, 1982, after the Tigers defeated Alabama in the Iron Bowl for the first time in nine years, sending Bear Bryant out on the wrong side of a 23–22 score. Photo courtesy of AP Images

'Bama's Benny Nelson busted through for an 80-yard touchdown run, and Joe Namath dove into the end zone from two yards out for the two-point conversion to pull within two at 10–8, but that was as close as the Crimson Tide got that day.

Jimmy Sidle was an All-America quarterback for Auburn in 1963. He told Clyde Bolton about his dream of snapping Alabama's four-game winning streak in the Iron Bowl. "I remember the first day I was at Auburn, several of us freshmen—Billy Edge, Tucker Frederickson, David Rawson, Mickey Sutton, Mike Alford, and me—were on the porch at Graves Center talking. Alabama had been beating Auburn, and we just sort of talked it over and said we were going to try to do something about that. It was just a bunch of kids talking, but we pumped ourselves up."

Auburn finished fifth in the nation, the Crimson Tide ninth.

1988: AUBURN 15, ALABAMA 10

With Reggie Slack throwing for 220 yards and tailback Stacy Danley rushing for 97 yards, Auburn topped the Crimson Tide 15–10. With the game tied 3–3, Ron Stallworth sacked Alabama quarterback David Smith for a safety, Win Lyle kicked his second field goal, and Vincent Harris scored on a one-yard run to give the War Eagles the win.

SIX-YEAR STRETCH, 2002–2007

Tommy Tuberville enjoyed a six-year stretch when he beat the Crimson Tide from 2002 to 2007. In 2002, when the Tigers enjoyed a 17–0 lead at the half, Auburn athletics director

David Housel was as friendly and cordial as ever. After a brief interview in the press box at halftime, he was asked if he had anything else to say. He smiled and parted with his usual, "Yeah, War Eagle, War Eagle now, and War Eagle forever!"

And that was at halftime. Rest assured Housel let loose with a grin from ear to ear following the Tigers' 17–7 upset of the Crimson Tide.

In the midst of the six-year run, after defeating Alabama for the fourth time, Tuberville angered 'Bama nation with his "one for the thumb" proclamation.

Before he left for Texas Tech, Tuberville beat Alabama seven times, the third-highest total after iconic coaches Bear Bryant, who enjoyed 19 victories in the series and Shug Jordan, who notched nine. Trailing Tuberville is Pat Dye, who recorded six wins.

'Bama fans think it's a good thing for Tuberville that he hightailed it for Tech, because if he stayed, Nick Saban and the 'Bama juggernaut he was assembling was going to take Tuberville behind the woodshed almost every year.

2005: AUBURN 28, ALABAMA 18

The 2005 Iron Bowl pitted two very good, championship-caliber teams that were still in contention for big-time bowls, No. 8 Alabama (9–1, 6–1 SEC) and No. 11 Auburn (8–2, 6–1). The two teams entered the contest with a combined won-lost record that compared favorably with some of the best in the longtime intrastate series. Whereas Alabama needed to

rebound from a painful loss to LSU, Auburn came into the game rejuvenated by its dramatic 31–30 road victory over then No. 9 Georgia, when John Vaughn kicked a 20-yard field goal with six seconds left that enabled the Tigers to escape Athens with the win.

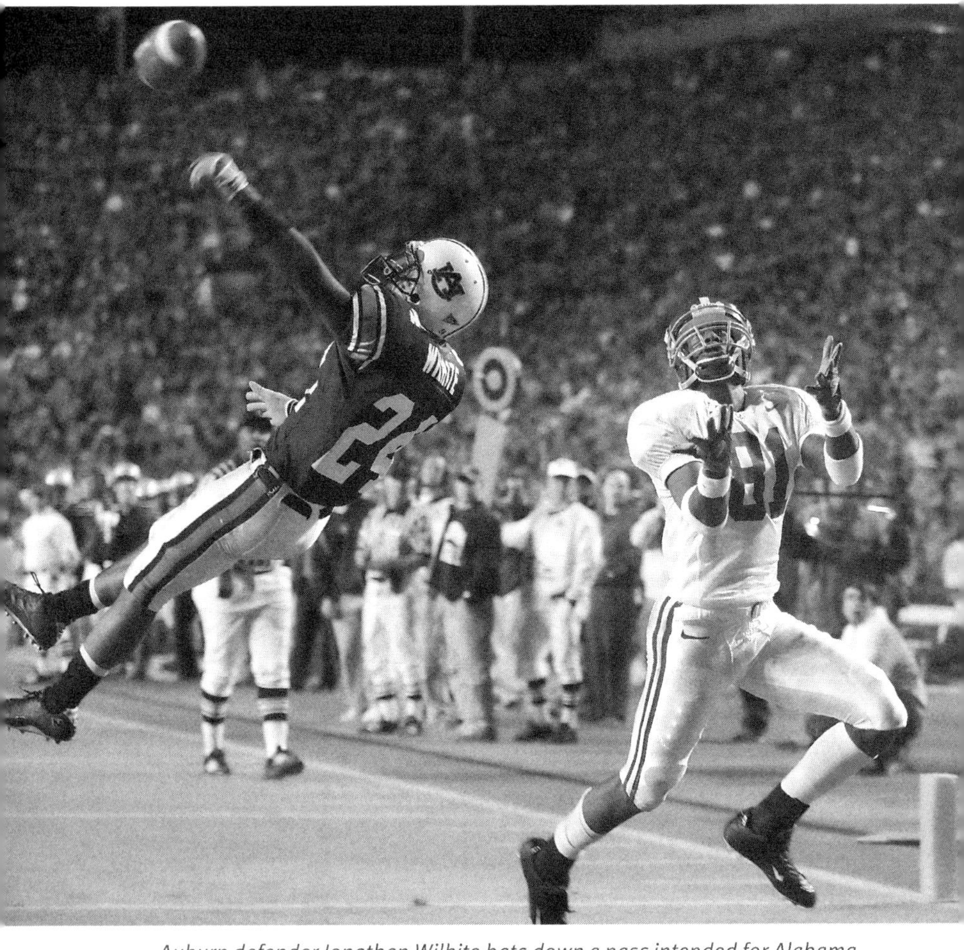

Auburn defender Jonathan Wilhite bats down a pass intended for Alabama receiver Keith Brown during the second half of the Tigers' 28–18 win in the Iron Bowl on November 19, 2005, in Auburn. Photo courtesy of AP Images

On the Plains, Auburn handed 'Bama its second straight loss, 28–18, relegating UA to the Cotton Bowl, where they would play Texas Tech.

Alabama fans hate this game because Auburn beat up the Tide quarterback, sacking Brodie Croyle 11 times. The War Eagles had as many sacks as Alabama had first downs. After the game, bumper stickers appeared with, "Did You Sack Brodie?"

The Tigers jumped out to a commanding 21–0 lead in the first quarter and never looked back.

After the game Tuberville pissed off Tide fans who thought he was rubbing it in when he sashayed over to the student section in Jordan-Hare Stadium and held up four fingers, signifying four consecutive wins over their hated cross-state rival. The result was that immediately bumper stickers and T-shirts came out with, "Fear the Thumb." Auburn fans loved the gesture and the opportunity to stick it to the Tide, while 'Bama fans thought Tuberville's grandstanding was classless.

The Tigers won again in 2006, 22–15, getting one for the thumb.

1995: AUBURN 31, ALABAMA 27

Alabama fans hate this game because it came down to one play that could have changed the outcome. Trailing 31–27, the Crimson Tide had its chance as it had the ball on the Auburn 22-yard line with the game winding down. With less than 10 seconds remaining, in a fourth-and-10, do-or-die situation,

quarterback Freddie Kitchens fired a pass that sailed out of bounds. And the Tide died.

Alabama fans hate this game because of a controversial call earlier in the series. With Alabama at the Auburn 22, Curtis Brown caught a pass in the end zone that the officials ruled out of bounds. Alabama claimed Brown had one foot in-bounds. The Tide accumulated 478 yards of total offense, but it couldn't get the 22 more yards it needed to win the game. 'Bama fans also hate this game because Alabama was on probation and therefore ineligible for a bowl game, so this was in effect Alabama's bowl game.

Auburn and its fans rejoiced as the win preserved their Iron Bowl streak at Jordan-Hare stadium.

1987: AUBURN 10, ALABAMA 0

This was Bill Curry's first Iron Bowl. The Tigers blanked the Crimson Tide 10–0. Curry very quickly found out just how important this game is to 'Bama followers. After the game, the press immediately reminded him that, as a coach, it was his eighth straight loss to Auburn (going back to his Georgia Tech head-coaching stint, where he went winless against the Tigers from 1980 to 1986).

The contest was a defensive struggle for the most part, although Auburn did compile 383 total yards and double the Tide's first-down total, 20–10. Harry Mose ran for a touchdown, and Win Lyle kicked a field goal. That was the extent of Auburn's scoring, but it was sufficient, as the War Eagles limited the Alabama offense to 183 total yards.

Auburn fans took pride because it was the first Auburn shut-out over Alabama since the Tigers' national championship season in 1957. Alabama fans wondered what the big deal was, what all the "War Eagles," the jumping up and down, and the celebrating was about. After all, it had taken Auburn 30 years to shut 'Bama out again. Whoopee.

In the meantime, the Crimson Tide had held the War Eagles scoreless seven times over the course of those three decades.

2000: AUBURN 9, ALABAMA 0

What really upset 'Bama fans about this game was that Auburn came to Tuscaloosa and not only defeated but, in the first Iron Bowl game played on the Alabama campus since 1901, shut out the Crimson Tide in Bryant-Denny Stadium. Getting beat on its own turf made the sting even more painful. The Plainsmen prevailed in a game dominated by defense that was played on a freezing, rainy day mixed with sleet. Damon Duval kicked three field goals to account for all the scoring.

'Bama fans hate this game because it was the third straight time that Auburn had blanked the Tide in Tuscaloosa. Furthermore, up to that point, Alabama had yet to score on the Tigers in games played in Tuscaloosa in the 1800s, 1900s, and 2000. Alabama finally scored against the Tigers in T-town in 2002, but still lost 17–7, the touchdown being their only points in three centuries.

Okay, Auburn likes to say it that way, but it's not nearly as bad as it sounds since the teams had up to that point only played in Tuscaloosa in 1895, 1901, and 2000.

1969: AUBURN 49, ALABAMA 26

Alabama faithful hate this game because Auburn snapped a five-game losing streak against the Tide with a 49–26 win that included an 84-yard touchdown on a fake punt by Connie Frederick. They also hate it because the Tigers tacked 49 points on 'Bama, the most ever scored on a Bear Bryant–coached team. That's sufficient reason to hate this game.

1957: AUBURN 40, ALABAMA 0

At 9–0, Auburn was the only undefeated and untied team in the country when they played Alabama. The Crimson Tide, on the other hand, was 2–6–1 and entered the contest having won just four of its last 35 games. It was the coldest day for an Iron Bowl game up to that point, with the temperature hovering around freezing. The weather didn't bother Auburn, as the Tigers heated up in a hurry, scoring two quick touchdowns to build a 14–0 lead seven minutes into the contest. By halftime, the margin had ballooned to 34–zip.

After recovering a fumble, Auburn scored on its first possession as Billy "Ace" Atkins plunged into the end zone from one yard out, and shortly thereafter ran six yards for another touchdown. Lloyd Nix then scored from the 2. Next Tommy Lorino picked off a pass from Bobby Smith, after it was deflected by Jackie Burkett, and scooted 79 yards for a touchdown that made it 27–0. Then Burkett got his own interception and scampered 66 yards for another touchdown. And just like that, it was 34–0.

The Tigers then took the second half kickoff and drove 62 yards for another score. Meanwhile, through all of Auburn's

TOP 5 RUSHING TDS SCORED *IN A* SEASON

	Player	Year	TDs
1.	Cam Newton	2010	20
2t.	Bo Jackson	1985	17
	Carnell Williams	2003	17
4.	Joe Cribbs	1978	16
5t.	Joe Cribbs	1979	14
	Stephen Davis	1995	14

AUBURN

fireworks, Alabama's offense stayed as cold as the weather, if not colder.

Auburn led the country in most defensive categories, and the 40–0 whitewash of the Crimson Tide, one of six shutouts recorded by the Tigers that season, only enhanced its reputation. Auburn was still the only undefeated and untied team in the nation, but the UPI voted Ohio State national champion. The Associated Press named Auburn national champion. Auburn also won its first SEC championship and recorded its first perfect season since 1913.

"That was a very unemotional club," Lorino told Clyde Bolton about the championship team that won with a ball-control offense and a tough-as-nails defense. "There was no emotion at all, just a workmanlike job."

The Crimson Tide absorbed its worst defeat in 50 years, and what made it all the more painful was that it was administered by Auburn. So one of Alabama's worst-ever teams got

hammered by one of Auburn's best-ever teams. That put an abrupt end to the J.B. "Ears" Whitworth era, a forgettable period of time in Alabama football history. After that debacle, Alabama desperately needed help and reached out to one of its own, Bear Bryant, who famously responded, "Mama called."

1986: AUBURN 21, ALABAMA 17

'Bama's Bobby Humphrey rushed for 204 yards, and the Crimson Tide took a 17–7 lead into the fourth quarter. But it was not enough, as Auburn tallied 14 unanswered points in the final 15 minutes of play to win.

With 32 seconds left, Lawyer Tillman, on a play where he wasn't even supposed to be in the game, let alone get the ball, took it on a reverse and ran seven yards into the end zone for the winning touchdown. It was the first rushing touchdown of his career, and it could not have come at a better time, if you're an Auburn fan. If you're an Alabama fan, it couldn't have come at a worse time.

AUBURN

TOP 5 RUSHING YARDS IN A SEASON

	Player	Year	Yards
1.	Bo Jackson	1985	1,786 yards
2.	Rudi Johnson	2000	1,567 yards
3.	Cam Newton	2010	1,473 yards
4.	Brent Fullwood	1986	1,391 yards
5.	Ben Tate	2009	1,362 yards

"I know I'll be hearing a lot of 'War Eagles' for the next 364 days," said UA coach Ray Perkins after the game. "But I'll just sit back and swallow it."

'Bama recoverd to wax Washington in the Sun Bowl 28–6. The Crimson Tide won big, but it would be Perkins' last game as coach at his alma mater. After denying all December that he was leaving, Perkins met with Alabama alumnus Hugh Culverhouse in a Birmingham motel to finalize a deal whereby Perkins would become head coach, general manager, and vice president for football operations of the NFL's Tampa Bay Buccaneers.

1954: AUBURN 28, ALABAMA 0

Alabama had a defense that was ranked fifth in the nation, but Auburn dissected it to the tune of 28–0 in winning the first of five straight games over the Crimson Tide. 'Bama's offense was struggling entering the game, and it continued to struggle as the Tide failed to score a point. Auburn quarterback Bobby Freeman rushed for 102 yards, passed for 64 yards, scored three touchdowns, and set up another with a 25-yard run in going through, over, and around the Tide's defense.

1955: AUBURN 26, ALABAMA 0

Against an Alabama defense that had been outscored 230–48, heavily favored Auburn easily handled the Crimson Tide in winning 26–0. It took a little while, but the Tigers' offense got on track toward the end of the first quarter. Starting on its own 20-yard line, the Plainsmen marched 80 yards to score when Howell Tubbs connected with Jerry Elliott on a 23-yard

scoring pass. Joe Childress' extra-point attempt was blocked by Knute Rockne Christian.

Then, starting from its own 10-yard line, Auburn drove 90 yards, and Tubbs and Elliott hooked up again, this time for nine yards. Childress' point-after kick made it 13–0 at intermission. In the second half, Childress bulled in for the Tigers' third touchdown. Another missed extra point, this time by Tubbs, left the score at 19–0. Tubbs added a three-yard run and Childress a PAT kick to make the final score 26–0. In the 1954 and 1955 games, Joe Childress rushed for 165 yards and scored two touchdowns.

'Bama fans also hate this game because it concluded a season in which the Crimson Tide finished 0–10 for the only time in its illustrious history. Worse yet for Tide fans was that Auburn took the lead in the series 10–9–1. At least the Tigers lost to Vanderbilt in the Gator Bowl, 25–13, though they still finished No. 8 in the national poll.

Future Alabama governor Forrest "Fob" James was a four-year letterman (1952–1955) and an All-America halfback for Auburn. Whereas Alabama's Bart Starr, who later went on to glory with the Green Bay Packers in their dynasty years under Vince Lombardi, had the misfortune of playing during the "Ears" Whitworth era, Fob had the good fortune of playing against Whitworth's teams. He carried the ball 50 times and gained 253 yard against the Tide, averaging 5.6 yards a carry.

Years later, in 1978, James successfully ran for governor of Alabama, beating Bill Baxley, an avid 'Bama supporter and a

good friend of Bear Bryant. According to David Housel and Tommy Ford, in their book, *Alabama-Auburn Rivalry Football Vault*, Bryant even campaigned for Baxley, running ads saying that Alabama didn't need an Auburn man as governor.

1956: AUBURN 34, ALABAMA 7

December 1, 1956, was a perfect day for football, at least for Auburn as the War Eagles scored 27 points in the second quarter en route to a 34–7 thrashing of the Crimson Tide for their third straight win over UA. On a fourth-and-6 situation, quarterback Howell Tubbs threw a six-yard pass to Jerry Elliott to get the Tigers on the board. Tubbs then tallied on an 11-yard run to make it 13–0, but his PAT attempt was no good.

Alabama's Don Kinderknecht then fumbled the kickoff, with Cleve Wester recovering for the War Eagles on the Tide 12-yard line. A run around left end advanced the ball to the 1. Then Alabama got a break when the Tigers fumbled, but the ball bounced into the end zone, where Billy Kitchens pounced on it for a touchdown to extend the Auburn lead to 20–0. An Auburn interception and a Tigers' touchdown pass pushed the lead to 27–0, and the rout was on.

Tommy Lorino scored on a 17-yard run and Tubbs added the extra point to close out the scoring. The Tigers' Bobby Hoppe only rushed eight times, but he rambled for 112 yards. James Loftin scored on an eight-yard run that enabled Alabama to avert another shutout.

In the 1956 and 1957 games, Billy Atkins, who also kicked extra points, burned Alabama for 18 points.

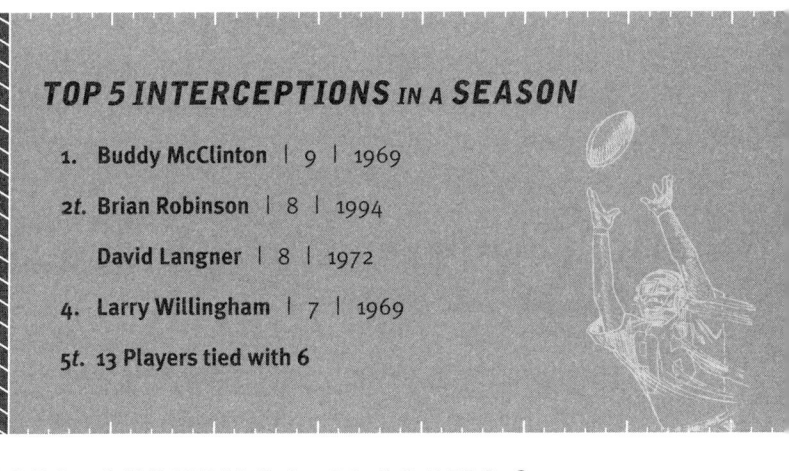

TOP 5 INTERCEPTIONS IN A **SEASON**

1. Buddy McClinton | 9 | 1969
2*t*. Brian Robinson | 8 | 1994
   David Langner | 8 | 1972
4. Larry Willingham | 7 | 1969
5*t*. 13 Players tied with 6

1958: AUBURN 14, ALABAMA 8

The Bear was back at 'Bama, but in his first of 18 matchups with Shug Jordan, Shug came out on top, 14–8. It was another cold day in Birmingham, but on its second possession, Auburn again warmed up quickly, jumping out in front 7–0 on Dick Wood's seven-yard pass to Jimmy Pettus. The score stayed that way until the first play of the fourth quarter, when James Reynolds powered in from the 1-yard line to extend the lead to 14–0. Marlin Dyess tallied for the Tide, and Bobby Jackson tossed a pass to Gary O'Stern to complete the two-point conversion to make it 14–8.

Auburn's only blemish that season was a 7–7 tie with Georgia. Many Tigers who played on both the 1957 national championship team and the 1958 squad that went 9–0–1 felt that the 1958 team was better overall. The national championship team was a predominately ball-control team on offense that primarily won with its defense, whereas the 1958 team had a more diversified offense that led the conference in passing and total offense.

Zeke Smith earned All-America honors both years and in 1958 won the Outland Trophy that is given to the best lineman in the country. Lloyd Nix, who played defensive back in 1956, switched to quarterback in 1957 and 1958 and engineered an offense that went 19–0–1.

The Tigers were on the prowl in 1956, '57, and '58, amassing a 24-game unbeaten streak, with only the tie to Georgia marring its record. Shug Jordan bettered Mike Donahue's string of 23 wins without a loss, with Donahue's streak also interrupted by a tie. A good reason for 'Bama fans to hate this one is that it completed a run of five straight victories for Auburn in the Iron Bowl, a stretch in which the Plainsmen outscored 'Bama 142–15 and shut the Tide out three times.

1892: AUBURN 32, ALABAMA 22

Although they weren't even alive, Alabama fans hate this game just because it was the first game between the two schools, and Auburn won. Auburn fans have no clue about this game, but they like to take pride in the fact that the Tigers stuck it to the Tide the first time the two teams clashed on the gridiron.

The first game was played in Birmingham at Lakeview Baseball Park, with a few hundred Auburn and Alabama fans in attendance. Despite a small crowd, the results were big news as the defunct *Birmingham Age-Herald* carried the game story on its front page.

Right from the get-go, there was disagreement. The game was played February 27, 1893, but Alabama records the game as the last game of the 1892 season, whereas Auburn lists the

game as the first game of the 1893 season. Shades of things to come.

1895: AUBURN 48, ALABAMA 0

Noteworthy about this game was that the Auburn coach was John W. Heisman, for whom the Heisman Trophy would later be named. After coming to the Plains following stops at Oberlin and Bucknell, Heisman was coaching his third game at Auburn and his first against Alabama. Neither team had acquired their nicknames yet.

With bigger and better players, Auburn shot out to a 22–0 lead at the half and continued the onslaught in the second half in the romp as they overpowered Alabama. Halfback Harry Smith busted through the porous 'Bama defense for several 50-plus-yard runs and scored three touchdowns. Details from the game are difficult to find. Alabama fans are very happy about that.

According to Housel and Ford in their book, it was the first game played in Tuscaloosa. The authors also noted that Auburn won the first game ever played between the two schools, the first game that was played in Birmingham, the first game that was played in Montgomery, and the first game that was played in Auburn.

'Bama fans are quick to point out that the Crimson Tide has won most of the games in between those games.

1949: AUBURN 14, ALABAMA 13

Auburn was going through a tough season, having won only one game while losing four times and salvaging three ties. Alabama entered the game on a five-game winning streak and, as a 19-point favorite, was expected to pound the Plainsmen. But somebody must have forgotten to tell the Tigers that they were supposed to lose because, in a huge upset, Auburn defeated the Tide 14–13. Billy Tucker, who would later be crippled by polio, kicked the game-winning extra point.

According to David Housel, Auburn historian as well as former athletics director and sports information director, the big win resulted in one Auburn student calling the Queen of England and declaring, "Auburn done beat the hell out of Alabama." Alabama finished with a 6–3–1 record, and Auburn closed out at 2–4–3, but the Tigers won the Iron Bowl.

1993: AUBURN 22, ALABAMA 14

This was the year that first-year Auburn coach Terry Bowden led the Tigers to a perfect 13–0 season, one that was tarnished a bit because the Tigers were on probation and ineligible for a bowl game. The War Eagles were hanging on to a slim 15–14 lead, with plenty of time for Alabama to score, when with 2:19 to go, James Bostic busted a 70-yard touchdown run to seal the deal.

Alabama still went to the SEC Championship Game, but fell to Florida 28–13. Then it was on to the Gator Bowl, where the Crimson Tide closed out the season with a 24–10 win over North Carolina.

1970: AUBURN 33, ALABAMA 28

This was the second straight down year for Alabama, but 'Bama fans also hate this game because the Crimson Tide squandered a 17–0 first-quarter lead. The Plainsmen came back to win 33–28 and saddle UA with another six-win season, subpar by Alabama standards.

When Auburn found itself down by two touchdowns and a field goal, All-America quarterback Pat Sullivan told star receiver Terry Beasley, "Get ready, Beez. We're going to win it just like when we were freshmen," referring to how the Tigers, trailing 27–0 in the freshman game (before they were allowed to play varsity), clawed their way back to defeat the Tide.

That they did again. By the end of the third quarter, the War Eagles had knotted it up 17–17. UA and AU traded field goals to keep it deadlocked at 20–20. Sullivan then tossed a 17-yard touchdown pass to Robby Robinett, with the extra point enabling Auburn to regain the lead, 27–20. Scott Hunter countered with a 54-yard scoring strike to George Ranager, and the follow-up two-point conversion pass to David Bailey put Alabama back in front 28–27.

Wallace Clark's three-yard blast into the end zone with three minutes remaining secured the win for Auburn.

1901: AUBURN 17, ALABAMA 0

After Auburn's 17–0 win in Tuscaloosa, the *Birmingham News* ran a headline: "A Tiger Claws Alabama." It was only the second time the press had used the Tigers nickname to describe

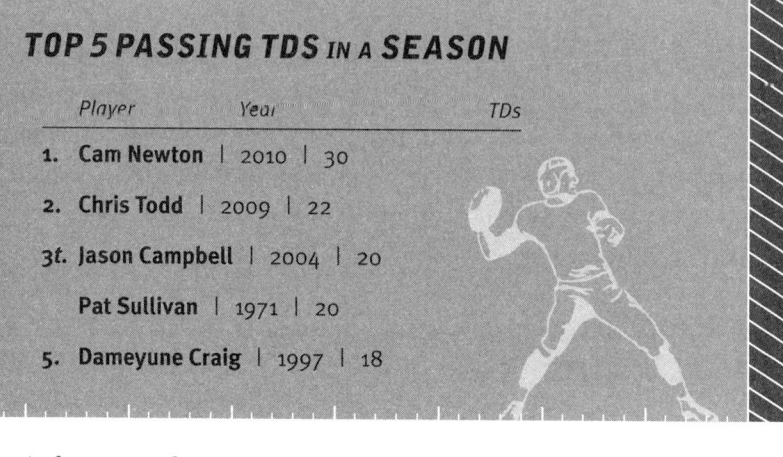

TOP 5 PASSING TDS IN A SEASON

	Player	Year	TDs
1.	Cam Newton	2010	30
2.	Chris Todd	2009	22
3t.	Jason Campbell	2004	20
	Pat Sullivan	1971	20
5.	Dameyune Craig	1997	18

AUBURN

Auburn, and it was the first time the name was used for a game within the series.

Alabama fans hate this game because, first of all, UA coach Mike Harvey played for Auburn in 1899 and 1900. Harvey invited his former teammates to play in Tuscaloosa. Bad mistake, writes Housel, Auburn's former sports information director and athletics director. UA did not get into Tigers territory the entire game. The following year, Harvey returned to Auburn as an assistant coach, and Housel states, "Auburn was not invited back to Tuscaloosa for 99 years."

1983: AUBURN 23, ALABAMA 20

Bo Jackson rushed for 256 yards, including runs of 69 and 71 yards. That wasn't fun to watch for Tide fans. 'Bama fans also didn't like it one bit that the win gave the War Eagles the SEC championship. While the Auburn Nation was giddy, 'Bama fans quickly pointed out that it was Auburn's first outright conference championship in 26 years.

1900: AUBURN 53, ALABAMA 5

First of all, Alabama fans who are interested in history and look back at this game hate it because of the lopsided score. If it makes 'Bama fans feel any better, the Tigers won all four of their games that season with ease and shut out the other three opponents. At least 'Bama scored five points.

2
TRADITIONS WE HATE

WHEN AUBURN FANS MOCK THE RAMMER JAMMER CHEER

When Alabama loses to Auburn, which is not that often, Auburn fans get giddy and mock the "Rammer Jammer Cheer" by modifying the lyrics to:

> *Hey, 'Bama!*
> *Hey, 'Bama!*
> *Hey, 'Bama!*
> *Rammer Jammer Yellowhammer*
> *We-just-beat-the-hell-out-of-you!*

Or worse yet:

> *Hey, 'Bama!*
> *Hey, 'Bama!*
> *Hey, 'Bama!*
> *Rammer Jammer Yellowhammer, go to hell, Alabama!*

Alabama fans hate that! Now, other schools do that too, but Auburn fans get the most joy out of doing it. Right behind

AUBURN

AUBURN'S 37 BOWL GAMES

6 Gator Bowls (1954 [twice], 1955 1971, 1972, 1974)
5 Sugar Bowls (1972, 1984, 1988, 1989, 2005)
3 Peach Bowls (1990, 1998, 2001)
2 Capital One Bowls (2003, 2006)
2 Chick-fil-A Bowls (2007, 2011)
2 Citrus Bowls (1987, 2001)
2 Cotton Bowls (1986, 2007)
2 Hall of Fame Bowls (1990, 1996)
2 Liberty Bowls (1965, 1984)
2 Orange Bowls (1938, 1964)
2 Sun Bowls (1968, 2003)
Bacardi Bowl (1937)
Astro-Bluebonnet Bowl (1969)
Tangerine Bowl (1982)
Independence Bowl (1996)
Music City Bowl (2003)
Outback Bowl (2010)
BCS National Championship (2011)

them are the Tennessee fans who get their kicks from changing the lyrics as well.

TOOMER'S CORNER

Fans of Auburn have a tradition of gathering at Toomer's Corner, at the corner of College and Magnolia Street in the center of town, to shower their beloved oak trees with toilet paper following Auburn football victories. The "rolling" of the two majestic, 70-year-old oak trees has been a part of Auburn football folklore for years. It is said to have begun back when

Toomer's Drug Store, an Auburn landmark for over a century, had the only telegraph in the city and, upon learning of an Auburn victory, employees rolled the trees with bathroom tissue. While that may grate on Alabama fans after the Tide loses to the Tigers, even Alabama fans were upset when Harvey Updyke, a self-proclaimed, diehard Alabama fan, took it upon himself to poison the trees.

A 62-year-old former Texas state trooper, Updyke called in the Paul Finebaum radio show and said he saw that Auburn fans had put what he called a "Scam" Newton jersey on the Bear Bryant statue. Responding to that he stated, "Well let me tell you what I did. I poisoned the two oak trees."

Updyke, who never even attended the University of Alabama, admitted and seemingly bragged on the air that the weekend following the Iron Bowl, he used the toxic herbicide Spike 80DF to poison the trees. When Finebaum asked Updyke if he had broken any laws by poisoning the trees, Updyke responded, "Do you think I care? I really don't."

By and large, 'Bama fans agreed that was taking the hatred level between the two schools way too far, so much so that the mean-spirited act by Updyke instigated the formation of a group of about 60,000 supporters called Tide for Toomer's, which donated $50,000 to the Toomer's Trees and Traditions Fund on March 29, 2011. Some time later, when he saw that what he had done had not only infuriated Auburn fans but Alabama fans as well, Updyke tried to explain his actions by saying, "I think there was too much 'Bama in me. I just wanted to get under their skin. I need to get my priorities straightened out."

Besides the physical damage to the trees, the unfortunate, cruel, thoughtless, and extreme act accomplished something that he and probably most Tide-Tiger fans never imagined. It paradoxically, if only for a short time, united many of the fans of the two rivals.

Not only were Auburn and Alabama fans angered and emotional over the poisoning, fans of other schools in the SEC were upset as well. Some people just don't know where to draw the line.

AUBURN'S BOWL HISTORY

1936 Bacardi	Auburn 7, Villanova 7
1937 Orange	Auburn 6, Michigan State 0
1953 Gator	Texas Tech 35, Auburn 13
1954 Gator	Auburn 33, Baylor 13
1955 Gator	Vanderbilt 25, Auburn 13
1963 Orange	Nebraska 13, Auburn 7
1965 Liberty	Ole Miss 13, Auburn 7
1968 Sun	Auburn 34, Arizona 10
1969 Astro-Bluebonnet	Houston 36, Auburn 7
1970 Gator	Auburn 35, Ole Miss 28
1971 Sugar	Oklahoma 40, Auburn 22
1972 Gator	Auburn 24, Colorado 3
1973 Sun	Missouri 34, Auburn 17
1974 Gator	Auburn 27, Texas 3
1982 Tangerine	Auburn 33, Boston College 26
1983 Sugar	Auburn 9, Michigan 7
1984 Liberty	Auburn 21, Arkansas 15
1985 Cotton	Texas A&M 36, Auburn 16
1986 Citrus	Auburn 16, Southern Cal 7
1987 Sugar	Auburn 16, Syracuse 16

AUBURN

THE TIGERS NICKNAME

Alabama fans understand and accept that Auburn people aren't too smart or original. Case in point: whereas Alabama has the unique nickname, the Crimson Tide, Auburn's athletic teams are called the Tigers. With 45 schools going by "Tigers," it's the third-most-common nickname in the country. Think about it, when a sportscaster or someone refers to the Tigers, who are they talking about—LSU, Clemson, Missouri, Memphis, Princeton, or some other school? Come

1988 Sugar	Florida State 13, Auburn 7
1989 Hall of Fame	Auburn 31, Ohio State 14
1990 Peach	Auburn 27, Indiana 23
1995 Hall of Fame	Penn State 43, Auburn 14
1996 Independence	Auburn 32, Army 29
1997 Peach	Auburn 21, Clemson 17
2000 Citrus	Michigan 31, Auburn 28
2001 Peach	North Carolina 16, Auburn 10
2002 Capital One	Auburn 13, Penn State 9
2003 Music City	Auburn 28, Wisconsin 14
2004 Sugar	Auburn 16, Virginia Tech 13
2005 Capital One	Wisconsin 24, Auburn 10
2006 Cotton	Auburn 17, Nebraska 14
2007 Chick-fil-A	Auburn 23, Clemson 20
2009 Outback	Auburn 38, Northwestern 35 (OT)
2010 BCS Title Game	Auburn 22, Oregon 19
2011 Chick-fil-A	Auburn 43, Virginia 24

AUBURN

Auburn has 37 bowl appearances, the 16th most in the country. Pretty good, but it pales next to Alabama's national record of 59 bowl appearances. The Tigers have 22 bowl wins, 12th best, but again well behind the Crimson Tide's best-in-the-land 34 bowl victories.

on, can't Auburn come up with something that sets them apart?

Auburn's battle cry is "War Eagle." At least the school's nickname is not the Eagles, because that's the most common nickname, with no less than 55 college teams sporting that nickname.

THE TIGER WALK

The Tiger Walk began in 1960 when, two hours before the kickoff of a home game, the Auburn players, led by their coaches, walked the one block down the hill from Sewell Hall to Jordan-Hare Stadium as their fans cheered them on. The tradition gained in popularity so that now, as the PA system blasts "Eye of the Tiger," thousands of people stand on both sides of Donahue Drive to cheer on and shake the hands of the players and coaches as they strut to the stadium. Before the 1989 Iron Bowl, the first time Alabama ever came to Auburn to play football, a record-setting crowd of about 20,000 people participated in the Tiger Walk. The Tiger Walk also takes place when the Auburn football team enters stadiums at away games. The Tiger Walk is a beloved Auburn tradition. Other schools have since initiated a similar thing.

The Tiger Walk is good and perhaps has been around the longest, but does it have the same ring as "the Walk of Champions?"

WAR EAGLE

Auburn's nickname is the Tigers, but the battle cry for the football team and the school is "War Eagle." Unique is that

Led by then-coach Tommy Tuberville, Auburn players march down the hill in the "Tiger Walk" prior to the 2005 Iron Bowl at Jordan-Hare Stadium in Auburn.
Photo courtesy of AP Images

AUBURN FIGHT SONG

War...Eagle, fly down the field, Ever to conquer, never to yield.
War...Eagle, fearless and true. Fight on, you orange and blue.
Go! Go! Go!
On to vict'ry, strike up the band,
Give 'em hell, give 'em hell.
Stand up and yell, Hey! War...Eagle, win for Auburn,
Power of Dixie Land!

a live eagle circles the stadium before the start of a football game, energizing the crowd.

There are several legends about the origin of the War Eagle battle cry, dating back to 1864. One story says Auburn's first eagle was War Eagle I in 1892. But an article published in 1960 said that, when Auburn first played Georgia in football in 1902, there was a Confederate soldier in the crowd who had a golden eagle with him, and the eagle got loose and began flying in a circle around the playing field. As the eagle soared around the field, Auburn fans screamed out, "War Eagle! War Eagle!"

Some say the "War Eagle" chant started at a pep rally. Others believe it came from the Eighth Wisconsin regiment. Regardless, there have been eight "War Eagles" to date, with the last three, Golden Eagles Tiger (War Eagle VI), Nova (War Eagle VII), and Spirit (a bald eagle, War Eagle VIII) being the eagles that have energized fans with their flights over Jordan-Hare Stadium.

Have to give it to Auburn for this one. Having an eagle trained to fly around the stadium is unique and exciting. But on

September 10, 2011, "Spirit" crashed into a luxury box window during his flight prior to the Mississippi State game. Ouch! The War Eagle must have had a bad headache after that maneuver.

AUBIE THE TIGER

The Auburn mascot is Aubie the Tiger, which originated with a cartoon character on the program for the 1959 Auburn–Hardin-Simmons football game and continued to be on the program for 18 years. The mascot made its first appearance as a costumed mascot in 1979 in a basketball tournament. It made its first appearance as the football mascot when it jumped out of a large box placed on the 50-yard line during halftime of the 1979 season opener against Kansas State, a game the Tigers won 26–18. The winner of six mascot national championships, the most of any mascot in the country, Aubie was one of the first college mascots inducted into the Mascot Hall of Fame. To that, Tide fans simply say, "You can have your mascot championships. We're more interested in winning national championships in football."

JORDAN-HARE STADIUM

Jordan-Hare Stadium was dedicated in 1939 and seated 7,500. In 1949 seating was increased to 21,500; in 1955 to 34,500; in 1960 to 44,500; in 1970 to 61,261; in 1980 to 72,169; in 1987 to 85,214; in 2000 to 85,612; in 2001 to 86,063; and in 2004 to its current capacity of 87,451.

In 1949 the stadium was named Cliff Hare Stadium, after a man who played on Auburn's first football team and went on

TOP 5 PASSING YARDS IN A CAREER

	Player	Years	Yards
1.	Stan White	1990–1993	8,016
2.	Jason Campbell	2001–2004	7,299
3.	Brandon Cox	2004–2007	6,959
4.	Pat Sullivan	1969–1971	6,284
5.	Dameyune Craig	1994–1997	6,026

to be a longtime chair of the school's Faculty-Athletic Committee. A dean of the Auburn School of Chemistry and Pharmacy, Hare also was president of the Southern Conference and the mayor of Auburn. In 1973 the stadium was renamed Jordan-Hare Stadium to honor Auburn coaching legend Shug Jordan.

Auburn has the 10th largest on-campus stadium in the country. It's a nice big stadium that the Tigers fill regularly, but guess what? Bryant-Denny Stadium, with 101,821, is the fifth largest stadium in the country. So nice try, Auburn. Trumped again.

AUBURN'S NATIONAL CHAMPIONSHIPS

Auburn has won national championships in 1957 and 2010. Now, why would Alabama fans love that? Simple, because two national championships pales in comparison to the 14 that the Crimson Tide have won. It doesn't even belong in the same book, let alone on the same page.

AUBURN

AUBURN ALMA MATER

*On the rolling plains of Dixie
'Neath its sun-kissed sky,
Proudly stands, our Alma Mater
Banners high.
To thy name we'll sing thy praise,
From hearts that love so true,
And pledge to thee our
Loyalty the ages through.
We hail thee, Auburn, and we vow
To work for thy just fame,
And hold in memory as we do now
Thy cherished name.
Hear thy student voices swelling,
Echoes strong and clear,
Adding laurels to thy fame
Enshrined so dear.
From thy hallowed halls we'll part,
And bid thee sad adieu;
Thy sacred thrust we'll bear with us
The ages through.
We hail thee, Auburn, and we vow
To work for thy just fame,
And hold in memory as we do now
Thy cherished name.*

—Composed by Bill Wood '24 (revised 1960)

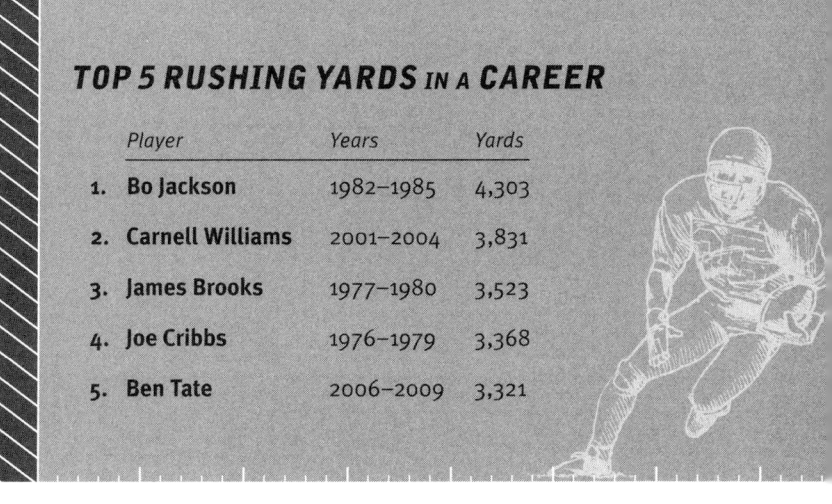

TOP 5 RUSHING YARDS IN A CAREER

	Player	Years	Yards
1.	Bo Jackson	1982–1985	4,303
2.	Carnell Williams	2001–2004	3,831
3.	James Brooks	1977–1980	3,523
4.	Joe Cribbs	1976–1979	3,368
5.	Ben Tate	2006–2009	3,321

But there's another reason too. Auburn didn't even win the 1957 national championship outright. They shared it with Ohio State. The Tigers were voted Associated Press national champions, and the Buckeyes were declared United Press International national champions, the UPI being the other major voting organization at that time.

Then there's the 2010 national championship, the one some say was somewhat tainted because of the Cam Newton controversy. You remember the story, how Cam's father was allegedly shopping him around for the best price. The joke was that Cam, who is responsible for taking the Tigers to the promised land and who went on to win the Heisman Trophy for his on-the-field heroics, was the best player that money could buy.

So Alabama fans love Auburn's two national championships because they're so very few, and because when they finally

win a championship—which is once every blue-and-orange moon—they can't even win it outright or clean.

Well, on October 13, 2011, after an extensive and drawn-out investigation, the NCAA stated that it determined that Auburn had not committed any major violations and the championship was legit. Okay, Alabama fans can still say it's only Auburn's second national championship. Big deal.

WRECK TECH PAJAMA PARADE

Legend has it that back in 1896, when football teams traveled by train to games, that some Auburn ROTC students pulled a prank on rival Georgia Tech by greasing the railroad tracks the night before the game. Due to the slippery tracks the train with the Georgia Tech team aboard was unable to come to a stop until it had gone five miles past Auburn. The Tech players had to walk the five miles back to town. The next day the Engineers got drubbed by Auburn 45–0.

The prank carries on to this day in the form of a downtown parade where Auburn students construct floats and, in their pajamas, walk through downtown Auburn. Alabama fans do not hate the Wreck Tech Pajama Parade tradition because it is not in reference to their school. They just think it's silly. Akin to rolling trees with toilet paper.

AUBURN CREED

I believe that this is a practical world and that I can count only on what I earn. Therefore,
I believe in work, hard work.

I believe in education, which gives me knowledge to work wisely and trains my mind and my hands to work skillfully.

I believe in honesty and truthfulness, without which I cannot win the respect and confidence of my fellow man.

I believe in a sound mind, a sound body and a spirit that is not afraid, and in clean sports to develop these qualities.

I believe in obedience to law because it protects the rights of all.

I believe in the human touch, which cultivates sympathy with my fellow men and mutual helpfulness and brings happiness for all.

I believe in my Country, because it is a land of freedom and because it is my home,

And that I can best serve that country by "doing justly, loving mercy, and walking humbly with my God."

And because Auburn men and women believe in these things, I believe in Auburn and love it.

—George Petrie (1945)

TOP 5 RUSHING TDs IN A CAREER

	Player	Years	TDs
1.	Carnell Williams	2001–2004	45
2.	Bo Jackson	1982–1985	43
3.	Joe Cribbs	1976–1979	34
4.	Stephen Davis	1993–1995	30
5.	Ronnie Brown	2000–2004	29

3

PLAYERS WE HATE

CAM NEWTON

Cam Newton only played one year, but what he accomplished during the 2010 season makes Newton one of the best players in Auburn history. He completed 185 of 280 passes for 2,854 yards and 30 touchdowns, rushed for 1,473 yards and a school single-season record 20 touchdowns, and even caught a pass for a touchdown. He accounted for 4,327 yards of total offense.

Newton triggered the second-half comeback that enabled the Tigers to climb back from a 24–0 deficit and overtake Alabama in the Iron Bowl. That alone puts Newton close to the top, if not at the top, of Alabama's "hate list."

Newton, 6′5″ and 248 pounds, won the Heisman, Maxwell, Walter Camp, Davey O'Brien, and Manning Awards and was named Associated Press Player of the Year. He's the reason Auburn won the national championship.

Then there's that little issue, that pay-for-play thing that his father was said to be involved in, but that Cam knew nothing

In 2010 Cam Newton amassed 4,327 total yards of offense, led Auburn to a come-from-behind win over Alabama, and won the Heisman Trophy—just a few of the reasons he's the most-hated Tiger. Photo courtesy of AP Images

about. Those in the anti-Newton camp would say he's the best quarterback money can buy. Others said that he would have to take a pay cut to play in the NFL.

Prior to the 2010 Iron Bowl in Bryant-Denny Stadium, the game song choices to be played over the stadium public address system included "Take the Money and Run" and "Son of a Preacher Man," which were directed at Newton. The music was unauthorized and the part-time employee who selected the songs to be played was fired. Again, like the poisoning of the oak trees, some people take the hatred thing too far.

Although the NCAA officially cleared Newton, some Tide fans still refer to him as "Scam" Newton. Picked No. 1 in the NFL draft by the Carolina Panthers, Newton broke Peyton Manning's rookie passing yardage record.

NICK FAIRLEY

An All-American and Lombardi Award winner in 2010, Fairley was not only the most dominant defensive tackle, but considered by many the meanest player in the country when he played. A very difficult player to block, Fairley notched 88 career tackles. In 2010 he made 60 tackles, 36 by himself. He also recorded 24 tackles for loss and a school-record $11\frac{1}{2}$ sacks for minus 74 yards.

Fairley was very good, no doubt about that. But some 'Bama fans feel that he wasn't the cleanest player. Therefore, if not at the top, he's near the top of the Crimson Tide dislike list.

AUBURN'S NATIONAL AWARD WINNERS

Heisman Trophy
Pat Sullivan (1971)
Bo Jackson (1985)
Cam Newton (2010)
Maxwell Award
Cam Newton (2010)

Outland Trophy
Zeke Smith (1958)
Tracy Rocker (1988)
Lombardi Award
Tracy Rocker (1988)
Nick Fairley (2010)
Jim Thorpe Award
Carlos Rodgers (2004)

PAT SULLIVAN

Pat Sullivan is one of Auburn's all-time best football players. He topped off a two-time All-America career by winning the Heisman Trophy in 1971. He quarterbacked the Tigers to Iron Bowl victories in 1969 and 1970, before absorbing a 31–7 setback in his senior year. As a senior he completed 162 of 281 passes for 2,012 yards and 20 touchdowns.

He later worked six years as an assistant at his alma mater on Pat Dye's staff. With no love lost between Alabama and the War Eagles, when Pat Sullivan came to Tuscaloosa, he was usually looked upon as among the enemy.

In 2001 Alabama had just thrashed Auburn 31–7, whipping the Tigers by the same score that Sullivan and his teammates experienced 30 years earlier. Two days after his alma mater got blown out, Sullivan was the speaker at the Tuscaloosa Quarterback Club meeting, though he would probably have preferred to address the club at another time. However, when

he spoke to this highly partisan group, Sullivan, also a two-time Academic All-American, was accepted for what he is, a former outstanding scholar-athlete and a gentleman. He was greeted warmly and with respect.

Sullivan recalled what it was like going through the process of picking a college, which he said came down to Alabama or Auburn. "That decision was so tough it was like wrestling with the angels," he said. "It was an awfully difficult decision, but probably the guy who helped me make up my mind more than anybody was Pat Trammell [the late QB of Alabama's 1961 national championship team].

Pat Sullivan, who won the Heisman Trophy at Auburn in 1971, had beaten Alabama in the 1969 and 1970 Iron Bowls, but came up short just after winning college football's most prestigious honor. Photo courtesy of AP Images

"He was so honest, so sincere, and he made me feel so comfortable. He told me, 'Pat, you know how much I want you to go to Alabama, but you need to go where you want to go.'

"Then my daddy told me, 'If you get hurt on the first play, go where you would still want to go to school.'"

Sullivan chose Auburn, where he started at quarterback for three years, guided the Tigers to a 26–7 record, twice earned SEC Player of the Year honors, and was named MVP of the Gator, Sugar, and Senior Bowls. And that's why he's included among the players Crimson Tide fans "hate," rather than love. Just a little decision like that. Yeah, right!

"Coach [Clem] Gryska was recruiting me, and the hardest thing I had to do was tell Coach Gryska that I wasn't coming to Alabama," said Sullivan. "That's because Coach Gryska is special."

Sullivan, who in his first college game only took four-and-a-half minutes before throwing his first touchdown pass, also told how he and former Auburn coach Shug Jordan were going to an NFL exhibition game in Birmingham between the Dallas Cowboys and the Kansas City Chiefs when their car overheated and a big escort with flashing lights approached.

"I asked Coach Jordan, 'Who is that?' Coach Jordan said, 'That's Coach Bryant. You can either ride with Coach Bryant, or walk with me.'" After coaching at his alma mater for six years, when the War Eagles went 52–16–3, and a stint as head coach at TCU, Sullivan became offensive coordinator and quarterbacks coach at the University of Alabama at Birmingham. He has been head coach at Samford University since 2007.

AUBURN PLAYERS IN THE
COLLEGE FOOTBALL HALL OF FAME (12)

Player	Inducted	Position
Mike Donahue	1951	Coach
John W. Heisman	1954	Coach
Jimmy Hitchcock	1954	Halfback
Walter Gilbert	1956	Center
Ralph "Shug" Jordan	1982	Coach
Pat Sullivan	1991	Quarterback
Tucker Frederickson	1994	Fullback
Bo Jackson	1998	Running Back
Terry Beasley	2002	Wide Receiver
Tracy Rocker	2004	Defensive Tackle
Pat Dye	2005	Coach
Ed Dyas	2009	Fullback/Kicker

AUBURN

Whereas there is bad blood between fans of the two schools, there is mutual respect among players and coaches from the cross-state rivals. "When I was appointed the head coach at TCU, [Alabama] Coach [Gene] Stallings called to offer congratulations," related Sullivan. "Coach Stallings was probably the second person who called. That meant a lot to me."

Sullivan, who in 1971 brought the Heisman Trophy to the Plains 72 years after its namesake stopped coaching Auburn in 1898, said that among his special memories was "just the privilege to play against Alabama. I think there is mutual respect. I don't think there is a better rivalry anywhere else in the country," he stated.

Sullivan said that he also treasures the friendships he made. "[Former star running back] Johnny Musso and I are still real close friends." He also considers former Alabama assistant coach Jim Fuller, whom he used to recruit against, a good friend.

The thrill of victory and agony of defeat also stick out in his mind. "One special memory [before freshmen could play on the varsity] was getting down 27–0 [against Alabama] and coming back to win," he said. "But nothing eats at me more than losing 31–7 in 1971 and getting beat out for the conference championship."

Sullivan's coach, Shug Jordan, told Clyde Bolton: "In 41 years of college football, I have never seen Pat Sullivan's equal as a complete quarterback." In Bolton's book, *War Eagle*, Bear Bryant is quoted as saying, "[Sullivan] does more things to beat you than any quarterback I've ever seen." Georgia's legendary coach Vince Dooley added, "[Sullivan] is the best that I've ever seen." Those are some sterling endorsements from a few people who know a little bit about football.

Sullivan is in the Alabama Sports Hall of Fame, Senior Bowl, Gator Bowl, and College Football Halls of Fame.

BO JACKSON

Bo Jackson is the best running back and considered by many to be the best player to ever play at Auburn. A two-time All-American and Heisman Trophy winner, he set the school single-season (1,786 yards in 1985) and career (4,303 yards) rushing records as well as the career touchdown record (43),

Auburn's Bo Jackson (34) dives over an Alabama defender for a touchdown in the fourth quarter of the 1982 Iron Bowl to lift the Tigers over the Tide, 23–22. It was the first Auburn victory in the series in nine years. Photo courtesy of AP Images

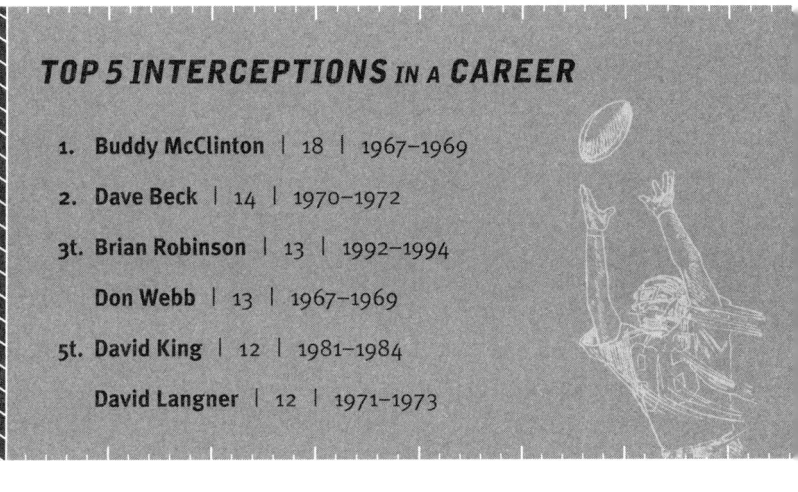

TOP 5 INTERCEPTIONS *IN A* **CAREER**

1. **Buddy McClinton** | 18 | 1967–1969
2. **Dave Beck** | 14 | 1970–1972
3t. **Brian Robinson** | 13 | 1992–1994
   Don Webb | 13 | 1967–1969
5t. **David King** | 12 | 1981–1984
   David Langner | 12 | 1971–1973

later broken by Carnell Williams who compiled 45. He averaged 6.6 yards per carry over the course of his college career.

Heavily recruited by Alabama out of high school, Jackson spurred the Tide for the Tigers. As a freshman in 1982 he went "over the top" to score the winning touchdown in the Iron Bowl to give Auburn a 23–22 victory and snap Alabama's nine-game winning streak in the series. As a sophomore he piled up 256 yards against the Crimson Tide as the Tigers won again, 23–20.

That's enough reason right there to earn a high place on Alabama's Auburn player "hate list." What probably saves Jackson from being closer to the top of the "hate list" is that 'Bama fans actually liked him a lot when he was supposed to block for Brent Fullwood but ran the wrong way, enabling Alabama to win the 1984 Iron Bowl when Fullwood was smothered short of the goal line. He was the MVP of the Sugar Bowl.

Jackson played professional football with the Los Angeles Raiders and professional baseball with the Kansas City Royals, and was an All-Pro in the NFL and an All-Star in the major leagues. Despite having his career cut short by injury, he is considered one of the best two-sport athletes ever. Jackson was also famous for his "Bo Knows" television commercials that were a big hit when he was in his prime.

AUBURN'S STABLE of RUNNING BACKS

Bo Jackson heads a list of star running backs who played at Auburn. They were all good, and therefore Tide fans hate them all.

Carnell "Cadillac" Williams

Carnell Williams earned All-America accolades in 2004 when he rambled for 1,165 yards and tallied 12 touchdowns. He concluded his career with 3,831 yards, the third highest total in Auburn history, and scored 45 touchdowns, breaking Bo Jackson's record. He earned nine SEC Player of the Week honors, most in conference history. He earned NFL Offensive Rookie of the Year honors in 2005.

James Brooks

Although he shared playing time in the backfield with Joe Cribbs and James Andrews, Brooks became an All-American. From 1977 to 1980 he scored 30 touchdowns and set Auburn records for kickoff-return yards (1,726) and all-purpose yards (5,596). He was a four-time Pro Bowler in the NFL and retired as the Cincinnati Bengals all-time leading rusher.

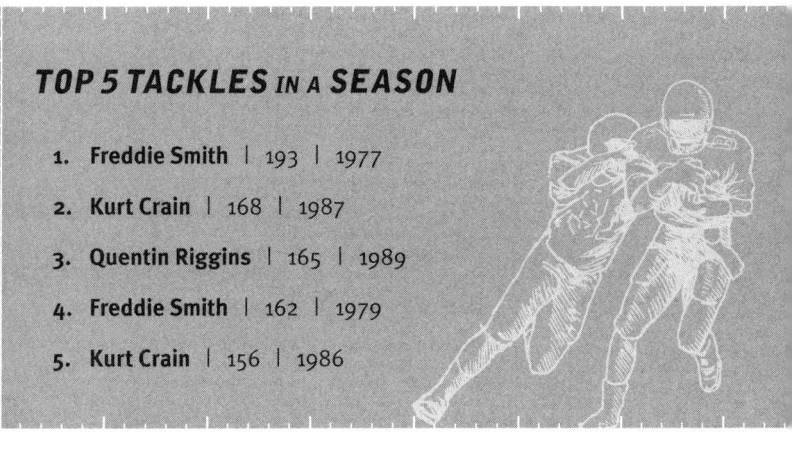

TOP 5 TACKLES *IN A* SEASON

1. **Freddie Smith** | 193 | 1977
2. **Kurt Crain** | 168 | 1987
3. **Quentin Riggins** | 165 | 1989
4. **Freddie Smith** | 162 | 1979
5. **Kurt Crain** | 156 | 1986

Stephen Davis

Stephen Davis was a big, fast running back who finished his collegiate career in 1995 fourth (now sixth) on Auburn's all-time rushing list with 2,751 yards, fifth in career rushing touchdowns (30), and tied for fifth in single-season rushing touchdowns (14). In the NFL, he led the Carolina Panthers to the Super Bowl.

Joe Cribbs

Despite splitting time at running back with James Brooks, Cribbs compiled 3,368 yards rushing, fourth all-time at Auburn, and scored 34 touchdowns. As a junior and senior in 1978 and 1979, he averaged more than 100 yards rushing per game and had two 1,000-yard rushing seasons.

Ronnie Brown

Like Brooks, Cribbs, and Carnell Williams, Brown's numbers are less than what they could have been had he not played at the same time as the "Cadillac." Despite starting only 21 of 37 games from 2001 to 2004, Brown still finished seventh (now

eighth) among Auburn's all-time rushers with 2,707 yards and fifth in rushing touchdowns with 28. He also had 58 receptions for 668 yards and two more touchdowns. In 2002 he ran for 1,008 yards and 13 touchdowns.

Brent Fullwood

Another in a long line of Auburn All-America tailbacks, in 1986 Fullwood ran for a school fourth-best, single-season 1,391 yards, scored 10 touchdowns, won the Wally Butts Award for the best running back in the Southeast, and finished sixth in the Heisman Trophy voting. If he hadn't played in the shadow of Bo Jackson, he would have put up even better numbers.

Alabama fans do like something about Fullwood, though. The Tide stuffed him short of a touchdown on the last play of the 1984 Iron Bowl when Jackson, who was supposed to block for him, went the other way.

Ben Tate

As a senior in 2009, Ben Tate rushed for a single-season 1,362 yards and 3,321 yards over the course of his career, both marks rate fifth highest in Auburn annals. He scored 24 touchdowns.

Rudi Johnson

Like Cam Newton, Johnson only played one year on the Plains, but it was a big year. In 2000 Johnson ran for more than 100 yards in 10 games, led the team with a school second-best, single-season 1,567 rushing yards, and scored 13 touchdowns in leading the Tigers to the SEC West championship.

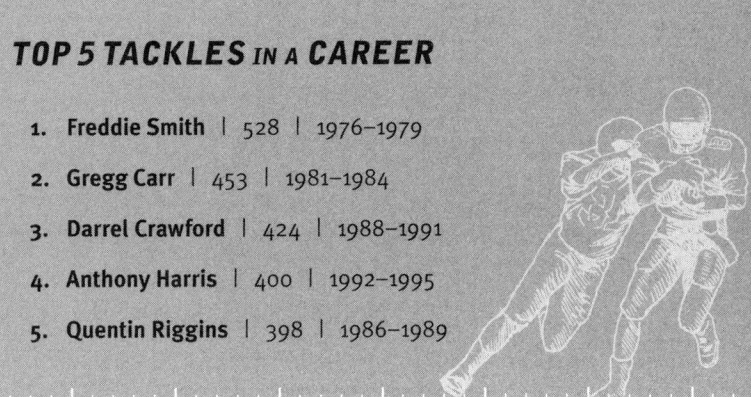

TOP 5 TACKLES *IN A* CAREER

1. **Freddie Smith** | 528 | 1976–1979
2. **Gregg Carr** | 453 | 1981–1984
3. **Darrel Crawford** | 424 | 1988–1991
4. **Anthony Harris** | 400 | 1992–1995
5. **Quentin Riggins** | 398 | 1986–1989

Fob James

Fob James played running back from 1952 to 1955. He was SEC Back of the Year and an All-American as a senior. He graduated as the school's leading rusher, a mark that has since been surpassed by several talented tailbacks that followed him on the Plains. James went on to become governor of the state of Alabama. 'Bama fans who voted for him may have had to hold their nose while casting their vote for a running back who caused the Tide a lot of problems. Can you imagine how hard it was for die-hard 'Bama fans to follow a leader from Auburn? Someone who was educated "down on the farm?"

TRACY ROCKER

The winner of the Outland Trophy and Lombardi Award, Rocker was an All-American and the Tigers' leading tackler with 100 total tackles, including 57 solo, 13 for loss, and five sacks. He also forced four fumbles. How can any 'Bama fan like players like Fairley and Rocker who enjoyed slamming Tide players to the ground?

TERRY BEASLEY

Terry Beasley was a two-time All-America end who had 2,507 career receiving yards and scored 29 touchdowns, the most by an Auburn wide receiver. Beasley was Pat Sullivan's favorite target, with the pass-and-catch combo referred to as the "dynamic duo." Beasley tied an NCAA record when he averaged 20.2 yards per catch in 1970.

TUCKER FREDERICKSON

Tucker Frederickson was as an All-American in 1964 when he also won the Jacobs Award as the Best Blocking Back in the SEC. He also played safety on defense during the era of one-platoon football. Fredrickson was runner-up in the Heisman Trophy voting. He was inducted into the College Football Hall of Fame in 1994. His coach, Shug Jordon, said Fredrickson "was the most complete football player I've ever seen."

ZEKE SMITH

Zeke Smith was a unanimous All-America offensive guard and Outland Trophy winner in 1958. He was named first-team All-America by the Associated Press, NEA, FWAA, *Sports Illustrated*, *Look*, *Time*, *Football Digest*, *Chicago Tribune*, and *Coach & Athlete* magazine.

CARLOS RODGERS

Carlos Rodgers registered 47 tackles, 37 of which were individual with five for loss, intercepted two passes, and broke up 10 pass plays en route to winning the 2004 Jim Thorpe Award.

4
COACHES WE HATE

TOMMY TUBERVILLE

Tommy Tuberville beat Alabama six straight times. Then he upset 'Bama fans by crowing, after their fifth win, "One for the thumb." Of course, 'Bama fans hate Tuberville. They think he's arrogant.

PAT DYE

According to David Housel, Auburn football's history guru, when Dye was being interviewed for the Auburn head football coaching job, he was asked, "How long will it take to beat Alabama?

"Sixty minutes," Dye responded confidently. He added, "I played at Georgia and I coached at Alabama...they are your two biggest rivals. I know what it takes to win, and I know what it takes to beat them." Dye's reply may have gotten him the job, writes Housel.

In 1982 Dye coached Auburn to its first win over the Crimson Tide in 10 years, with Housel pointing out the far-reaching significance of that by stating, beyond just football, Auburn's

Auburn head coach Pat Dye celebrates with his team on the sideline in 1982.
Dye led the Tigers to a 6–6 record in the Iron Bowl from 1981 to 1992, including
four wins in a row in the mid-1980s. Photo courtesy of Getty Images

entire institutional confidence was bolstered. Clem Gryska
was an assistant with Dye on Bear Bryant's Alabama staff from
1965 through 1973. "I'm not an Auburn fan," stated Gryska,
"but I'm a Pat Dye fan. He's exactly what Coach Bryant stood
for, and what Alabama stands for."

Dye said, "I learned from the master. Our goal [at Auburn] every
year was to win the national championship. We never did."

TERRY BOWDEN

Terry Bowden won his first 11 games as Auburn's coach in 1993, including a victory over the Crimson Tide. If you're a 'Bama fan, there's nothing there to like, except that Auburn was on probation that season and ineligible to play in a bowl game. Now Alabama fans liked that—a lot.

In a short period of time, Bowden made his mark on the Plains, beginning with that perfect season. He guided the Tigers to 20 straight wins, the longest in school history. He compiled an overall 47–17–1 record for a .731 winning percentage. Tide fans may not like that, but they should respect his accomplishments. Bowden won three out of the five Iron Bowls that he coached in. 'Bama fans hated that, and for good reason.

MIKE DONAHUE

Mike Donahue coached at Auburn from 1904 until 1922 and enjoyed a very successful run, winning 99 games, while only

AUBURN'S TOP 5 COACHES

	Coach	Record	Years
1.	Ralph (Shug) Jordan	176–83–6	1951–1975
2.	Mike Donahue	99–35–5	1904–1906; 1908–1922
3.	Pat Dye	99–39–4	1981–1992
4.	Tommy Tuberville	85–40	1999–2008
5.	Jack Meagher	48–37–10	1934–1942

AUBURN

losing 35 and tying 5. But from first impressions, few would have predicted that success when Donahue first showed up on the Plains. Only 5′4″ tall, Donahue was diminutive and had red hair and blue eyes. "He looked more like a mother's son than a football coach. When the 200 or so students waited at the train station to meet their new football coach in 1904, they shook their heads in disbelief. The students had expected a John Wayne. Instead, they had gotten a Mickey Rooney," wrote Clyde Bolton in *War Eagle: A Story of Auburn Football*.

On top of that, many had trouble understanding Donahue because he had a northern accent accentuated with an Irish twang. "They had no way of knowing this petite little man would become known as 'Iron Mike,' leading Auburn to its greatest days on the gridiron, including a national championship [designated by the Billingsly Poll] in 1913," stated David Housel in his book *Auburn Football Vault*.

Donahue, considered "the father of the Auburn football program," coached Auburn to five Southern championships, three official Southern Intercollegiate Athletic Association championships, and two more Southern championships awarded by the news media. Three of his teams went undefeated, while seven of his 18 teams lost no more than one game. Starting with the 1913 season through the sixth game of the 1915 season, Donahue's teams were dominant, winning 22 games without a loss. The only blemish during that period was a 0–0 tie with Georgia in the next-to-last game of the 1914 season. Twenty-one of 23 teams failed to score against the Tigers. Ed Danforth of the *Atlanta Journal* wrote, "You were nobody until you had beaten Auburn. That was the place card for the head table."

Housel, who in *Auburn Football Vault* covers the time period 1892 to 2007, believes that the 1913 and 1914 Auburn teams and the 12-year run between 1908 and 1919 may have been the best in Auburn history.

Zipp Newman of the *Birmingham News* wrote, "[Donahue] was the War Eagle!" Donahue Drive runs adjacent to Jordan-Hare Stadium.

AUBURN JOKES WE LIKE TO TELL

Alabama fans love to tell jokes that make fun of their Auburn counterparts. The jokes come from everywhere, so it's hard to credit who makes them up. Plus there are so many of them, and new jokes pop up every year and sometimes every week. The following are just a sampling of Auburn jokes, many of them taken off various websites and others passed along in conversation.

> *Question*: What is a seven-course dinner at Auburn?
> *Answer*:   Stewed possum and a six-pack.

Auburn stands for: Alabama *U*sually *B*eats *U*s *R*ed *N*ecks
   or
Alabama *U*sually *B*eats *U*s *R*ound *N*ovember

*

A first-grade teacher explains to her class that she is an Auburn fan. She asks her students to raise their hands if they are Auburn fans too. Not really knowing what an Auburn fan was, but wanting to be liked by their teacher, their hands fly into the air.

AUBURN'S 4 UNDEFEATED SEASONS

1957 (10–0)
1993 (11–0)
2004 (13–0)
2010 (14–0)

Like the 2010 national championship, SEC championship, and
Western Division championship, Auburn's titles are the most recent,
so Tide fans will concede those.

AUBURN

There is, however, one exception. A little girl named
Jane has not gone along with the crowd. The teacher asks
her why she has decided to be different. "Because I'm not
an Auburn fan," she replies.

"Then what are you?" asks the teacher.

"I'm a proud Alabama fan!" says the girl. The teacher is
a little perturbed now, her face getting red.

She asks Jane, "Why are you an Alabama fan?"

Jane answers, "Well my dad and mom are Alabama fans,
so I'm an Alabama fan too," she responds.

The teacher is angry now. "That's no reason," she says
loudly. "What if your mom was a moron and your dad was
an idiot? What would you be then?"

Jane smiles and says, "Then we'd be Auburn fans."

*

A couple who were Auburn fans owned a dog. During the
football season they invited several of their friends over to
their house to watch some of the really big Auburn games.
The first of the big games that the couple's friends came over

to watch was the Auburn-LSU game. Auburn beat LSU, and the couple's dog started doing numerous flips and neat tricks. "Wow!" exclaimed their friends. "How in the world did you teach your dog to do all those flips? We've never seen a dog that can do anything like what we've just seen."

The couple responded, "We did not teach our dog any of those flips or tricks. He just does them on his own." None of their friends believed them, but were still very much impressed.

The next game that the couple's friends came over for was the AU-Georgia game. Auburn beat UGA, and the dog did even more impressive flips and tricks. Their friends asked again, "How is your dog able to do all of that neat stuff? Surely you had to teach your dog to do all of those tricks." Again, the couple responded in the same way, saying that they did not teach the dog to do any of the things that he was doing.

Next, their friends asked, "Well, if the dog does all of these impressive things when Auburn beats LSU and Georgia, then what in the world does the dog do when Auburn beats Alabama? They must be some really good tricks."

The couple responded, "We have no idea. Our dog is only eight years old."

*

A football fan walks into a small store in Birmingham. He spots a bottle labeled "Alabama Football Player Brains," $5 an ounce. He asks the clerk if there are any other bottles. The clerk replies, "Well, we've got Tennessee brains for $10 an ounce, and Auburn football brains for $1 million an ounce." The man asks, "Why the big difference in price?" The clerk answers, "Do you know how many Auburn football players we have to kill to get an ounce of brains!"

*

Question: What do you call a genius at Auburn?

Answer: A visitor

*

A guy goes into a bar and asks the bartender if he wants to hear a good Auburn joke. The bartender says, "Before you tell it, you should know that I am 6′2″ and weigh 225, and I'm an Auburn fan. See that guy at the end of the bar? He's 6′4″ and weighs 250, and he's an Auburn fan too. And see the guy at the other end of the bar? He's 6′6″ and weighs 280, and he's an Auburn fan too! Now, do you still want to tell your Auburn joke?"

The guy says, "Nah." To which the bartender smiles and says, "What's the matter? Are you chicken?" The guy says, "Nah, I just don't want to have to explain it three times."

*

An Auburn man had 50-yard-line tickets for the Auburn-Alabama game. As he sits down, a man comes down and asks if anyone is sitting in the seat next to him. "No," he says, "the seat is empty."

"This is incredible," said the man. "Who in their right mind would have a seat like this for the Iron Bowl, the biggest sporting event in the world, and not use it?"

The Auburn man says, "Well, actually the seat belongs to me. I was supposed to come with my wife, but she passed away. This is the first Auburn-Alabama game we haven't been to together since we got married in 1964."

"Oh…I'm sorry to hear that. That's a shame! But couldn't you find someone else, a friend or relative, or even a neighbor to take the seat?"

The Auburn man shakes his head. "No, they're all at her funeral."

*

Question: How do you get the Auburn graduate away from
            your door?
Answer: Pay him for the pizza!

*

Auburn's new fight song:

> *War Eagle!*
> *Crank the John Deere.*
> *Break out the Red Man.*
> *Shotgun a beer.*
> *War Eagle!*
> *Inbreeds delight.*
> *Go, go, go back to the trailer!*
> *Fire up the grill.*
> *Savor the night's road-kill.*
> *War Eagle!*
> *Big Cow College.*
> *Cesspool of Dixieland!*

*

A 'Bama grad, a Tennessee grad, and an Auburn grad have
been captured by Iraqi forces and are about to be executed
by firing squad. First the 'Bama alum is blindfolded and
placed in front of the firing squad. The Iraqi officer says,
"Ready, aim…" The 'Bama alum yells, "Sandstorm!" and
all the Iraqis hit the dirt and the 'Bama alum runs away.
The Tennesse guy is placed in front of the firing squad. The
officer says, "Ready, aim…" The Tennesseean shouts, "Tor-
nado!" All the Iraqis again hit the dirt while the Volunteer
escapes. The Auburn guy thinks this is great. The officer
says, "Ready, aim…" and the Auburn grad screams, "Fire!"

*

Bear Bryant (right) with his friend and coaching rival Shug Jordan

Poor Au*barn*! Cows, hayseeds, hay-rides, trailers. "Barn-ers" have to constantly remind people that Auburn is in Alabama, not Georgia.

*

Why do Alabama fans hate Auburn? Because they are like a possum. They play dead at home, and get killed on the road.

*

Question: What's the difference between Wheaties and Auburn?

Answer: One belongs in a bowl, and the other doesn't.

*

Question: Why does the football team play on a natural field at Auburn?

Answer: Because the cheerleaders need a place to graze.

*

Question: What's the best sign in Auburn?

Answer: TUSCALOOSA 120 MILES

*

An Auburn football player goes to take his final exam. The questions require a yes or no answer. After staring at the test for several minutes, he becomes frustrated and starts flipping a coin, answering the questions with a yes for heads and no for tails. The football player finishes the test long before the rest of the class. He then starts flipping the coin again. When the teacher finally asks him what he's doing, the Auburn football players responds, "I finished the test early, so I'm rechecking my answers."

*

Talking to his athletics director, the Auburn coach pleaded, "I need a raise."

The AD responded, "Coach, you make more money than the entire English department. How can I justify giving you a raise?"

AUBURN

AUBURN'S 7 SEC CHAMPIONSHIPS

1957
1983
1987
1988
1989
2004
2010

Alabama fans respond to that with, is that all?

"I'll show you what I have to put up with," the coach replied, opening his office door and calling in his star player. "Son," the coach said to the player, "run over to my office and see if I'm there."

"Sure, Coach." Twenty minutes later, the winded athlete returned. "No, sir, Coach," he panted, "you ain't there."

Thanking the player and sending him back to practice, the coach turned to his AD and asked, "Now do you understand?"

"I sure do," the athletics director agreed. "The dumb SOB could have phoned."

*

A ventriloquist, with his dummy, was making fun of Auburn fans who were sitting at a bar. An angry Auburn fan stood up, rolled up his sleeves, and yelled, "I resent that!" The ventriloquist started apologizing. The Auburn fan interrupted him and said, "You stay outta this, I'm talking to the guy on your lap!"

*

A country bumpkin family from Auburn decides to go to New York for the first time. Maw, Paw, and their son go into the Empire State Building. As they're walking around, they notice the elevator. Never having seen one before, they stand in front of it bewildered. While staring at it, an old lady in a wheelchair rolls up, pushes the button, the door opens, she rolls herself inside, and the door closes. The Auburn hick family watches as the numbers for each floor light up as the elevator goes up. They continue to watch as the numbers go down again. The door opens and out walks this gorgeous blonde with a great figure. Just beautiful!

Paw looks at his son and says, "Quick boy, shove yer Maw in there!"

*

There was this AU teacher who was yelling at his class because they were so incredibly lazy, "I wouldn't be surprised if 50 percent of you flunk this math class," he said. One of the students put up his hand. "But professor," he said, "there aren't that many in this class."

*

An Auburn man goes to Georgia, buys a lottery ticket, and wins $10 million. He goes to Athens to verify his ticket number and claim his money. The Aubie states, "I want my $10 million."

The man replies, "No, sir. That's not how it works. We give you a million today, and then you'll get the rest spread out for the next nine years."

The Aubie says, "Oh, no. I want all my money *right now*! I won it, it's mine, and I want it now." Again the man slowly explains that he would only get $1 million that day and the rest over the next nine years. The Aubie, furious with the man, screams out, "Look, I want my money now! If you're not going to give me my $10 million *right now*, then I want my dollar back!"

*

An Auburn football player broke his leg raking leaves. An Alabama player asked him how he did that. The Auburn football player, responded: "I fell out of the tree."

*

An Auburn football player and his date were walking in a park. His date suddenly says, "Awww, look at the dead birdie." The Auburn player stops, looks up, and says, "Where?"

*

AUBURN'S 7 SEC WESTERN DIVISION CHAMPIONSHIPS

1997
2000
2001
2002
2004
2005
2010

Alabama fans again respond with, is that all?

A U B U R N

Bubba just started the third grade in a new school. The teacher asks each student to count to 50 to determine the academic level they were at. Some couldn't count to 10, while some counted as high as 30. Others couldn't get past 20. Bubba counted all the way to 100 without any mistakes.

Bubba was so excited he ran home and told his father how well he had done. His father nodded and told him, "Son, that's because you're from Auburn."

The next day the teacher asked the students to recite the alphabet. Some made it through several letters, and others made it almost halfway through the alphabet. But Bubba rattled off the alphabet with no problem. Bubba again told his father how well he did in school. Bubba's father again explained, "Son, that's because you're from Auburn."

The next day, after physical education, the boys were taking showers. Bubba noticed that, compared to the other boys in his grade, he seemed overly "well endowed." Not sure why, he said to his father. "Dad, all the boys have little

tiny ones, but mine is 10 times bigger than theirs. Is that because I'm from Auburn?" he asked.

"No, son," explained his dad, "that's because you're 18."

*

What do Camp Greenleaf, Centre, Davidson, George Washington, Georgia Navy P-F, Manhattan, Marquette, Maxwell Field, Southeastern Louisiana, Santa Clara, and Sewanee have in common? They all have all-time winning records in football against Auburn.

5
OTHER GAMES WE HATE

THERE ARE SOME 'BAMA FANS and players who hate Auburn, but despise Tennessee even more. Okay now, are you ready for this?

On August 21, 2008, posted on YouTube was this interview conducted by B.L. Wright with a student on the topic "I Hate Tennessee." It was recirculated on the Internet prior to the 2011 Alabama-Tennessee game:

"I hate Tennessee, first of all because they're Tennessee. I just hate Tennessee. They're low-down, they're dirty, they're snitches. I hate Philip Fulmer.

"I just dislike Auburn, I hate Tennessee. I hate their colors. It's a throw-up color orange. It's a puke orange. It looks like the inside of a pumpkin, and I hate pumpkins. I hate Tennessee. I hate Neyland Stadium. It looks like a garbage workers' convention. I just dislike Auburn. I hate Tennessee. They're sore losers because they're not Alabama. I just hate Tennessee. I just can't stress that enough."

Okay, now tell us how you really feel. Again, if you listen to this rant, it's hilarious.

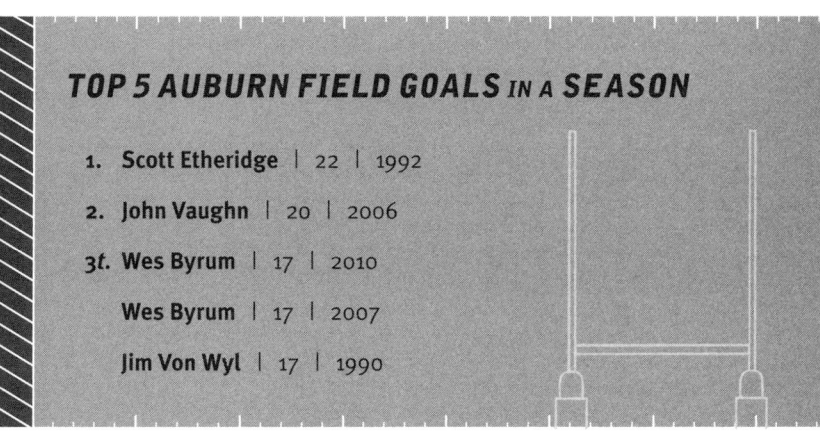

TOP 5 AUBURN FIELD GOALS IN A SEASON

1. Scott Etheridge | 22 | 1992
2. John Vaughn | 20 | 2006
3t. Wes Byrum | 17 | 2010
    Wes Byrum | 17 | 2007
    Jim Von Wyl | 17 | 1990

AUBURN

Roger Shultz, who played in the first Iron Bowl ever played at Auburn in 1989 as well as on the Tide team that beat the Tigers in 1990, said that he dislikes Auburn, "but I can't stand Tennessee. That's because for many years Tennessee was our biggest rival. I just always wanted to beat Tennessee more, and when I played, we never lost to Tennessee." Shultz played on UA teams from 1986 to 1990. "Back then, I said that, 'We ought to pay property tax on Neyland Stadium because we own it.'"

Here's a little story to further the point: Two boys are playing baseball on a playground when one is attacked by a rabid Rottweiler. The other boy quickly grabs a baseball bat and swings it hard and hits the dog, breaking the dog's neck.

A newspaper reporter who happens to be walking past the playground sees the incident, and runs over to interview the boy for a story.

He starts his story, "Young 'Bama Fan Saves Friend from Vicious Animal."

"But I'm not a 'Bama fan," the little hero replies.

"Sorry, I just assumed you were," says the reporter, and he starts his story again. "Little Auburn Fan Rescues Friend from Horrific Attack."

But the boy says, "I'm not an Auburn fan, either."

The reporter says, "I assumed everyone in the state was either for 'Bama or Auburn. So, what team do you root for?"

The boy states, "I'm a Tennessee fan."

The reporter then crosses out everything that he had written and starts again, "Little Hillbilly Bastard Kills Beloved Family Pet."

Okay, you get the point.

Alabama fans are not fond of Tennessee's string of wins from 1967 to 1970, 1982 to 1985, or 1995 to 2001. They especially dislike the ones that got away, such as the five-overtime 51–43 setback in 2003, one-point losses in 1968 (10–9) and 1984 (28–27), the two-point loss in 1985 (16–14), and four-point loss in 2004 (17–13). A play here and there, and those would have been Ws.

THE NEXT-WORST THING

Next to Auburn, Alabama hates to lose to Tennessee. Here are a few losses that still sting.

October 25, 2003: Tennessee 51, Alabama 43 (5 OTs)

Alabama hates to lose to anybody, especially Auburn and Tennessee. Alabama and Tennessee are the two most successful football programs in the Southeastern Conference. Historically, the storied series between the two southern powerhouses ranks among the best rivalries in college football.

On October 25, 2003, the Crimson Tide played Tennessee in Tuscaloosa, but unlike past matchups when both teams were great or very good, this would be a game between an Alabama team with a losing record and a Tennessee team coming off two straight defeats. But on that afternoon, the two teams played a five-overtime thriller at Bryant-Denny Stadium that ranks right up there with some of the best games ever played between the two schools.

After five and a half hours, Tennessee in an epic struggle before 83,018 mesmerized fans, finally prevailed over the Tide 51–43 to narrow the gap in the all-time series between the archrivals to 43–36–7.

The game started out relatively slow and, with Alabama leading 6–3 at the half, seemed destined to become another defensive battle like so many other UA-UT games in the past. It picked up momentum in the third and fourth quarter, with the score tied 20–20 at the end of regulation. Then the contest continued, and continued, and continued, and continued, and continued, and ended up being the highest-scoring affair in the 86-game series between the institutions, one in which neither team deserved to lose and, in the end, Tennessee refused to lose. Despite the Tide's uncharacteristic 3–6 record (1–4, SEC) and the Vols' mediocre 3–2 conference mark (5–2 overall),

this game in the minds of many will go down as another 'Bama–Big Orange classic.

"Going way back, the Alabama-Tennessee game used to be a defensive and special teams game. Whoever had the best punter controlled the game," said Clem Gryska, a longtime Bear Bryant assistant coach who was then working in the Bryant Museum. "This wasn't a typical Alabama-Tennessee game because there were so many points scored.

"It was definitely a classic. It is probably in the top five games in the Alabama-Tennessee series," stated Gryska.

The late Bert Bank, who had been involved in broadcasting Alabama football games since 1951 and who followed the Crimson Tide since before Bryant was a player in the 1930s, said, "It's got to rank as one of the top games in Alabama-Tennessee history, I think. We've never had a game with Tennessee like this before. This was the longest game in Alabama

TOP 5 AUBURN FIELD GOALS IN A CAREER

1. **Wes Byrum** | 60 | 2007–2010
2. **John Vaughn** | 50 | 2003–2006
3t. **Damon Duval** | 45 | 1999–2002
    Win Lyle | 45 | 1987–1989
5. **Al Del Greco** | 42 | 1980–1983

AUBURN

AUBURN

LONGEST AUBURN FIELD GOALS MADE

	Player	Distance	Opponent	Year
1t.	Philip Yost	57 yards	W. Kentucky	2003
	Neil O'Donoghue	57 yards	Tennessee	1976

history. It's never happened before, and the fact that it's with Tennessee makes it more significant. People from both schools will remember this game for many years to come. They will remember it for a long, long time."

Players from both schools will not forget it either. The sound of "Rocky Top" played yet again at the end was long-awaited and refreshing to the Vols and their faithful, but it grated and will continue to grate on 'Bama players and fans whenever they recall this struggle.

"This is the most physically drained that I've ever been after a game, and I'm emotionally drained as well," stated 'Bama quarterback Brodie Croyle, who endured the marathon while playing with an injured shoulder.

His counterpart, Casey Clausen, the QB for the victorious Vols, said, "It was a great game. Once you get into overtime, it's the last man standing. It's gut-wrench time, and it becomes a matter of who wants it more."

Robert Peace, who recorded 16 tackles (11 solo) for Tennessee, stated, "I'm exhausted, but excited. This game will go down as a Tennessee-Alabama classic. Both teams were exhausted, and both teams weren't ready to quit."

Muscle Shoals native Jason Allen, who had 12 tackles and a blocked field goal against his home-state school, said, "Wow, this is the longest game that I've ever played in. Both teams fought hard all the way, and we just ended up on top."

Or, as Alabama offensive coordinator Joe Kines put it: "It was a 15-round boxing match. We'd hit them, and they hit back a little harder."

Alabama athletics director Mal Moore, who had been involved in many, many Alabama-Tennessee games going back to his days as a player for the Tide in the early 1960s and then as a longtime coach under Bryant, called it "another in a series of many exciting games between two great institutions. It was different because of the five overtimes, and without question it will long be remembered for that. There's no question it was an exciting game played with a lot of emotion and a lot of ups and downs. There was great effort by our players, and we had our chances to win the game."

Crimson Tide cornerback Charlie Peprah summed it up: "It's a tough loss. Five overtimes. No one deserved to lose. Nobody wants to lose."

Although Alabama did not win, Crimson Tide players can one day look back and say that they played in what truly will go down as one of the all-time great games in a great series.

It may be one of those events that someday, 10 or 20 years from now, 150,000 people will say they were in Bryant-Denny Stadium for that historic five-overtime game, even if the stadium at that time had a capacity of 83,818. And if they weren't, they probably wished they were.

October 16, 1982: Tennessee 35, Alabama 28

This was Bear Bryant's last season, and Alabama had won its first five games and was ranked No. 2 in the country. The Vols came from behind to defeat the Tide 35–28. 'Bama had a chance to pull it out in the last minute but couldn't connect on three passes into the end zone.

'Bama Nation hates this game for a lot of reasons. The Bear lost his last game against Tennessee, a team that he considered his main rival for many years. The Big Orange handed the Crimson Tide its first loss of the season, and in doing so snapped Alabama's 11-game winning streak in the series.

October 26, 1996: Tennessee 20, Alabama 13

This was the first time that the Alabama-Tennessee game was not played on the third Saturday in October. The Volunteers were ranked No. 6 and 'Bama No. 7. The score was tied 13–13 late in the game. With three minutes left to play and the Vols facing a second-and-12 situation at the UA 21-yard line, Jay Graham busted through for a 79-yard touchdown run that broke the Tide's back. 'Bama responded by driving down the field and threatened to tie the game, but UT defensive end Leonard Little jarred the ball loose from quarterback Freddie Kitchens. The Big Orange recovered the fumble to preserve the win.

WE ALSO HATE THESE TIGERS

The Alabama-LSU game is developing into another major rivalry, which the 2011 season and BCS title game only intensified.

From 1971 to 1999 Alabama won at LSU 14 times in 15 games with the 1988 game ending in a 14–14 tie, causing former Crimson Tide center Roger Shultz, who played during that streak, to quip: "The Tide don't lose in 'Ba-ton Rouge.'"

However with LSU's football fortunes on the rise and Tennessee's on the downtick, and with former LSU coach Nick Saban now at Alabama, the 'Bama–Bayou Bengals game has gained in importance, and in recent years has surpassed the UT game in significance.

November 5, 2011: LSU 9, Alabama 6 (OT)

As far as a regular season game, it doesn't get any bigger or better than the 2011 LSU game. LSU and Alabama, the No. 1 and No. 2 teams in the nation went head-to-head in Bryant-Denny Stadium in a game that marked the first time that the top two teams in the country had faced off during the regular season since the Ohio State Buckeyes met runner-up Michigan in 2006, and the first time that it had ever happened in the Southeastern Conference. The two SEC powerhouses were on a collision course ever since the season began. The contest had conference and national implications, with the winner taking over first place in the SEC West and gaining the inside track to the BCS National Championship Game.

LSU celebrates after eking out a 9–6 overtime win against Alabama in the first meeting of the two teams during the 2011 season. Photo courtesy of AP Images

The two national heavyweights entered the historic showdown unbeaten (8–0, 5–0 in the SEC) and both were coming off a bye week, where they had a chance to rest, recover from injuries, and prepare for this epic battle of the titans. Even though both teams had three games left on their schedule after their battle in Bryant-Denny, the game was looked at as a de facto

national championship game, or a semifinal to the BCS title game, a designation more commonly used to describe the SEC Championship Game. It was a game for the ages.

People had anticipated the game all season long, and when it finally arrived, ticket prices shot through the ceiling. Of the approximate 3,000 tickets that remained available through FanSnap.com and TiqIQ.com (two search engines that list tickets to sporting events sold via the internet), FanSnap CEO Mike Janes told the *Tuscaloosa News* that the week before the game prices had skyrocketed to $804 for a ticket face-valued at $70. The average asking price was $789, which was 5 percent higher than what the SEC Championship Game ticket was going for.

The Tuscaloosa Tourism and Sports Commission estimated that, besides the almost 102,000 people who packed Bryant-Denny Stadium, another 40,000 people who didn't have tickets hung around the area just to take in the atmosphere. Whereas most Alabama football games pump an additional $15 million into the Tuscaloosa economy, Auburn, Tennessee, and LSU games bring in $17 to $18 million dollars, with the state gaining an extra $23 to $25 million compared to $21 to $22 million gained from a game against a team with less drawing power, University of Alabama economist Ahmad Ijaz told the *Tuscaloosa News*.

They billed it "The Game of the Century." CBS negotiated with ESPN to broadcast the game in its 7:00 PM prime time slot. ESPN came to town a day early to begin its *GameDay* show. To prepare for what was going to be an extraordinary event, Tuscaloosa did "more of everything."

Beyond the top two teams in the country squaring off and all the ramifications that entailed, there was the Saban factor. When Saban coached at LSU from 2000 to 2004, not only did he win a national championship, but he beat the Crimson Tide four out of the five times that he faced them. Since taking over at Alabama in 2007 he had split four games with LSU. LSU fans still had not gotten over Saban bolting the bayou and a few years later resurfacing at SEC rival Alabama.

As if the game needed more hype.

The 2011 Alabama-LSU game drew the most people to Tuscaloosa for a football game in UA history, with the *Tuscaloosa News* estimating that as many as 200,000 fans descended on the city. Fans of both teams had been waiting for this game since the season started. With a 7:10 PM start time, the excitement began mounting in the early morning and continued throughout the day, peaking just prior to kickoff when the decibel level in the stadium reached 110.3, as the Crimson Tide ran out of the tunnel onto the field.

The game lived up to its billing. It was a great defensive battle between two of the best defensive teams in the country. Neither team scored a touchdown in four quarters of play plus an extra session.

'Bama fans hate this game because LSU won 9–6 in overtime, and because it put a serious crimp in Alabama's aspirations for a second national championship under Saban. It turned into a field-goal-kicking contest, and the Crimson Tide came up short, and sometimes wide. UA sophomore Cade Foster missed from 44, 50, and 52 yards, the last kick coming in

overtime after the offense was stopped and a penalty pushed the ball back to the 35-yard line. Meanwhile LSU's Drew Alleman was successful on three shorter field-goal attempts, none longer than 30 yards, with the game-winner in overtime coming from 25 yards.

"It's every kicker's dream, and I got to live it," Alleman said after the game. "Three field goals for all the points, I'll take it. It felt great, but it was a great team effort."

Early in the game, after Foster was off on his first two field-goal attempts, backup Tide kicker Jeremy Shelley had his 49-yard field-goal attempt blocked. At the 3:53 mark of the second quarter, Shelley made a 34-yard field goal to put Alabama on the board. Alleman answered with a 19-yarder as time expired to make it 3–3 at the half. With 7:56 left in the third quarter, Foster got another opportunity, and this time connected from 46 yards to put the Tide back in front, 6–3. Then with 14:13 to go in the fourth quarter, Alleman responded from 30 yards to knot it back up at 6–6.

There was a critical game-changing call in the fourth quarter that 'Bama fans hate. With a little more than 11 minutes remaining, operating out of the wildcat formation, Crimson Tide wideout Marquis Maze threw a long pass that tight end Michael Williams seemed to go up in the air and catch at the LSU 1-yard line, but somehow LSU safety Eric Reid managed to take the ball away from Williams before the players hit the ground. The ruling was an interception and video replays upheld the call. After the game, 'Bama coach Nick Saban said of the play, "[It was] a possible touchdown that turns out to be an interception."

TOP 5 AUBURN RECEIVING YARDS IN A SEASON

	Player	Year	Yards
1.	Ronney Daniels	1999	1,068
2.	Terry Beasley	1970	1,051
3.	Darvin Adams	2009	997
4.	Darvin Adams	2010	963
5.	Frank Sanders	1994	910

So, at the end of regulation, nothing was settled, with the score deadlocked at 6–6. The Tide had the ball first in overtime, but went backward. Two incomplete passes and a substitution infraction followed by Sam Montgomery's sack of quarterback AJ McCarron pushed UA back to the 35-yard line and made the field-goal attempt long-distance and low-percentage.

Whereas the penalty against Alabama made the kick difficult for Foster, when LSU got the ball, a 15-yard run by Michael Ford set Alleman up for an easy 25-yarder—and that was the difference that raised the Bayou Tigers' SEC and national championship hopes, and put a monkey wrench in 'Bama's aspirations.

CBS announced that the contest was its second highest-rated game ever, behind only the November 25, 1989, Notre Dame–Miami game. Great game between two great teams, but plenty of reasons for 'Bama fans to hate it.

November 3, 2007: LSU 41, Alabama 34

Ordinarily Auburn and Tennessee are considered the biggest games of the year. However, perhaps the most hyped-up game in Saban's first year was when No. 3–ranked and SEC preseason favorite Louisiana State came to Tuscaloosa. After winning the national championship at LSU in 2003 and then later leaving for the Miami Dolphins, this was Nick Saban's first game against his old team. His successor at LSU, Les Miles, playing with what some said were Saban's blue-chip recruits, had a 34–6 mark with three straight top five rankings, the best three-year start in school history.

Regardless, LSU faithful were still resentful that Saban had left them and resurfaced at, of all places, Alabama. Because of the Saban factor, they flocked to the game and weren't bashful about expressing their feelings toward their former coach. They made noise from the time they arrived until they left town, creating an environment that ratcheted up the excitement level leading up to and carrying over into the game that at least matched the Iron Bowl.

LSU entered the game with a 7–1 record, and Alabama was 6–2 and had moved up to No. 17 in the national polls. Feeding off the revved-up feelings of the fans of both teams, the Tide and Tigers battled each other to the bitter end. "There couldn't have been a more electric atmosphere in Tuscaloosa. It was, by far, the loudest place I've been to in five years," stated Matt Hayes of the *Sporting News*.

When it was over, the Bayou Bengals had put a 41–34 hurt on the Crimson Tide, beginning 'Bama's season-ending four-game free fall.

The Cajuns who came up from Baton Rouge were ecstatic. For them it was payback time. They would feel even better two months later when Miles took the Tigers to another national championship, four years after Saban showed them the way to the promised land.

NONCONFERENCE GAMES WE HATE

December 31, 1973, Sugar Bowl: Notre Dame 24, Alabama 23

Alabama doesn't like to lose to anybody, especially Auburn and Tennessee. Out of conference, Notre Dame might be at the top of Alabama's hate list. Why? Because Notre Dame enjoys its unique national mystique, and Alabama is 1–5 against the Fighting Irish since its first-ever meeting with the team in the 1973 Sugar Bowl.

The 24–23 loss in the Sugar Bowl was particularly painful for Crimson Tide fans because it cost Alabama the Associated Press national championship. The win enabled Notre Dame to jump from third to first place in the polls to win the AP national championship. Alabama still was the UPI national champion because that poll was conducted before the bowl games. Still, the setback to Notre Dame diminished that honor.

September 6, 2003: Oklahoma 20, Alabama 13

The Mike Shula Era was off to a satisfactory start after a convincing 40–17 win over South Florida. Then Shula was confronted with a huge game against Oklahoma. Crimson Tide fans, of course, were fully aware of Alabama's rich football history—the record 12 national championships, the 21 conference championships, the 29 bowl victories in 51 bowl games, and the 755 total victories that at the time placed

Alabama No. 5 on the all-time victory list. There was Bear Bryant, of course, the standard by which all college football coaches are compared, who at the time of his retirement had amassed more victories (323) than any other NCAA Division I college coach. Then there are the other 'Bama football legends—Joe Namath, Kenny Stabler, Lee Roy Jordan, and a slew of others going all the way back to Johnny Mack Brown, Don Hutson, and Harry Gilmer, through Cornelius Bennett, Derrick Thomas, and Shawn Alexander.

Many visiting teams, especially if they were escorted to the Bryant Museum, would come into Bryant-Denny Stadium in awe of the famed Crimson Tide tradition. That wasn't the case when the No. 1–ranked Sooners came to town. With its seven national championships, 38 conference championships, 23 victories in 36 bowl games, 726 total victories, and a then No. 9 ranking on the all-time victory list, Oklahoma was not the least bit intimidated. Before Bear Bryant became the Coach of the Decade for the 1960s and 1970s, Oklahoma's Bud Wilkinson dominated football in the 1950s, with his Sooners winning what is still a national record 47 straight games from October 10, 1953, through November 16, 1957. After Wilkinson put the program on a pedestal, coaches such as Barry Switzer continued the Sooners' success story, with Bob Stoops, then in his second year at the helm, winning Oklahoma's last national championship in 2000, eight years after the Tide's last title in 1992. Oklahoma had produced three Heisman Trophy–winning running backs (Billy Vessels in 1952, Steve Owens in 1969, and Billy Sims in 1978) and more than its share of stars going back to Tommy MacDonald, Lee Roy Selmon, and Roy Williams, a safety who was the first player to win both the Nagurski Trophy and the Thorpe Award in the same year.

Whereas the loud roar that emanates over the load speakers while the Bryant-Denny scoreboard shows the elephant menacingly swinging its trunk back and forth might intimidate lesser opponents who stopped to look and listen, the Boomer Sooner Schooner stagecoach that circles Memorial Stadium stirring up that sea of red in Norman probably has the same effect on some of Oklahoma's more impressionable opposition. While Alabama has an illustrious football heritage, Oklahoma has a very proud and storied tradition of its own.

Crimson Tide quarterback Brodie Croyle was looking forward to the challenge of playing a team with as much history and hype as Alabama. "Oklahoma speaks for itself," he said following the win over South Florida. "We've got some unfinished business. Oklahoma is going to come in here No. 1 with the No. 1 defense—some say they're supposed to have the best defense that ever stepped on a college field. You couldn't ask for a better stage than that."

So the scene was set. Shula was going to face his first real big challenge, with the opportunity for his first signature win. However, it wasn't to be as Oklahoma defeated the Crimson Tide 20–13. Even though the Tide lost, Shula, who in the NFL had coached in the AFC and NFC Championship Games, had experienced the Super Bowl, and attended many Orange Bowl games while growing up in Miami, stated, "None of those games compared to the atmosphere in Bryant-Denny Stadium today."

January 1, 2000, Orange Bowl: Michigan 35, Alabama 34 (OT)

The reason that this game is listed is because on December 17, 2011, the *Sporting News* selected it as the sixth-best bowl

game of the BCS era. The season began with a dark cloud over the Alabama program as rumors circulated that Coach Mike DuBose was involved in an inappropriate relationship with his secretary. Then in the third game, the embattled coach came under more fire as the Crimson Tide lost a stinker in Birmingham to Louisiana Tech, 29–28. On the last play from scrimmage, Tech's backup quarterback Brian Stallworth fired a 29-yard hope-and-a-prayer pass into the end zone that Sean Cangelosi caught for the game-winning touchdown, sending shockwaves reverberating around Legion Field.

That was Louisiana Tech, mind you, not LSU. And it was the second straight time that the Tide had lost to the Bulldogs, something that's just not acceptable at Alabama. DuBose's critics coiled.

DuBose and 'Bama rebounded as the Crimson Tide didn't lose again until Tennessee beat them 21–7 in Bryant-Denny.

TOP 5 AUBURN RECEIVING YARDS
IN A CAREER

	Player	Years	Yards
1.	Terry Beasley	1969–1971	2,507
2.	Tyrone Goodson	1993–1997	2,283
3.	Karsten Bailey	1995–1998	2,174
4.	Courtney Taylor	2003–2006	2,098
5.	Frank Sanders	1991–1994	1,998

AUBURN

Alabama beat bitter rival Auburn 28–17 in the Tide's first-ever win in Jordan-Hare Stadium and finished first in the SEC West. After edging Florida 40–39 in overtime in Gainesville during the regular season, 'Bama drowned the Gators in the SEC Championship Game 34–7, saving DuBose's job, at least for the time being.

Alabama brought a 10–2 record into the Orange Bowl against Big Ten power Michigan. The game was intriguing because it matched two of college football's most historic programs and featured a player on each team who would go on to win the Most Valuable Player Award in the National Football League—the Crimson Tide's All-America running back Shaun Alexander and Michigan's star quarterback Tom Brady.

Alabama was ahead 28–14 in the third quarter before Brady, who would go on to win two MVPs with the New England Patriots in 2007 and 2010, brought back the Wolverines to knot up the game.

Alexander, who won the MVP while playing for Seattle in 2005, ran for 161 yards on 25 carries with three touchdowns on the day, including a 50-yard scamper in the third quarter to put Alabama up 21–14.

'Bama missed what would have been a tying point-after-touchdown kick in overtime, which gave the Wolverines the 35–34 win in the first overtime game in Orange Bowl history. Alabama ended up No. 8 in the nation, and DuBose was named SEC Coach of the Year.

January 2, 2009, Sugar Bowl: Utah 31, Alabama 17

The *Sporting News* picked this game as the ninth best in the BCS era, meriting its listing here. In Nick Saban's second season in Tuscaloosa, Alabama, won its first 12 games, only to lose its last two, 31–20 to Florida in the SEC Championship Game and 31–17 in a huge upset to Utah in the Sugar Bowl.

Coming out of the little-known and little-respected Mountain West Conference, Utah stunned the Crimson Tide in a surprisingly easy win over the heavily favored Tide. The No. 7 Utes shocked 'Bama by bolting to a 14–0 lead before late-arriving fans had a chance to find their seats in the New Orleans Superdome. Then, before they had a chance to get settled in, Utah struck again, extending its advantage to 21–0 with 4:01 left in the first quarter. Alabama did close the gap to 21–17 early in the third quarter, giving Tide fans reason to feel optimistic, but Utah responded with a seven-play, 71-yard drive that squelched the momentum and enabled the nine-and-a-half-point underdog Utes to pull off the upset.

Alabama is not accustomed to losing to Utah, and therefore 'Bama fans were not happy about this one, so it probably deserves a place among the games that it hates. Still, the season gave 'Bama Nation an inkling of what was soon to come.

ABOUT THE AUTHOR

DONALD F. STAFFO did not attend Alabama or Auburn. But he has covered Alabama football for the last 27 years, including the last 24 years for the Associated Press. He was a writer for *'Bama Magazine* for 17 years and a correspondent for the *Tuscaloosa News* for 10 years and the Gannett News Service for three years. For the last 10 years he has covered the Crimson Tide for the *Northport Gazette* and for the last three years for *Touchdown Alabama Magazine.*

Don is the author of 10 books and more than 2,000 articles. He has written three other books on Alabama Football— *'Bama after Bear* (Sevgo Press, 1992), *Alabama Football: Stallings to Saban* (American Press, 2009), and *Alabama Football: Saban Leads Crimson Tide to the 2009 National Championship* (American Press, 2010)—with some information from the research done and interviews conducted for those books included in this work. He has written articles on Alabama football for *USA Today* and the *Alabama Alumni Magazine*, among other publications. He has written about 27 Iron Bowl games for various media outlets. This is his 32nd year as a sports journalist.

Don will be beginning his 45th year in education and his 28th year as professor and health and physical education department chair emeritus at Stillman College in Tuscaloosa. A

former college and high school coach and athletics director, he is the recipient of four national awards, one district award, four state awards, five distinguished alumni awards, five institutional awards, and has been inducted into three halls of fame. He is one of only four people in the country to receive the three highest national awards given by the American Alliance for Health, Physical Education, Recreation, and Dance.

Don earned his PhD from Ohio State University, MA from Western Kentucky University, and his BS from the State University of New York at Brockport.

He and his wife, Dr. Marilyn Staffo, have been married for 37 years and are the parents of two married daughters, Andrea and Deanna. They have one granddaughter, Ava.